The Great Admirals

Weidenfeld and Nicolson
London

Richard Hough

The Great Admirals

ISBN 0 297 77308 9

House editor Esther Jagger
Designed by Behram Kapadia for
George Weidenfeld and Nicolson Limited
11 St John's Hill, London SW11

Layout by Gill Mouqué

Colour Separations by Newsele Litho Ltd.

Filmset and printed Offset Litho in Great Britain by
Cox & Wyman Limited, London, Fakenham
and Reading

PREVIOUS PAGES
HMS *Superb*, flagship
of the C-in-C
Mediterranean.
Painting by F. H.
Mason, 1918.

Contents

Contents

Maps

Introduction

The art of the admiral has been an unchanging one since Salamis. Only the style of fighting has altered. Neither Admiral Halsey nor Admiral Beatty was called upon to lead a boarding party. Had they done so, they would no doubt have laid about them with sword and pistols as enthusiastically and effectively as Drake or Nelson. Robert Blake was never called upon to order a task force's evolutions according to radar plots and radioed scouting reports, but would have applied his tactically canny mind to the problems of carrier warfare as well as 'Electric Brain' Spruance in the Second World War.

The art of the admiral is the art of decision-making, of judging odds and alternatives according to assessments of *matériel*, weather, intelligence, quality of morale and so on. Decisiveness is a supremely valuable quality in an admiral, bringing with it success as deserved as Nelson's at the Nile, when he astonished and intimidated the French by sailing straight into Aboukir Bay *immediately* on arrival. Spruance won at Midway by committing all his bombers *immediately* on the morning of 4 June 1942. Procrastination is the thief of success in naval warfare, as poor Villeneuve demonstrated at Trafalgar, and Graves at Chesapeake Bay.

The art of the admiral is also the art of keeping 'your head when all about you are losing theirs'. Time and again the importance of good scouting and intelligence is shown in battle reports. A good admiral has ensured that he has good scouts, and, in his turn, correctly and swiftly acts upon the intelligence he receives without becoming fussed. A good admiral is an opportunist.

There are factors over which the admiral has little control, like the quality of his ships and guns. The German battle cruiser commander at Jutland recounted that his losses would have been catastrophic if British shells had not been so faulty. All the courage and skill in the world could not have saved Cradock at Coronel or Medina Sidonia at Gravelines. The ships were not up to the job.

Nor can the luck factor be overestimated. For Nelson, luck became a habit. He came to accept good luck as a companion to his skill and audacity. It rarely failed him. For Villeneuve and Jellicoe, misfortune dogged the wakes of their flagships. If you study their portraits, this is not all that surprising. They have unlucky faces.

There are golden and dark ages for admirals as for architects. The worst period was between the downfall of Bonaparte, who never understood seapower, and the Second World War, a period of 125 years. The first one hundred years were almost entirely uneventful, when generations of admirals retired without ever hearing a shot fired in anger.

The worst fighting period was undoubtedly the First World War, when admirals lost their freedom and initiative, and had been trained to preserve rather than risk their ships, and were beset by doubts. Unreliable intelligence and often unwise instructions were uncertainly transmitted over the ether by high command playing with its new and dangerous toy, the wireless. This was the age of interference and the busybody.

So much emphasis had been placed on the value of the unprecedentedly expensive and complicated *matériel* that commanders shrank back from taking risks. They had all been brought up in fear of the new weapons, the underwater mines and torpedoes.

By the Second World War, conditions were much better for the admiral. There was much less timidity all round. This time the new weapons – the aerial torpedo and bomb – were underestimated and at first treated with scant regard. Even after Taranto and Pearl Harbor, which showed that supremacy at sea was meaningless without control of the air too, the British prime minister (and Winston Churchill was as experienced a navalist as you could find) still thought the balance of power in the Pacific could be restored by battleships.

Interference with the man on the spot continued (e.g. Nimitz at Leyte Gulf, Pound with Convoy PQ17) but headquarters staff had learned greater discretion.

The sea war was run with greater efficiency in spite of the growing multiplicity of weapons, and the world-wide complexity of operations. The art of the admiral was more exercised than ever before, and (with some unhappy exceptions) shone brightly.

The admirals included in this book are only representatives of their period, their service and their wars. All of them were notable commanders who operated, or created, substantial fleets. These 21 admirals, who fought from Lepanto in 1571 to Leyte Gulf in 1944, are sufficient in number and in the range of their fighting and weapons (from pikes to oxygen-powered torpedoes) to provide at least an historical framework of naval events and personalities over 400 years.

RICHARD HOUGH
1977

9

1 Galleons and Galleasses

Don John of Austria
1547–78

Strong gongs groaning as the guns boom far,
Don John of Austria is going to the war,
Stiff flags straining in the night-blasts cold,
In the gloom black-purple, in the glint old-gold,
Torchlight crimson on the copper kettle-drums,
Then the tuckets, then the trumpets, then the cannon, and he comes.
Lepanto, *G. K. Chesterton (1874–1936)*

No figure in history is more redolent of the romance of naval warfare than Don John of Austria, hailed by many during his lifetime as the saviour of Christendom. This tall, handsome, brave admiral was the illegitimate son of the Emperor Charles v and his beautiful mistress, twenty-two-year-old Barbara Blomberg, whose noble nature, 'silky hair, white skin, large eyes, and low musical voice'[1] enchanted all who met her. All the auguries were favourable when Don John was born early in 1547. Even the day itself, 24 February, seemed to the emperor to be especially appropriate, for it was his own birthday, the anniversary of his crowning as Holy Roman Emperor by the Pope, and of his greatest victory over the French at the Battle of Biocca.

Before the age of one, the infant was taken from his mother and placed by the emperor in the care of one of his own closest friends, Luis Quixada, a Castilian nobleman and soldier. His childhood was discreet and obscure. Quixada's childless wife, Magdalena, was the greatest influence during Don John's early years. This excellent woman gave him love, and the education he would need for his life as a priest, which the emperor had decreed for him.

It soon became evident that the church was not for this active, lively boy who dreamed of military glory, and who, when he was not riding his horse in mock cavalry charges, was studying the laws of chivalry and military science. When the emperor learned of the developing nature of his son, he agreed that he should be allowed instead to train for a military career, no doubt recalling at the same time the joys of his own military conquests.

Shortly after this, late in 1555, the Emperor Charles v quit his throne with the intention of devoting the rest of his life to religious studies. He remained in poor health, but gained comfort from the quiet, contemplative life he now enjoyed, and by visits from his fast-growing son.

But it was not until 1559, after the ex-emperor's death, that the boy learned of his real identity. Legend tells of a meeting with his half-brother, King Philip of Spain, of his kneeling at his feet and being asked, 'Know you, young man, whom you had for a father?' And, when the boy turned with a puzzled expression to Quixada, receiving the answer from the questioner:

12

'Take courage, my child. You are the offspring of a hero. The Emperor Charles v, who now dwells in heaven, was your father and my own.'

From this time, the boy was to be known as Don Juan (or John) of Austria, addressed as 'Excellency', and accorded many of the honours and privileges of royalty. His military training was intensified, and there had never been a more receptive and enthusiastic student, although his half-brother like his father considered that a life within the church was more appropriate for the boy and still hoped that there might one day be a change of heart.

Not a bit of it. By the time he was eighteen, and bursting with zeal for military campaigning, he attempted to join an expedition to help defend the island of Malta against Turkish attack. The king forbade it, claiming the boy was too young. Don John disobeyed his orders, and was only recalled at the last minute by a personal letter from his half-brother threatening disgrace if he did not return to the court. Four years of frustration followed this failure and humiliation over the Malta expedition, and it was not until Don John was twenty-two that he first saw action. By then, however, he had reached the exalted rank of captain-general of the sea and commander of all Spain's fleets.

This high-speed promotion was quite usual. Under Spain's hierarchical system, rank in the fighting services had to correspond with social rank. It was considered demeaning for soldiers to serve under an officer of comparatively low social standing. Only a grandee was suitable for the higher ranks, and it was appropriate and in accord with the laws of chivalry that the son of the great emperor should command Spain's navy, even if he was a bastard. Besides, he had as constant adviser a vice-admiral of great experience and wisdom to make up for any deficiencies he might suffer in the science of sea warfare.

The period of sea fighting in which Don John made his reputation was a transitional one, and Lepanto, which crowned his career, was the last link with Mediterranean galley warfare as it had been practised since the days of Xerxes and earlier.

The galley of the mid-sixteenth century had developed little since Salamis. Its motive power was sail when conditions permitted, oars when there was inadequate wind and in battle. Its striking power was the ram, which was used to commit as much damage as possible before the soldiers engaged in hand-to-hand combat:

> ... And each against his neighbour
> Steers his own ship: and first the mighty flood
> Of Persian host held out. But when the ships
> Were crowded in the straits, nor could they give
> Help to each other, they with mutual shocks,
> With beaks of bronze went crushing each the other,
> Shivering their rowers' benches ...

Thus wrote Aeschylus on Salamis.

Don John, noble bastard and 'saviour of Christianity'.

13

The evolutions of sea warfare in the Mediterranean were similar to those of the cavalry on land, who would manoeuvre for a favourable position and then charge with lance before engaging in close combat. Each galley's company was clearly divided between those who powered and managed the ship, and those who did the fighting. The oarsmen were customarily slaves, often captured from the enemy. The enlightened and efficient Venetians introduced freemen as oarsmen, who left their benches in combat and fought along with the soldiers. Slings and mechanical artillery were sometimes additionally used but the damage they caused was marginal. With the advent of explosive artillery, new problems were created for the galley's architect. They came gradually because there was strong prejudice against gunpowder and guns, just as there was prejudice against steam power 300 years later. Gunpowder could well do more damage to the ship firing the gun than to the enemy.

By Don John's day, the cannon's awful power could no longer be denied. The bigger galleys might carry two three-ton bombards, flanked by smaller guns, in the prow. With luck and judgement, these could wreak havoc seconds before the ram sliced deep into the enemy galley's hull. Cannon-armed galleys were an anachronism, like the steam-*and*-sail driven battle-ships of the mid-nineteenth century and the Japanese battleship-carriers of the Second World War. The galley was a dying breed in Don John's lifetime, although still occasionally seen a hundred years later and a formidable vessel when skilfully and determinedly handled.

Also suffering a decline in Don John's time was the unity of Christendom. The Reformation had split the once unified nations into two hostile camps, and two of the strongest powers, Venice and Spain, were in a condition of affluent slackness. The opening up of America by the *conquistadores* had been a stunning achievement, but the wealth that had accrued from it had sharpened nationalism in Spain. Venice was preoccupied with keeping the eastern Mediterranean open for her life-dependent trade with the East, and Spain, with equal parochialism, was concerned only with the western Mediterranean and her rich trade with the Americas. This disunity coincided with an ever more aggressive stance by the Ottoman Empire. When the ferocious Selim II succeeded to the Ottoman throne in 1566, plans were made for the conquest of Cyprus and other Mediterranean islands, and for war against Spain.

Two great figures were chiefly responsible for the salvation of Christendom over the next years. The first was Pope Pius v, who was determined to lead a new crusade against the infidels in order to recover Christian unity and create a Christian league. By powerful persuasion, cunning and horse-trading, he succeeded magnificently. The second was Don John, destined to lead the allied Christian forces against Moslem power.

At the outset of his active military career, Don John personified all the virtues of the age of chivalry before the decay of Spanish militarism symbol-

Pope Pius V, who brought accord to Christian nations in order 'to destroy the common enemy'.

ized by Cervantes's caricature in Don Quixote. His fair colouring and proud bearing alone made him stand out. In addition, he was stylish and authoritative in his manner, and, rare among great leaders, was blessed with intellectualism, modesty and simplicity. His letters to his half-brother, for example, are described as lucid and without frills. He was unreflective and refreshingly decisive in command. He loathed all negotiation because it involved intrigue.

Don John's first voyage as C-in-C took place in the summer of 1568 when, in his lavishly embellished galley, he led 33 craft out from Carthagena into the Atlantic to escort the pricelessly valuable Spanish Indian fleet over the last leg of its voyage home. The four-months'-long cruise was little more than a demonstration of strength, a showing of the flag. A land campaign followed, and now at last there came the opportunity for Don John to test his mettle and show his courage and skill as a warrior. A major rebellion among the Moors of Granada had broken out and in February 1569 the king offered his half-brother the command of the royal forces to quell this insurrection. It was a bloody, confused campaign, beset by hardship and unspeakable cruelties on both sides. The Moors fought ferociously. For Don John, the worst moment in the long campaign occurred a year later when Luis Quixada, fighting at his side, was wounded and thrown from his horse. The elderly warrior, Don John's guardian, friend and mentor since he could remember, died later, to the commander's great grief.

It was not until November 1570, with the death of the Moorish 'Little King', Aben Abu, and the extinguishing of the last flames of revolt, that Don John was able to give up his command. Already his eyes were set on greater achievements than the suppression of rebellions – the command of a great

Christian force that would hurl back the military power of Islam in a glorious crusade.

The pattern of Don John's destiny was unfolding in all its gallant and romantic splendour. Six months after his return to court and after a series of agonizing failures to reach an agreement, the Holy League was proclaimed at the Vatican in Rome. The republic of Venice and the kingdom of Spain were sufficiently reconciled to agree to join forces with other allies in the fight for Christianity, both against the Moors of Algiers, Tunis and Tripoli, and the Turks in Europe and Asia. Between them, the allies were to provide 200 galleys, 100 auxiliary vessels, 50,000 foot soldiers, 4500 horsemen, and arms to match. Spain was to bear half the cost, and the Pope and Venice one-third and two-thirds respectively of the remainder.

On this same day, 24 May 1571, Don John of Austria's ultimate ambition was to be realized:

> Pope Pius v, to our well-beloved son in Christ, health and Apostolic benediction.
> Almighty God, the author of all good, has been pleased that with His divine favour the League should be concluded ... which, having come to so good an issue, it appeared to us right to congratulate Your Nobleness on the occasion, as by these letters we do, being assured that our message will be welcome and agreeable to you ...
> Greatly do we rejoice to behold you thus prosperously navigating this our sea, that together with the fleets of the other members of the League you may make a beginning of the destruction of the common enemy ...

Nobody could doubt Don John's powers of leadership. His men would go anywhere with him and fight at his side against impossible odds. One historian of this period has written that 'he seemed to personify the crusading ardour of the Pope. His inspiring presence swept men off their feet, and made them temporarily forget their own selfish aims in an overwhelming enthusiasm for the common cause.'[2] He was a commander in the tradition of the great *conquistadores*.

But Don John had yet to prove himself a master of military diplomacy as well as of military science and leadership. Time and again the negotiations leading to the signature of the Holy League had broken down. Finally, when the Venetians were forced to concede that the supreme commander should be nominated by Spain, they also gained the point that no decisive act must be taken without the consent of the leaders of all the other contingents. This was a piece of military nonsense which the twenty-five-year-old captain-general of the sea would have to deal with.

Don John's appointment coincided with a new pressure on the cause of Christendom in the eastern Mediterranean. Selim had struck a serious blow at Venice by the capture of Nicosia in Cyprus. His forces had been thrown back outside the island's other great city and fortress of Famagusta, but within days of the signature of the Holy League they were back, renewing their attack on this centre of Venetian trade, strength and military power. Confident of the disunity of the Christians, the Sultan believed that he was at last on the brink of a series of Islamic victories that would clear the enemy from the whole of the eastern Mediterranean.

Don John departed from Madrid on 6 June 1571 and anchored in Naples Bay on 9 August after many halts *en route* to collect and consolidate his forces. Here he formally received the banner of the League and a letter from the Pope which begged him to attack and destroy the enemy as speedily as possible. The allied assembly point was Messina in Sicily, on the Straits of Messina which separate that island from the toe of Italy. At this point there arrived vast numbers of ships and men, frigates and brigantines from Spain, galleons from Venice, more than 200 galleys, and, most formidable of all, six great Venetian galleasses. Viewed from the hills above Messina, this vast crusading armada, manned by 50,000 galley slaves, or free oarsmen, and sailors, with a complement of 30,000 soldiers, appeared to be invincible. The grand total of 316 men-of-war presented a brave and spectacular sight of which the Pope, and the officers of the Vatican who had negotiated so patiently and determinedly to bring about this gathering of allied forces, could be proud.

But Don John was well aware of the fierce divisions of loyalty in his fleet, the jealousies that must lead to outbreaks of violence even before the enemy was sighted. Every day that passed increased the disunity. On one occasion the elderly Venetian commander, Sebastian Veniero, had three Spaniards hanged following an outbreak of violence. Don John had then to prevent his own men from turning their guns on to the Venetian flagship.

As the final preparations to sail were made, Don John, against strong opposition, played his ace card by drastically mixing the nationalities among the ships, shuffling Venetians among Spanish vessels, Sicilians among Vatican, Italians among Maltese, Spanish and Genoese. It was rather as if the Americans, British, Free French, Dutch and Australians had swapped around their ships' crews in 1945 for the final assault on Japan. But the advantages were manifest – especially the advantage that it diluted the authority of all the commanders except Don John himself.

During the last days of August and the first days of September, Don John established the formation and battle plan of his armada. Like the man himself, these were straightforward and sound. The main fighting force was of three divisions each of about 63 galleys, with his own division in the centre. In support, he had two commanders of his own – Veniero, so that he could keep an eye on him, and Marco Colonna of the papal contingent. On his left, Don John placed the Venetian Augustino Barbarigo, and on his right the Genoese Giovanni Andrea Doria. A vanguard of eight galleys was under the command of the Sicilian Don Juan de Cardona, and the rearguard of 30 more galleys was commanded by that great leader, the Marquis of Santa Cruz.

All this was tactically sound and traditional. But Don John's percipience

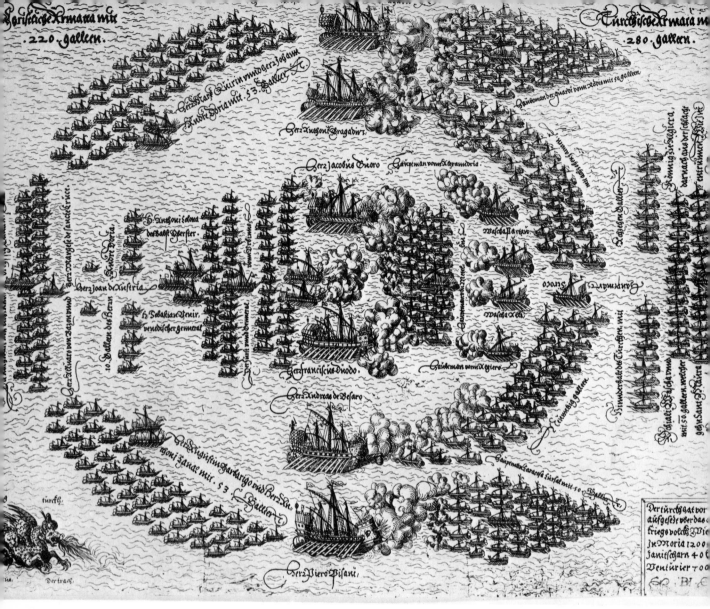

Lepanto, formal plan of battle. It was not as tidy as this.

and wisdom as a commander were shown in a number of important ways. First, he announced to all Christian slave oarsmen that they would be pardoned and freed if the enemy were defeated. His second radical decision was to order the removal of the beaks of all the galleys in order to allow the bow guns a wider and freer range of fire. The third was to give the heavy Venetian galleasses a much more positive and aggressive role than was traditional. Two were assigned to each of the three divisions, and they were placed in the van with orders to crush with their powerful artillery as many of the enemy galleys as they could before the main force came up in support.

By this decision alone, Don Juan had ensured a place in naval history for the coming battle with the Turkish fleet. Artillery had been accorded an enhanced priority as never before. The crude thrust of pike and sword, the firing of slings and catapults and muskets, were never again to be the final arbiter in major fleet actions.

Meanwhile the Turkish fleet, commanded by Ali Pasha, had assembled under the shelter of the fortresses of Lepanto, situated in what is now called the Gulf of Corinth. Encouraged by a report which substantially underestimated the size of the Christian fleet, Ali Pasha sailed westwards through the narrows on 6 October.

Although numerically superior, Ali Pasha's fleet was less well protected and more lightly gunned than Don John's. It had nothing to match against the Venetian galleasses, which mounted probably as many as ten heavy cannon, a dozen or more lighter guns and a number of railing pieces. A well commanded and manned galleass among Turkish galleys and galliots (small galleys) was like a twentieth-century tank let loose among infantrymen. Ali Pasha's fleet was also suffering from complacency after some recent easy victories.

Don John's fleet, in spite of earlier divisions, was fired by religious fervour quite as powerful as the Moslems', and in the few weeks since it had been formed had acquired a strong regard and loyalty for its commander. Moreover, in the last few days before the engagement, it had received news of the enemy's recent success at Famagusta, of the sacking and pillaging of the town, of the murder or enslavement of the garrison, the sacking of the cathedral and the scattering of the contents of the Christian tombs. Worst of all, the hero of the earlier defence against the Turkish attack, Bragadino, had been revoltingly and publicly tortured, and skinned alive on orders from Ali Pasha himself. As the Christian fleet sailed forth to seek out the enemy, every man was filled with a raging lust for revenge for this humiliation and outrage.

Early on the morning of 7 October, the two fleets sighted one another, both of them surprised but not intimidated by the numbers of the enemy. In a last gesture of inspiration, Don John embarked from his galley, the lavishly equipped and decorated *Reale*, into a smaller, faster ship, and was rowed round his fleet standing at the prow, a crucifix held in his right hand.

The two great armadas clashed at midday, the galleasses at once doing terrible execution among the leading Turkish galleys. Barbarigo on the left was the first to be fiercely engaged, and although he did crippling damage to the Turkish right wing, his own galley was twice captured and retrieved, while he was mortally wounded.

In the centre, Don John's *Reale* was the primary target of the Turks' attack. Here, too, the fighting was ferocious, with Don John in the centre

OVERLEAF Lepanto: 'Scarlet running over on the silvers and the golds/Breaking of the Hatches up and bursting of the holds. . . .'

> . . . pounding from the slaughter-painted poop,
> Purpling all the ocean like a bloody pirate's sloop,
> Scarlet running over on the silvers and the golds,
> Breaking of the hatches up and bursting of the holds,

Thronging of the thousands up that labour under sea,
White for bliss and blind for sun and stunned for liberty.[3]

On the right, the Turkish commander of the van was beheaded and his body cast back into the bloodstained sea. In the centre, Ali Pasha was sorely wounded, and although he offered treasure in exchange for his life, he got short shrift. In seconds, his head was held aloft on the end of a pike for all to see. Only on Don John's right was the victory incomplete. Andrea Doria was temporarily outmanoeuvred, the knights of Malta sorely pressed and their commander killed. But Santa Cruz, with brilliant timing, moved in with the reserve to save a rout, and put the Turkish commander, Ulick Ali, to flight.

By evening victory was complete. Don John had inflicted on the Moslems one of the most decisive defeats of all time. With the loss of almost all their fleet, the death of some 30,000 men and the release by the Christians of 12,000 of their slaves, the Turks had suffered a terrible blow, moral as well as material.

'Don John has saved Christendom.' The news reached Venice on 17 October and the people went wild with excitement. Expressions of religious fervour spread with the news across Europe, from cities to towns to the smallest villages. Pope Pius v instituted a perpetual festival in honour of the day of salvation. Sculptors and painters worked at their craft to create permanent monuments to the victory at Lepanto, and the victor, Don John.

> *Vivat Hispania!*
> *Domino Gloria!*
> Don John of Austria
> Has set his people free!

Don John deserved all the credit lavished upon him. Many of his commanders had counselled caution. There had been a strong feeling among the more timorous that they should withdraw in order to keep the combined fleet 'in being' as a threat and lever. Defeat, it was argued, would be the end of Christendom.

Lepanto, the first great fleet action between surface ships to be dominated by artillery, makes an interesting contrast in aggressive decisiveness with the last similar great fleet action 350 years later at Jutland.

The fact that the Holy League crumbled from dissension and perfidy, making it impossible for Spain to follow up the tactical and strategical success of Lepanto, in no way diminishes Don John's momentous achievement. The young warrior had been granted a unique opportunity at Lepanto to show his greatness as a commander, and fate had been splendidly generous. But Don John's fortunes, like those of the Holy League, declined into anticlimax. He had some military successes in the Low Countries, a thankless arena for campaigning, and died of the plague there in September 1578.

The Duke of Medina Sidonia

1542–99

Don Alonso Pérez de Gusman el Bueno, Twelfth Señor and
Fifth Marques de Sanlucar de Barramada, Ninth Conde de Niebla
and Seventh Duque de Medina Sidonia

I t is an untidy irony of history that one of the most fateful military
expeditions ever to set forth was led by a man with little military and no
naval experience, who had accepted the command unwillingly. A
further twist to the irony is that the Spanish expedition's failure to
liberate England from the Protestant yoke could not really be blamed on
this unfortunate duke.

The speed with which England rose from its insignificant status as a mist-
shrouded island off the continent of Europe, inhabited by peasants and
governed by Norman barons, was faster even than that of the recent
Japanese rise to power and wealth. The English renaissance was so swift that
it was almost as if a westerly gale had swept over the island, clearing the mist
and cloud, bringing skies of crisp sunshine which awoke the nation and set
the blood racing.

The return of Francis Drake from his three-year-long circumnavigation in
September 1580, loaded with Spanish treasure, conveniently marks the high
point of what has since been known as 'the Elizabethan age'. Suddenly, it
seemed, spirits were buoyant, art, industry and commerce flourished as
never before, and with brash self-confidence the queen's subjects dared, and
succeeded, and so gained ever greater rewards. It was this spirit which fired
England to defy the Spanish super-power, which with the conquest of
Portugal in 1580 gave King Philip II Catholic sovereignty over the greater
part of the known world.

The political, dynastic, economic, commercial and religious conflict
between the Spanish empire and England had been drifting along, with no
set pattern but with sudden outbreaks of violence and periods free of
incident, for several years before King Philip made the decision to put an end
to it all and embark on the holy military crusade, 'the Enterprise of England'
as he called it. There had been no declaration of war at any time. In fact,
King Philip could not be certain that there even *would* be war. His plan, if
it could be called a plan, was to despatch up the English Channel the most
formidable force he could muster, consisting of the largest ships with the
most intimidating configuration (what the French later called 'fierce face'
men-of-war), loaded to the gunwales with the cream of Spain's soldiery.

This armada was to sail in arrowhead formation, which would make it
look more numerous and ferocious than it really was and which was a good

'My health is not equal
to such a voyage.' The
Duke of Medina
Sidonia.

23

King Philip II of Spain, the most powerful man in the world in 1588.

defensive formation in any case, and *close inshore* so that as many English people as possible could see it. It was judged that the news of the Spanish descent upon English shores would spread like wildfire – and so it did, from beacon clifftop to beacon hilltops and in minutes to London, the sudden blaze of kindling flashing its flames of warning. At worst, King Philip calculated, the news would demoralize the enemy. It would certainly encourage the Catholics. At best, it would lead to a successful Catholic uprising without the need for Spanish intervention.

The Enterprise was as much an operation of intimidation as invasion; although, if the need arose, a military landing would take place. The armada's only firm commitment was to link up with the Duke of Parma's forces in the Low Countries. Every other contingency would be acted upon as it arose, according to the outcome of the sea battle, the state of the weather and the reaction of the English. In modern jargon, the Duke of Medina Sidonia was instructed to play it by ear.

Plans for the creation of an armada had been first discussed in detail in 1585. By March 1586 the scale of the enterprise had been worked out in all its formidable size and strength – about 550 ships and almost 100,000 men. This was scaled down over the following months, and the final count was 130 ships, including 65 galleons instead of 150, 32 smaller fighting ships, 4 galleys and 4 galleasses and the rest made up of storeships. The number of seamen and soldiers was reduced to 30,000.

The appointed c-in-c was the Marquis of Santa Cruz who had fought so skilfully at Lepanto and who, with the death of Don John, was regarded as the greatest Spanish naval leader. In building or acquiring the ships, in victualling them for six months, in assembling and training the men, Santa Cruz faced a formidable task, made even more difficult by the king's parsimony. Moreover, he was not in the best of health, and in February 1588, within weeks of the planned departure of the Enterprise, this excellent nobleman died.

In appointing the Duke of Medina Sidonia as his successor, the king was guided by so many advantages that no alternative was considered. Medina Sidonia, the senior duke of Spain, and probably the richest man too, possessed vast estates and wielded great influence. He was known to many as 'the good'. But, while not an especially ruthless or cruel nobleman, he knew very well how to look after himself, was ambitious and possessed a keen eye for the main chance. English historians especially, relying on the mockery of triumphant contemporaries after the Armada's retreat, belittled his prowess as a military leader, and described him as a pacific duke. Drake called him an amateur gentleman from the olive groves of Port St Mary – although that was not even his town:[4] he made do with the profit from his olive groves while he went on military campaigns.

Medina Sidonia was captain-general in Andalusia as early as 1580, and had even been seriously considered as successor to Don John as supreme commander at sea. In Spain at least he was credited with driving Drake from Cadiz after the devastating English raid in 1587, and a year earlier rumour had it that he was to command the Enterprise in place of Santa Cruz, whose administrative ability and drive on land was not equal to his prowess in battle.

Sidonia was a superb organizer and administrator. There was no more respected or noble grandee, a paramount asset under the Spanish tradition of command, and a great encouragement to his men, from the highest officer to the lowliest seaman. They were further encouraged by his wealth. Everyone fights better in the knowledge that he is going to be fed and paid properly.

Sidonia had two further advantages which the cunning and devious king took into account, and a third which has been little considered and will be mentioned later. While Santa Cruz was hated by the Portuguese for his successful campaigning against them before the surrender, Medina Sidonia was popular in that proud and once independent nation, and his wife was half Portuguese. As the Portuguese were providing, resentfully, the greater number of the galleons and many of the sailors, it was important to keep them sweet. Sidonia was also, paradoxically, known and liked by the enemy. The duke was generous with English traders and had granted special trading rights to them in Andalusia, to his own considerable profit. If there was to be an invasion, and England was conquered, it was helpful for the conqueror to be known as an anglophile, especially if he had to appoint himself a temporary regent under some future truce.

The fact that Sidonia had no experience of fighting at sea was of no more consequence than Don John's inexperience before Lepanto. He would have veteran commanders at his side, and he would not contemplate questioning their judgement. Nor did he.

No one was surprised at the appointment, and few realized that he did not want it. His first attempt to wriggle out of it came in a letter to the king's secretary:

My health is not equal to such a voyage [he wrote], for I know by experience of the little I have been at sea that I am always seasick and always catch cold ... Since I have had no experience either of the sea, or of war, I cannot feel that I ought to command so important an enterprise.

Sidonia was no coward. He just had no confidence in the outcome of the Enterprise. In fact, he believed it would end in disaster because of the superior fighting ships and fighting qualities at sea of the English, their superior guns, their knowledge of Channel waters, their advantage in fighting close to their bases and in defence of their homeland, and the insuperable difficulties in making a landing and sustaining a prolonged campaign on foreign soil.

Nor did he want war with England. He believed it to be against the interests of the Spanish empire, and certainly against the interests of the Duke of Medina Sidonia, the greater part of whose wealth depended on foreign trade, and trade with England at that. 'How much more would a negotiated peace have suited him than these fruitless hostilities!'[5] These fruitless hostilities were also going to be hard on his pocket. And so they proved to be, to the extent of no fewer than eight million *maravedis*.

Finally, presupposing the failure of the Enterprise, Medina Sidonia judged that, as its leader, his reputation would be ruined and for ever after the proud name of his family would be associated with defeat and humiliation.

Philip brushed aside all objections. In one way the death of Santa Cruz had been fortuitous because it provided the king with the opportunity of despatching the duke from his estates for many months. He was aware that Sidonia was becoming too wealthy and too powerful for comfort. His wealth was notoriously vast, his personal military forces a considerable anxiety. The command of the Armada would at once diminish his wealth, his influence and his power. And the old fox was right.

The early experiences of the Armada were not propitious. Sidonia had had little more than two months from the date of his appointment to the fleet's assigned day for sailing. Santa Cruz had left it in a state of disarray, demoralized by delay and poor victuals, incomplete and ill-equipped. The new commander, backed by long experience of quartering fleets, did what he could in the time to correct the situation. But, pressed on by the king, and by the knowledge that every day's delay was adding to the cost, most of which he would bear, and to the preparedness of the English, he embarked and hoisted sail before his Armada was fully equipped and ready.

Led by the duke's flagship, the *San Martin*, the Armada dropped down the Tagus from Lisbon on 4 May 1588. It made a brave, formidable and gaudy picture, with the brightly coloured flags and long pennants, the painted sails, the new tall castles fore and aft on the galleons also newly carved and painted, and with cannon booming from the ships and the forts.

There was nothing secret about the size of the fleet and its intentions. For purposes of propaganda and intimidation, all Europe had been advised, down to the number of vessels and men, the number of guns and pikes. And thousands watched from the banks of the river as the Enterprise of England sailed off, great galleon after great galleon, the 25 *urcas* or storeships, the smaller fighting vessels as well as the mighty galleasses, which had been so decisive in the last great religious crusade of 1571.

Unfortunately, when at last the fleet got to sea fourteen days later, the wind was unfavourable, and after being forced south in the opposite direction to their intended course, Sidonia found himself, a month after the embarkation, just off the Tagus again, with nil progress to report. At last the wind obliged, and on 31 May the first few sea miles on the long voyage to the English Channel were logged.

'. . . till the great Armadas come'. The departure from Lisbon of 'the Enterprise of England'.

The next event in the chapter of misfortunes was a westerly gale, so violent that the Armada was scattered, and the *San Martin* put in at Corunna. From here, as his brave men-of-war limped in, Sidonia made one last effort to have the Enterprise cancelled. The king, of course, would have none of it. His commander therefore took advantage of this unscheduled call to re-provision with fresher food and water, discharge the sick and injured and take on more ammunition and crew, so that when another start was made on 12 July, the fleet was in better heart and better shape than before in spite of its misfortunes.

This time wind and weather were favourable, and one week later a look-out at the *San Martin*'s masthead sighted the mainland of England. 'There-upon the Duke hoisted his Pope-consecrated banner at the main – Christ Crucified, with the Virgin Mother on one side of him and Mary Magdalene on the other. The Crusade had begun.'[6]

Impressive as it appeared, and formidable as was the fighting capacity of the Spanish soldiery on board, the Spanish Armada was in fact a vast, clumsy and inflexible convoy, dependent for its security on its protective formation of six groups of fighting ships about the *urcas*, the loss of which would seal the Enterprise's fate. For this reason Sidonia lay to on sighting the Cornish coast and waited for stragglers to catch up and take position in the formation – galleasses in the van as at Lepanto. (The galleys had found the northern waters impossible: three had put back and one sank.)

Sidonia first sighted enemy sail for sure, and in numbers, at dawn on Sunday 21 July. So slow had been his progress that the English fleet had overnight succeeded in getting to seaward and windward of him (the weather gage), and was bearing down on his starboard formation. With a speed and dexterity quite unfamiliar to Spanish seamen, the low-profile English fighting ships came on in succession, fired a broadside from their long-range culverins, put about and fired their other guns.

Rapidly, the English galleons worked across the rear of the Armada to the extreme port formation, and set about this tight pack, causing disarray, dismay and even panic among the Spanish commanders. There was not much co-ordination or order in the English attacks, which were more a series of tip-and-run raids than planned attrition, but the results brought about their intended purpose, demoralizing the enemy and breaking up, though only temporarily, the solid arrowhead formation.

In spite of these disruptions, between the time when he sighted the English coast on 19 July and veered away from the southern tip of the Isle of Wight on 25 July, Sidonia succeeded in his prime aim of keeping his fleet intact, and in trailing his cloak along half the length of England's southern shoreline. He could claim no victory, or even any serious damage to the enemy. But he survived, with little loss, and from the evening of 25 July, after a day of brisk fighting which had denied him the opportunity of landing on the island if he had so wished, until the afternoon of 27 July when

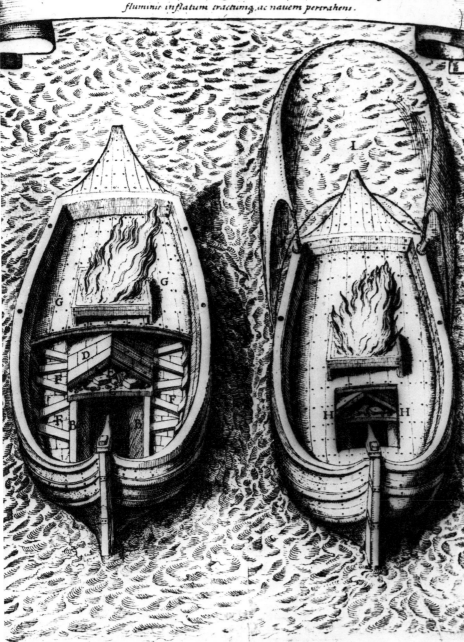

Nauis incendiaria cum cuniculo.

A. Fundamentū cuniculi ex calce, et lateribus, altum ped. 5 latum 1 bellico puluere oppletum. B. Parietes sup. fundamento, lati ped. 1 alti 3. C. Operimentum ex praegrandibus lapidibus. D. Tectum ex similibus qui saxis acuminatum. E. Tecti camera ferreis marmoreisq́, globis, et catenis, et molaribus constipatum.
F. Quadrati lapides cuniculi latera arctè firmiantes. G. Tabulatum nauis cuniculum occultans, et incen dium praeferens. *Nauis cum inuerso uelo.*
H. Cuniculus sub tabulato nauis. I. Velum praegrande subter mediam nauem alligatum, et à cursu fluminis inflatum tractumq́, ac nauem perrrahens.

The dread fireship. Packed below were chains, rocks, iron ball shot, and gunpowder to distribute them.

he anchored his ships off Calais, the Invincible Armada appeared to live up to its name. Its progress was slow and stately, but not a shot was fired by the four shadowing English squadrons – those of Drake, Hawkins, Frobisher and the Lord High Admiral, Lord Howard.

Sidonia was increasingly concerned at the absence of firm news from the Duke of Parma. But the Enterprise had so far succeeded far beyond his expectations.

Sunday 28 July marked the turning-point in the duke's fortunes, and those of his great fleet. The first bad news concerned Parma. Sidonia's own secretary, sent ashore on reconnaissance, reported it as unlikely that the reinforcements could reach them in less than two weeks. Then Sidonia received a message from the sympathetic French governor of Calais warning that his ships were anchored in a vulnerable position – just how dangerous Sidonia recognized at midnight.

The tide was setting up-Channel, the wind was freshening from the south-west, when there appeared from the ranks of the blockading English fleet the first flickers of flame, which grew higher and drew nearer on the brisk wind.

Fireships as a weapon against an anchored fleet went back to the earliest days of sea warfare. Nothing was more vulnerable to fire, nothing more combustible, than a wooden man-of-war with its sun-dried decks, its tarred rigging, its unprotected gunpowder, and no one was more aware of the dangers of fire and explosion at sea than those who manned these vessels. Compounding this fear was superstition, and this was increased with darkness, and for these sailors the suspicion that something even worse than fire was about to descend upon them – perhaps even the dreaded *maquinas de minas*, the 'mine machines', which had committed such terrible execution among the Spanish at the siege of Antwerp three years before.

Sidonia claimed later to have been prepared for this eventuality, and to have had pinnaces out ready to grapple any fireships. But the speed of the ships, their size and the extent of the flames made interception impossible even by the bravest. How right the governor of Calais had been! There was time only for Sidonia to order his ships to proceed to sea and return to their anchorage when the danger has passed, a tidy-sounding performance in theory, but in practice a panic-stricken, chaotic business.

A number of commanders had anticipated the order as the flames drew nearer, the ships 'spurting fire and their ordnance shooting, which was a horror to see in the night', as one eyewitness reported, recalling the horrors of the mine machines. It was only primed cannon going off in the heat, and not one of the Spanish ships was ignited, the fireships passing through and piling up on the French shore to burn themselves out.

However, eight merchantmen had succeeded where for a week the English squadrons of fighting ships had exhausted their ammunition and failed to break up the Spanish Armada. Sidonia watched in horror from the

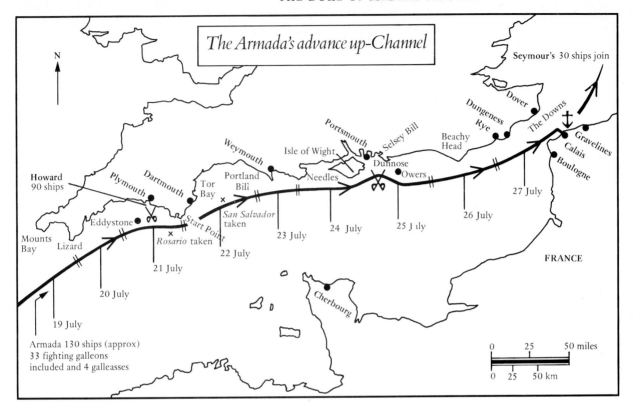

The Armada's advance up-Channel

Seymour's 30 ships join

Dover
Dungeness
Rye
The Downs
Gravelines
Calais
Boulogne

Beachy
Head

27 July

26 July

FRANCE

Portsmouth
Selsey Bill
Isle of Wight
Dunnose
Needles
Owers

25 July

24 July

Weymouth
Portland
Bill
San Salvador
taken

23 July

Howard
90 ships
Plymouth
Dartmouth
Tor
Bay

Eddystone

Start Point
Rosario taken

22 July

21 July

Mounts
Bay
Lizard

20 July

19 July

Armada 130 ships (approx)
33 fighting galleons
included and 4 galleasses

Cherbourg

0   25   50 miles
0   25   50 km

San Martin as his ships cut their precious anchor cables and collided, damaging rigging and spars in their attempt to reach the security of darkness and the open sea. His flagship was one of only five galleons to return and re-anchor – the other four being Portuguese, always the steadier and more experienced seamen. The rest of the Armada were to be seen at dawn on Monday 29 July strung out along the banks of Zealand between Gravelines and Dunkerque, a strong west to north-west wind threatening to drive them on to the shore, their possible retreat to the bolt hole of Spanish-held Antwerp cut off by the Dutch.

Sidonia observed also the fateful, inevitable closing in for the kill of the English squadrons, reinforced now by a fifth, that of Lord Henry Seymour, who had held back in the 'Narrows' awaiting this moment. Bravely, Sidonia sailed out to meet them, supported by the four Portuguese ships, hoping by glorious self-sacrifice to deter the whole English fleet from falling upon the rest of the fleet struggling to reach the safety of the open sea.

The cream of the Armada was soon fiercely engaged, but most of the English galleons passed them by, intent on richer, softer prey beyond, and Sidonia put about to join the main engagement to the east.

The Battle of Gravelines is correctly regarded as one of the most decisive in history, and its result was far more lasting than that of Lepanto. Here, off the dangerous Flemish lee shore, to the panic and disruption created so

33

cheaply by a few fireships was added the pounding, splintering broadside weight of the finest gunners with the finest weapons on board the best-built and best-manned fighting ships in the world.

Like the earlier brushes, this was no tidy engagement with neat evolutions traceable at the end of the day of destruction. No one has ever attempted to depict the battle by diagram. It was, in fact, a series of mainly individual engagements, and only a small proportion of the Armada was even involved. Encouraged by evidence of enemy shortage or complete lack of heavy shot, the English for the first time closed in. Witness Sir William Wynter, who wrote in his report: '.. out of my ship the *Vanguard* there was shot 500 of demi-cannon, culverin and demi-culverin; and when I was farthest off in discharging any of the pieces, I was not out of shot of the harquebus, and most time within speech of one another.'

For the first time, the Armada began to receive serious injury from the English guns. At least one ship was sunk by gunfire, and probably others, too, while more were forced ashore to be seized by the eager Dutch, who gave short shrift to the crews.

At the height of this desperate engagement, Sidonia, it was said, insisted on climbing the rigging of the hard-pressed *San Martin* in order to gain a better view of the state of his fleet. Below decks, the divers were striving to stop up leaks with tow and lead plates. From Sidonia's hazardous perch, he would have seen nothing but smoke and ruin about him, his ships struggling with two enemies simultaneously – the lee shore and the English gunners. He saw no evidence of serious damage to any English galleon.

By the end of the day a dozen or so of his ships, many of them the best that he had, including two of the royal galleons of Portugal, had gone. But many more than this were gravely damaged: some were partly dismasted with their rigging torn to ribbons, there were gashes on the waterline, dead littering the decks and the injured lay uncared for.

By 9 pm on that Monday, 29 July, the Armada was all but done for, just as Sidonia had feared. On the following day, with the wind still strong from the north-west and still threatening to drive the ships on to the shore, the English held off, as if watching and waiting gleefully for the cruel sea to complete their own handiwork.

For Sidonia and his commanders, it seemed that only prayer could save them; and later in the day the Lord answered them. Their run of bad luck broke, the wind bore to the south-west, and the tattered, scattered fleet came round and set sail for the north-west, its rear protected again by the gallant *San Martin*.

Shadowing relentlessly, the English galleons followed at a distance. Europe was soon to learn, from false report, that the Armada had inflicted a stunning victory on the English, that 40 English galleons had been lost, that Drake had been taken.... It was to be some time before the world learned that the Enterprise against England had failed, had been blown asunder by the force of northern gales and the skill and courage of northern seamen.

Many weeks more were to pass before some of the details of the fate of Sidonia's Armada became known. Others are not known to this day. Ships were last seen, battered and bowling before a gale-force wind, and never heard of again. In their attempt to force a passage around the north of Britain, galleons sank with all hands at sea or were thrown up on to the coast of Ireland and elsewhere. Frozen by sub-arctic weather, starved and diseased, the plight of the survivors was the most terrible aspect of the great Catholic defeat.

For the Duke of Medina Sidonia, the fate of his Armada was even worse than he had feared. When at last, in mid-October, the *San Martin* sailed into Corunna harbour with half its company dead or dying, the duke was so ill from dysentery and starvation that it was six days before he could even get ashore. When at last he could be lowered into a pilot boat, it was seen that he was still too weak to sit upright. It was seen, too, that he and his gentlemen staff were 'all apparelled in black like mourners. The like lamentation was never in any country as in Biscay and Asturia.'[7]

King Philip was magnanimous towards his failed c-in-c. In relieving Sidonia at last of his unwanted command, he excused him from attending court and the traditional kissing of hands. 'Return in peace to your estates,' Sidonia was ordered. And this is what the wretched duke did, late in October, in a curtained horse litter.

The Duke of Medina Sidonia recovered his health and lived for another eleven years. If King Philip could derive any satisfaction from the outcome of the Armada tragedy (and he seemed curiously phlegmatic about its fate), it was that the most powerful and richest nobleman in Spain had been reduced in wealth, power and stature. The duke had indeed been cut down to size. Nothing could prevent the association of his name with defeat and humiliation.

But history should give him his due, though it rarely has. He had his moment of triumph when he ordered his intact Armada to drop anchor outside Calais. Nor has anyone denied him his great courage. And if the defeat is to be laid anywhere but at the feet of King Philip of Spain, the finger points at the demoralized and hysterical Spanish commanders who panicked at the sight of a few fireships and proved themselves unable to face English gunfire. Where had the spirit of Pizarro and the *conquistadores* gone?

Lord Charles Howard of Effingham
1536–1624

I protest before God, and as my soul shall answer for it, that I think there never were in any place of the world worthier ships than these are, for so many. And as few we are, if the King of Spain's fleet be not hundreds, we will make good sport with them.
Lord Howard to Lord Burghley before the Armada, 1588

The c-in-c of the English fleet in the Armada battles of 1588 had little more experience of the sea than the Duke of Medina Sidonia. Nor had he any experience of fighting. Furthermore, his supreme rank in the campaign derived directly from his exalted social rank. Here the similarity sharply terminates, because at this point you have to dig deeper into the respective class and caste systems in King Philip's Spain and Queen Elizabeth's England, at least as it applies to maritime affairs.

The strength of the class structure in the English navy lay in its flexibility and resilience. It was far beyond the bounds of possibility for a Spanish seaman from humble stock to rise and become the most famous of all commanders as Francis Drake did. The strength of the Spanish class structure, contrary to the English, was its rigidity. No one in Spain disputed Sidonia's fitness to command the Enterprise and his subordinates never disputed his orders, at least not until those desperate days in the North Sea when half of his commanders refused to obey his instruction to lay to and await the enemy. (He held a summary court-martial, at which all 20 were sentenced to be hanged. The corpse of one was paraded through what remained of the Armada, hanging from the yard-arm of a pinnace.)

Drake's qualities, alone and unaided by influence or wealth or, of course, rank, led to his becoming second-in-command of the English fleet in 1588. But not for one moment did he, or anyone else, think he might be supreme commander. The flexibility of the English class system had given him the opportunity of rising to this dizzy height. But he had made so many enemies on the way up that he could not go right to the top. Under the English system at least you could rise if you had the leadership qualities. But it called for exceptional powers of ruthlessness as well as skill and courage. And that meant enemies. It still meant enemies up to at least the First World War: chips and epaulettes on the shoulder are synonymous among naval officers who have come up the hard way.

For the role of supreme commander there could be only one choice, the lord admiral of England, Lord Charles Howard of Effingham. If, unlike Sidonia, he was not the premier duke, he was related to the Duke of Norfolk. He was also related to Queen Elizabeth I, Ann Boleyn being his first cousin. His rank was hereditary, or almost, in the undefined English way. His father,

36

DESTR. NA. REPOS.

HONI. SOIT. QVI. MAL. Y. PENSE.

A° 1596.

incibilem tibi (Carole digne Philippi
hani victam Deus:. Arma Medynæ
Maris æstus, Numine sacro
tui: Sed Honoribus amplis,
ducem reducem videmus onustum.

his grandfather, and two of his uncles had all been lord admiral in their time. In terms of the twentieth-century British Royal Navy, Howard was at once first sea lord, first lord of the admiralty, commander-in-chief and chief of staff. He was responsible for everything except the victualling, manning and upkeep of the fleet.

At the time of the Armada of 1588 Howard had been in office for only three years and was making up for his lack of knowledge and experience with the same speed that Winston Churchill showed as first lord in 1912. Like Churchill 350 years later, Howard possessed a sharp mind, boldness and inherited aristocratic self-confidence. Unlike Churchill, but like Eisenhower in 1944, he was universally loved and respected and was a wise listener. Some of his subordinates had doubts about his ability to tame and get on with Drake. He had none. 'Sir, I must not omit to let you know how lovingly and kindly Sir Francis Drake beareth himself,' he wrote to Walsingham shortly before the sailing of the Armada, 'and also how dutifully to her Majesty's service and unto me, being in the place I am in ...'

The affection he attracted from his subordinates extended to the humblest seamen. Like all great commanders, he took at least as much interest in the well-being of the lowest ranks as he did in the ability of the highest ranks. Besides doing all that he could for the good feeding (and drinking) of the lower deck, Howard showed exceptional concern for the ships in which they sailed. Fortunately, he had come to office in the golden age of English warship architecture and construction.

By contrast with the Spanish and Portuguese galleons, the large English fighting ships of the second half of the sixteenth century were leaner, lower and nippier. They had long since grown out of the Iberian practice of extravagantly built-up fore and aft castles, intended for the benefit of the soldiers. The English were not interested in soldiers. Their interest was in the sailors. With the English emphasis on manoeuvrability, speed and gun-fire, castles were old-fashioned and a handicap.

English galleons in 1588 were the first in the long line of gun platform capital ships which have lasted through the centuries, though rockets have now largely replaced the guns. The Spanish fighting ships of 1588 were the last of the troop carriers. In the eyes of a Spanish grandee, steeped in the traditions of chivalry and man-to-man combat, the culverin and cannon were vulgar nonsense. Gunnery was 'an ignoble arm'. Little more than 300 years later, the English were saying the same sort of thing about the torpedo and the submarine – 'underhand, unfair and damned un-English', commented a future first sea lord.

In spite of the queen's continuing hopes of peace, by the autumn of 1587 it was clear to all her advisers that there was a real likelihood of a winter attack from Spain, perhaps combined with a crossing by the Duke of Parma with his powerful force in the Low Countries – and perhaps, too, a third attack from Scotland. Howard arranged his dispositions accordingly, with the main fleet under his direct command, Frobisher and Hawkins commanding squadrons under him, and Drake with his own division, virtually an independent command, although with direct responsibility for the conduct of the fighting.

Shortly before the arrival of the Armada all the ships of these four commands were based in the west of the Channel. A fifth division under Seymour was to operate at the east end in order to counter any attack from Parma. After a long winter of uncertainty and discontent, with the queen constantly vacillating in her policy and plans, Drake at last received permission from her to take the fleet to sea with Howard in order to accomplish what he had long desired – a strike at the enemy in his own waters, just as he had so sorely damaged the Spanish fleet at Cadiz the previous summer. The gale that had scattered Medina Sidonia's Armada prevented Howard and Drake from making any headway towards Spain, and when they got back to water and re-victual at Plymouth new orders were awaiting them from the queen prohibiting another expedition.

Howard remained implacably opposed to disobeying the royal orders, while backing his second-in-command's forceful arguments in favour of another strike. By the time the queen had changed her mind again, it was too late. The Armada had reached the Channel unopposed, and Howard's fleet was caught napping in port.

By luck and good seamanship they extricated themselves from the trap in which Sidonia had unknowingly caught them, and by sublime seamanship got the weather gage on the enemy and entered upon the first attack of a week's spasmodic fighting along half the length of the Channel.

Lord Howard fought as bravely and doggedly as any during the long Armada battles as if he were a veteran of sea warfare. Only once did his natural judgement fail him seriously, and that was off Calais after the fire-ships had done their work, and the moment had come for a mass assault on the scattered and fleeing Spaniards. Instead, the lord admiral diverted his ship, the mighty *Ark Royal*, towards the tempting target of a stranded galleass which, rudderless, had been cast upon the shore.

He had other tasks to perform during that epochal week in July 1588. In the excitement of the early battles the English gunners had been extravagant in their consumption of powder and shot. Soon some of the men-of-war had no ammunition left. Howard despatched pinnaces daily to scour stores and forts along the English coast for precious ammunition, and saw to it that the galleons husbanded their supplies and kept sufficient reserves for the inevitable final and crucial battle. He was certainly at fault in allowing himself to be distracted by that juicy galleass and in encouraging his men to 'have their pillage of her'. But he made up for this failure by ensuring that Drake, Hawkins, Frobisher, Seymour and the rest who kept their sights on the main body of the armada possessed enough (just enough) ball and shot and powder to batter the Spanish galleons off Gravelines.

DORCET

SHIRE

Waymouth

Sandesfoote castel

Lulworth

Corf castell

St Aldams

Portlande castel

Portlande Bill

SE

Medina Sidonia's blunt
arrowhead proceeds
implacably up-Channel.

The Scale of

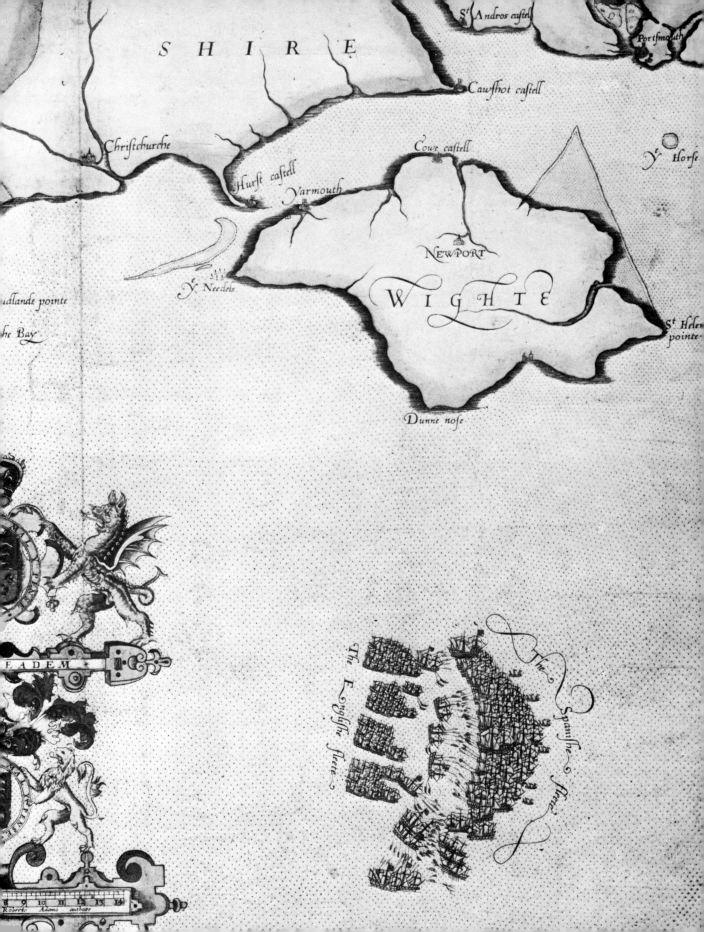

S H I R E

St Andros castell

Portsmouth

Cawshot castell

Christchurche

Hurst castell

Yarmouth

Cowe castell

Yͤ Horse

Newport

Yͤ Needels

WIGHTE

St Helen pointe

dlande pointe

he Bay

Dunne nose

EADEM

The Englishe flete

The Spanishe flete

9 10 11 12 13 14
Roberto Adamo author

HERUS Eq auratus MARTINUS BOLI

42

Another of his many duties was to give credit where it was due, for reasons of justice as well as good morale. On 26 July, within sight of the great becalmed Armada, Howard knighted Frobisher and Hawkins and four others.

All the way from Corunna, the wind had dictated the fortunes and misfortunes of the Armada. Its influence continued, as powerfully as ever, after Gravelines, when the damaged but still formidable Armada was swept up into the North Sea, and Howard began his long pursuit. He could do little more. His fleet was now out of ammunition. So was Sidonia's. Neither side knew it, but both were equally helpless to commit any further damage to the other at sea.

It was not until they were off the Scottish coast on 2 August, with the wind blowing strongly from the north-west now, that Howard decided that there was no longer any danger of the Armada reversing its course and renewing its threat to England. Now at last he could safely leave it to go to its fate.

It was a long time before he, or anyone else, learned how fearful its fate had been. Howard, like his commanders and his men, was a bitterly disappointed man. Even after Gravelines, he was unaware of how much damage the fleet had done to the Armada; and he could not know how savage nature was to be to the enemy as the sails faded into the mists of the North Sea. Howard knew that the immediate threat of invasion had been ended. But after the expenditure of so much ammunition, after the long pursuit, after the demonstration of so much courage and tenacity, there was little enough reward. And there was no doubt that the Spaniards would be back, in greater strength and with the measure of the English this time.

It was very much the same during the closing stages of another critical attempt to defeat this island, in 1940, when the airmen who fought off the Luftwaffe felt no sense of triumph that they were saving the nation and making history; only that they were tired and the enemy's strength seemed limitless. But at least those who fought in 1940 received their just reward. It was harder in 1588 when the men who had fought so valiantly and returned so hungry and disease-ridden were offered neither acknowledgement nor food nor money, and many were left to die in the streets of the ports to which their ships returned.

Howard and Drake did what they could to help. Howard spent a great deal of his own money paying the men their due in face of his ungrateful and parsimonious sovereign's failure to do so. Three days after his return, he was writing passionately to Burghley, 'Sickness and mortality begins wonderfully to grow amongst us; and it is a most pitiful sight to see, here at Margate, how the men, having no place to receive them into here, die in the streets.' There is a practical as well as a compassionate note in a later communication to the Queen's secretary of state:

OPPOSITE Martin Frobisher, stalwart sea-dog, knighted by Howard in the midst of the Armada operations.

43

It was too pitiful to have men starve after such a service. . . . Therefore I had rather open the Queen Majesty's purse something to relieve them, than they should be in that extremity for we are to look to have more of their services; and if men should not be cared for better than to let them starve and die miserably, we should be hardly get men to serve.[8]

Amongst the hierarchy there was concern only for another sickness, and the failure of Howard and his men to cure it: 'So our half-doing', wrote Walsingham, 'doth breed dishonour and leaves the disease uncured.'

As at Jutland in 1916, Howard could not know that the outcome of the apparently indecisive engagement was, negatively at least, a triumph: Spain never tried again.

When the news filtered through that northern gales and the wicked coasts of Ireland had completed the job Howard and his men had begun, there was rejoicing. But it remained subdued and cautious while the Duke of Parma still threatened from across the Channel. It had been a victory; but only history was to give it its proper recognition and stature.

Although in most accounts of the defeat of the Spanish Armada, Lord Howard is not given sufficient credit for the victory (Drake, as usual, stole the limelight), the year 1588 is properly regarded as the high point in his long life of service to the crown. But he remained lord admiral for many more years, and this was a troubled time for the nation and an active time for the navy. With the defeat of the Armada, the English were recognized as the premier fighters at sea, and naval mastery called for the exercise of skill and wisdom in this highest of appointments. Lord Charles Howard of Effingham never failed his country or the navy.

Sir Francis Drake
?1540–96

Drake nor devil nor Spaniard feared,
    Their cities he put to the sack;
He singed His Catholic Majesty's beard,
    And harried his ships to wrack.
He was playing at Plymouth a rubber of bowls
    When the great Armada came;
But he said, 'They must wait their turn, good souls,'
    And he stooped and finished the game.

Henry Newbolt (1862–1938)

What made this peppery, strutting, jaunty little Devonian the greatest seaman of his age? Greed, ambition, the satisfaction of leadership and the delight of the proletarian in overcoming the handicaps of his class, the need to excel, patriotism and love for his queen – all these factors were strongly influential. But the most powerful of all was the sustained anger of religious zeal, for which the fate of his father provided the combustive force.

Francis Drake was one of 12 children born to Edmund Drake and his wife, who were modest yeoman farmers at Crowndale near Tavistock in Devonshire. As a young boy he witnessed the persecution of his father for his strong Protestant beliefs, and at length the entire family was driven from its home.

The humiliation and suffering of a loved father is something a passionate boy never forgets; nor will he ever forgive those responsible. The family settled briefly at Gillingham in Kent, living in the hulk of an old ship. His father became a lay preacher to the men working at Chatham dockyard, but he could not for long escape the storm of conflict between the Protestant forces of Reformation and the Catholic forces of counter-Reformation during the reign of Catholic Mary. Edmund Drake lost his precarious job and his hulk and was lucky not to lose his head.

Francis was about thirteen (no one knows for sure when he was born) when Queen Elizabeth I came to the throne, and slowly and painfully civil and religious stability were restored to the nation. He became an apprentice seaman. Like most Devonians, the Drakes had connections with the sea. His father had briefly been a sailor as a young man and the family was connected with the seafaring family of Hawkins. Francis served for some years on Thames coastal craft, acquiring experience in the difficult waters of the North Sea and Channel. In 1567, after an earlier and uneventful crossing of the Atlantic, he was invited by his relation John Hawkins to join him on a slave-trading voyage with four ships from Plymouth.

Drake was born at the right time, with the right fervour and enterprise,

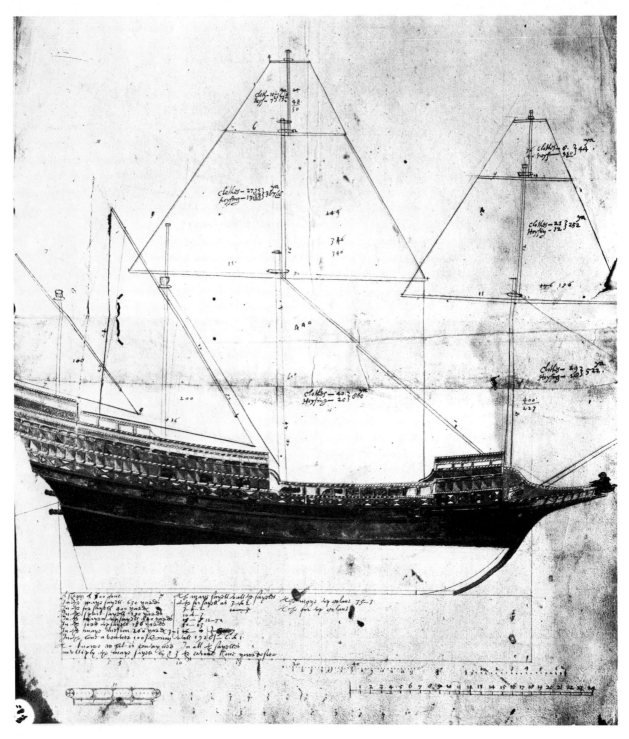

English galleon at the time of the Armada. Drawing from the Pepysian Library, probably by master shipwright Matthew Baker.

the right skill and pertinacity, to achieve fulfilment in the Elizabethan renaissance. The outcome of this disastrous voyage, during which Hawkins was sneakily outwitted and defeated by the Spaniards, hardened the resolve of the young man. Many of Drake's shipmates met horrible deaths at the hands of the inquisition. The fire of anger and hatred of all Catholics, and of Spanish Catholics in particular, first ignited at a tender age, had risen to a white heat by the time Drake was a mature young man.

Drake's powers of leadership and seamanship were rapidly recognized at a time when resolute commanders were in demand by enterprising merchants, backed by the high-risk money of courtiers and noblemen, in search of new trading markets. Syndicates were formed by shareholders eager to gamble on the outcome of a professional seaman's voyage. Nor were these promoters in the least particular about the legality of the business. It required nerve and self-confidence in the promoters as well as in the captain and his crew who ventured into waters that were unknown or mainly hostile. It was just this risk-taking, invigorating spirit that created the nation's golden age in Elizabeth's reign.

Many fortunes were lost in sponsoring the Elizabethan trading-exploring corsair expeditions. But, as always, success bred success, and Drake was soon attracting the cream of bold Devon seamen and the promotion money of syndicates alike. On his return from one of his most intrepid and rewarding voyages to the Caribbean in 1573 he reported that he had seen the Spanish treasure fleet homeward bound out of Nombre de Dios – a heady sight for any corsair – and glimpsed Magellan's *Mar Pacifico* from the top of a tree high on the spine of the Panama isthmus; and had 'besought Almighty God of his goodness to give me life and leave to sail once in an English ship in that sea'.

Several years were to pass before Drake's prayer was answered. The voyage that was to take him to this ocean called for immensely complicated and devious preparation. A courtier named Thomas Doughty, whom later Drake was to hang for mutinous conduct, was chiefly instrumental in getting authority for the voyage and for effecting for Drake an audience with the queen.

Queen Elizabeth was an ardent admirer of her loyal, aggressive little captain, and spoke to him of her 'divers injuries of the King of Spain, for which she desired to have some revenge'. At the same time, for reasons of domestic as well as foreign diplomacy, she did not wish her support (let alone the extent of her personal investment) for the voyage to be known – even to her closest ministers. And, she added cheerfully, she would execute anyone who passed the news on to the Spanish king.

Drake's voyage to the Pacific, and his subsequent circumnavigation of the world, is one of the great maritime achievements of all time – greater in many ways than Magellan's circumnavigation 50 years earlier, because Drake survived the voyage and came back a rich and famous man and

THE Famous West Indian voyadge made
by the Englishe fleete of 23 shippes and Barkes
wherin weare gotten the Townes of S. IAGO:
S. DOMINGO, CARTAGENA and
S. AVGVSTINES the same beinge begon
from Plimmouth in the Moneth of September
1585 and ended at Portesmouth in Iulie
1586 the wholecourse of the saide Viadge
beinge plainlie described by the pricked line
Newlie come forth by Baptista B.

Hochelaga Canada

Norumbega

Virginia

Florida

Augustine

Baye of Mexico

Iamaica   Hispaniola Ilande   S. Iohns

S. Domingo

Cartagena

WEST INDIA

Scale of 300 Leauges

The Occean commonlie called
the South Sea

Panama

Lima

The Cuntrey of Peru

North

Sea Cannye

Some times 15 Degrees to the Southwarde or P 10 d
Plus for the Searuce of Magellanus

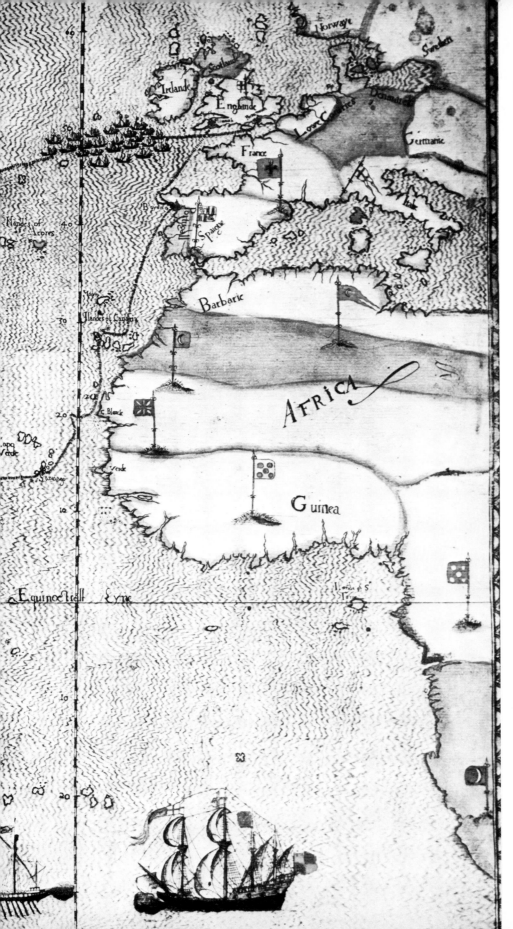

Drake's voyage to the
West Indies, 1585–6.

achieved immense advantage for his nation and religion and did commensurate damage to the nation's enemies.

In terms of navigation without charts and with only the most primitive of navigational aids (no means of telling the longitude); of victualling for months at a period when little or nothing was known of preservatives and dietetics; of frustrating the enemy at sea and on shore, and keeping mutiny at bay in his own ships – in all these respects and many more, Drake's voyage from November 1577 to September 1580 was a *tour de force*. His plundering of the Spanish South American colonies, his capture of treasure at sea, brought, it was said, sufficient profit to the expedition to pay for the fitting out of the English fleet to oppose the Armada eight years later. For every guinea (including the queen's one thousand guineas) invested in the expedition, the profit was a multiplication of 47. From this time Drake was known to the Spanish as *El Draque*, the dragon; and his effect on the morale of Spanish and Portuguese sailors is incalculable.

And what of the last lines of the Newbolt tribute at the head of this chapter? With the defeat of the Armada in 1588 there were born numerous legends. Drake was a romantic who achieved greatness in a romantic age and was his own best publicity agent. There is no reason why he should not have been playing bowls. If the story is a total fabrication, he would be the last to deny it. He is known to have been ashore at the time and he enjoyed 'a rubber of bowls'. If he felt a sense of urgency he was the last person to reveal it publicly – and no doubt he had a large audience, before whom he would enjoy this opportunity of showing his self-confidence by a gesture of bravado.

Frobisher was the only man to question Drake's conduct during the Armada action. This bold Yorkshireman's squabble with Drake went back over many years of corsair work together or in competition. On the night of 22 July, close to Berry Head, Drake led the fleet and guided it by a single stern lantern. Suddenly this was extinguished, and widespread confusion resulted.

It was not until later the next day, with the Armada making valuable and unimpeded headway, that Drake rejoined Howard. He had, he said, seen sails in the night, passing down-Channel. Judging them to be Spanish and fearing they would get the weather gage on them, he had set off in pursuit, extinguishing his lantern in order to conceal his course from the Spanish look-outs on the one hand and the English on the other, who would otherwise follow him instead of pursuing the main body of the enemy.

He later discovered that the sails were harmless merchantmen; he also, by happy chance, discovered a partly crippled Spanish galleon – a flagship no less, which he proceeded to capture without combat and to his great financial benefit. It was Drake's luck again. You could not call it anything else, unless your name was Martin Frobisher. You certainly could not say that Drake had his eye on the main chance, not at this critical juncture. Later, off Calais,

'... "They must wait
their turn, good souls,"
/And he stooped and
finished the game.'
Drake on Plymouth
Hoe. The Armada has
been sighted and the
alarm signal is being
made.

RIGHT Sir John
Hawkins at 44.

OPPOSITE Turkish
galley at Lepanto.

OVERLEAF
LEFT The launching of
the fireships against the
Armada.

ABOVE Philip II of
Spain in his St Quentin
armour.

BELOW Miniature of
Drake by Nicholas
Hilliard.

he did not give the stranded and treasure-laden galleass a passing glance; instead, he was the first to throw his *Revenge* against the main body of the enemy fleet.

Drake would have done better to die at the height of his greatness and glory, like Nelson. He lost favour with the queen after the Lisbon disaster and became, of all things, a politician and committee man. King Philip had learned his lesson, rebuilt his fleet, instituted convoys, and turned on the offensive by raiding and burning Cornish seaports.

On 28 August 1595, with the queen's delayed and reluctant approval, Drake sailed on what proved to be his last voyage, sharing the command

with his veteran cousin, Sir John Hawkins. Like their first voyage together, it was a disaster. Ports that had once been ripe for the picking were now heavily fortified. Drake missed a treasure fleet by hours – his luck had fled with the Spanish ships. Some of his best friends were killed in futile attacks. Sick at his failure but still defiantly crying, 'We must have gold ere we see England again,' the little captain was seized with dysentery, which had already killed old Hawkins. He died in his cabin on 28 January 1596.

The glory of the Drake legend has endured, through Newbolt (who is quoted further below) almost to modern times. But a recent history of British naval power, by a young university historian anxious to make his mark, tells us only that Francis Drake and his fellow sea-dogs quickly gained an unenviable reputation for their brutality, greed and willingness to rob anyone. *O tempora! O mores!*

> Drake he was a Devon man, an' ruled the Devon seas,
>   (Capten, art tha sleepin' there below?),
> Rovin' tho' his death fell, he went wi' heart at ease,
>   An' dreamin' arl the time o' Plymouth Hoe,
> 'Take my drum to England, hang et by the shore,
>   Strike et when your powder's runnin' low;
> If the Dons sight Devon, I'll quit the port o' Heaven,
>   An' drum them up the Channel as we drummed them long ago.'

OPPOSITE Dutch ships painted by van der Velde.

2
The Fire and
the Broom

Admiral Maarten Harpertszoom Tromp
1597–1653

Maarten Tromp.

We met fifteen ships and frigates of the Parliament, among which was an Admiral's, which I intended to speak with, taking in all my sails except both my topsails, which we lowered to the middle of the mast. As soon as we were within cannon-shot he shot a ball over our ship. We answered not. He shot another, to which we answered with one. At once he gives me a broadside, being within musket-shot, and shot all his broadsides through our ship and sails. Some of our men were wounded, some with the loss of their arms, some otherwise; whereupon we presently gave him our broadside. . . .

Tromp on the Battle of Dover, 1652

The rise of the Dutch navy followed closely on that of the English navy and it defeated the Spaniards at sea even more soundly and decisively than Lord Howard had done. It was therefore appropriate that Holland's greatest admiral, Maarten Tromp, was born in the year following the death of Francis Drake.

Like Drake, Maarten Tromp fought with the memory of his father's fate close to his heart. Maarten's father was a ship's captain, who had taken his son to sea at an early age, a common practice among the Dutch. When Maarten was still only twelve, his father's ship had fallen prey to an English pirate in the Mediterranean. In the action that followed, the father was killed, and Maarten was forced into slavery as a cabin boy. Two years passed before he could escape back to Holland. He subsequently joined the naval service, rose rapidly in rank, and at the age of twenty-seven was in command of a frigate.

Like Drake again, the hour and the man coincided. In the same year that Drake cast his eyes for the first time upon the Pacific Ocean, the hardy, audacious Dutch were enjoying their first major success against the Spanish off the Zuider Zee, and their long struggle with their Spanish overlords gained renewed encouragement from the success of Drake and his fellow commanders against the Spanish Armada in 1588. The achievement of the Dutch in holding off the might of Catholic Spain at sea and on land, while building themselves up as the greatest trading nation, was as remarkable as the creation of any empire. The accomplishment was all the greater because it was based on maritime power, for the Dutch had an unfavourable coastline, no natural resources for shipbuilding (timber had to be brought in from Scandinavia), a population of less than a million and, like Germany later, a disadvantageous geographical position.

The Venetians and Portuguese had long before learned the price Europeans were prepared to pay for the riches of the East – the cloves, the pepper

PREVIOUS PAGES Dutch galleons at the time of the wars with England.

and nutmeg, the frankincense and indigo, camphor and mace and opium, to make dull diets palatable, to overcome foul odours with sweet scents, and to relieve pain. These all cost little on one side of the world and could be sold at vast profits on the other side.

Like the Portuguese before them, the Dutch traders obtained concessions, built trading posts and claimed monopolies in the consumable treasures of the East with the zeal and sometimes the ruthlessness practised by the Spanish in the West in their acquisition of precious minerals. Their laden trading vessels soon became the target for pirates, privateers and corsairs. The Dutch navy was created from the need to protect this trade, especially against the Spanish and Portuguese, who were as bitterly opposed to seeing the Dutch grow rich and powerful as they were to their rebellious Protestantism.

Between the Dutch and the Spanish it was the usual struggle for power and commerce, inflamed by sharp religious division. But the decay of the Spanish empire, dating from even before 1588, was biting even deeper. The English had shown that the Spanish were not unconquerable at sea. The Dutch confirmed it by their defeat of a Catholic fleet at Gibraltar in 1607. Ship-to-ship actions usually resulted in a Dutch victory.

During these years of maritime conflict, Tromp was gaining in experience and stature. His powers of attracting the loyalty of the common seamen were in the Drake class, and he had the same swashbuckling self-confidence as the Englishman.

Fresh vigour was meanwhile given to the Dutch cause by the capture by Piet Hein of the Spanish silver fleet off Cuba in 1628, a success in the best tradition of Cavendish, Frobisher, Grenville and others, which also enriched the Dutch to the tune of fifteen million florins.

By 1639, at the time of his first great fleet action, Tromp had been pro-moted c-in-c ('lieutenant-admiral') of the Dutch fleet. He introduced a new offensive spirit which resulted in the total destruction of a Spanish squadron off Gravelines. Next, he saucily blockaded Dunkerque, the chief Spanish-held port for the war of attrition against the Dutch rebels. King Philip IV of Spain was forced to prepare hastily an armada on the scale of the 1588 Enterprise, complete with 24,000 soldiers in 50 transports, a number of them hired English ships, all under the command of Admiral d'Oquendo in the *Santiago*.

The pattern of disaster for the Spanish fleet was only marginally less catastrophic than that of half a century earlier. Tromp kept himself well informed of the progress of the Armada by means of reconnoitring vessels, and off Selsey Bill swept down fearlessly upon d'Orquendo with a mere 18 men-of-war, making for the Spanish flagship. There was a brisk action in which the Dutch did so much damage to the Spanish fleet that d'Orquendo put himself at the mercy of the English and sought refuge off Dover, close to an English naval squadron under the command of Sir John Pennington.

With Tromp hovering close by, now with his fleet reinforced, Pennington

Battle of the Downs,
21 October 1639. For
once the English
just watched.

ordered the Spanish soldiers out of the English ships, a dangerous and
possibly diplomatically compromising act – but Pennington was a Dutch
sympathizer and had once fought alongside Tromp against the Spanish. This
was not approved of by King Charles I's pro-Spanish court, an indication of
the confusion of loyalties that religious and commercial conflict brought
about at this time.

Tromp now proceeded to blockade the Dover roadstead instead of Dunkerque, and sent messages back home for further reinforcements if the states
wanted a decisive victory. Meanwhile, he teased d'Orquendo mercilessly,
at one time offering him 500 barrels of gunpowder in case shortage of
ammunition was the reason for his failure to meet the challenge of combat.

Tromp's patience was the first to break. On 21 October 1639, he ordered
his fleet to attack, regardless of losses and diplomatic complications. The
Battle of the Downs, as it came to be called, was an overwhelming Dutch
victory. Tromp, suddenly a hero of Spain's enemies, was disappointed only
at his failure to destroy d'Orquendo's flagship, which escaped in mist, and
to capture the admiral. The *Santiago* got into Dunkerque and later slunk
home to Spain, like the *San Martin* after the 1588 disaster.

Ascendancy over the Spanish at sea, more than any other factor, led to the
peace of Westphalia in 1648 in which Spain at last acknowledged the

independence of the United Provinces – the Netherlands – and the validity of Dutch conquests in the Far East.

In spite of their common religion, and in many respects common temperament, the Dutch and the English were certain to clash in their competitive interests. Physical clashes were limited for some years to ship-to-ship fighting in faraway places, mostly in the East where the Dutch brooked no interference with their monopolies. English traders became incensed that they had increasingly to rely on Dutch ships to carry their cargoes. Dutch herring fleets cast their nets without authority close to the English shore. For their part, the Dutch were always conscious that because of their geographical position, the English with a superior navy could literally cut off their trade: the English demand that acknowledgement must be made to their sovereignty of the seas by 'dipping the flag', and insistence on the right to search neutral ships for contraband in time of war, added a further bitter taste to the slight.

The last provocation that eventually led to hostilities was the English Navigation Act of 1651 in which it was decreed that imports into England from Asia, Africa and America must all be carried in English ships, and that imports from Europe must be carried only by English ships or ships belonging to the nation that produced the goods. This virtually signed the death warrant to the large and immensely profitable Dutch carrying trade. It was clear by the end of 1651 that both sides were spoiling for a fight and the First Dutch War really began on 12 May 1652 when a Dutch admiral, escorting a convoy of merchantmen up-Channel, refused to dip his flag to an English naval captain when challenged. An exchange of shots ('I do believe I gave him his bellyful of it,' remarked the English captain cheerfully) led to Dutch compliance.

Word of this action soon reached Tromp who was cruising further up-Channel in his flagship *Brederode*, 54 (guns), with 40 men-of-war as a covering force against any English belligerence. He had already faced a delicate situation when forced by the weather into the roadstead off Dover. A gun on Dover Castle fired several shots to remind the Dutch admiral of the need to strike his flag, and Tromp felt justified in ignoring it.

The English commander, Robert Blake, flying his flag in the *James*, 48, with 11 men-of-war, was beating against a north-easterly off Folkestone. He had already received warning of likely trouble and was cleared for action when he caught sight of Tromp's 40 or more sail bearing down fast upon him from the east.

After the battle, both commanders liked to convince themselves and their governments that the other had provoked the action and fired first (see the quotation at the beginning of this chapter). Tromp and several of his ships at once closed on and surrounded the English flagship, giving it a severe battering, killing the master and some 50 of his men, before the other English ships could come to the aid of the flag.

ABOVE English galleon, Dutch Wars period.

RIGHT The Three Days' Battle between the veteran antagonists (and personal friends) Maarten Tromp and Robert Blake in February 1653. Blake was badly wounded and lost three ships.

Tromp was not only highly experienced as a result of his old battles with the Spaniards, and imbued with self-confidence: he greatly outnumbered the English and had the advantage of the wind while the English ships were close-hauled against it. But he soon discovered that he was up against a different calibre of foe from the Spaniards. The English fought fiercely and their gunners had not lost the superiority they had acquired 80 or so years earlier. As they fell, Tromp saw that their places were taken by others, often by fishermen who put out from nearby harbours to give support to their countrymen. Later in the afternoon, a further squadron of English ships joined the battle, and although still outnumbering the enemy, Tromp was thankful to haul to the wind and withdraw to the Flemish coast. The Battle of Dover, as it came to be known, was indecisive. But there could be no doubt that Tromp had suffered more heavily, with the loss of two ships, than the English under Blake.

An official declaration of war followed some half-hearted attempts to find a diplomatic solution to the quarrel between the two northern nations. The English at once went over to the offensive, clearing the valuable Dutch herring fleets from her shores and cutting off not only Dutch trade up the Channel, but also with the Baltic. Nothing went right for Tromp. An attack on an English squadron off Deal was beaten off, and an offensive expedition against Blake in the North Sea met fierce gales which broke it up and scattered it. The Dutch admiral returned to find himself in disgrace. He resigned his command and disappeared from public view.

However, the sea war with England went from bad to worse under his successors, and the states were thankful to turn back to their veteran hero in October 1652. The Dutch lived by trade and the tourniquet of the English blockade was bankrupting the great trading houses. Tromp was ordered to prepare a great convoy, to be protected by an overwhelming number of men-of-war, to break through the English Channel squadrons and at the same time damage them as savagely as possible.

Before talking about numbers – and the naval escort alone was to number about 80 ships – it is right to talk about size, especially by contrast with English fighting ships. The Dutch built smaller than the English. They had to because of the numerous shoals and sandbanks off their coast and the shallowness of their harbours. Their ships were therefore limited to two gun-decks by contrast with the bigger English warships' three gun-decks, right up to the famous *Sovereign of the Seas*, a three-decker of prodigious size – 1637 tons displacement – which lived up to her name for 60 years.

Like the English galleons at the Armada battle, the Dutch fighting ships were fast and manoeuvrable. But by contrast, and in spite of the English example, Dutch naval thinking still did not put first emphasis on the gun instead of the boarding party. This offset the advantage of the speed and nippiness of their well-designed ships with their excellent rig and straight sides instead of the heavy tumble-home of English men-of-war.

In fact, the two antagonists were very evenly matched in *matériel* as well as fighting quality. Both Tromp and Blake, however, suffered from internal dissension, the Dutchman because of rivalry and jealousy between the five states, the English commander because of strife between solid Commonwealth loyalists like himself and those with active Royalist sympathies.

Tromp sailed with his fleet, numbering about 400 sail in all, on 24 November 1652. This vast armada was spotted from the church tower at Margate before contrary winds sent it back to shelter. At the next opportunity, Tromp sailed without the merchantmen. He had learned of the weakness in numbers of his enemy, and had decided on a purely offensive action in the hope of destroying Blake once and for all.

In a bloody four-hour mêlée off Dungeness on 30 November, with much hand-to-hand fighting in which Tromp played a full part, his secretary dying at his side, the Dutch won a clear victory, as they should have done with a two to one advantage, and several English ships with Royalist captains keeping clear of trouble. Blake was right to offer his resignation (which was smartly rejected by Cromwell), and Tromp right to claim success, justifying the legend – or truth? – of his sailing with a broom at his masthead.

But Tromp had not swept the seas clear of the English navy. He had merely destroyed or captured a handful of ships, and although he got his convoy through safely, it was clear that he had gained no clear advantage, and the English were as fighting-fit as ever.

Eleven weeks later, on 18 February 1653, the two commanders (who, incidentally, both liked and admired one another) clashed again in the Channel in a ding-dong contest which lasted off and on for three days. This time the odds in numbers were more even. Blake was badly wounded early on, and three English ships were captured, but the tide of battle slowly turned to the English advantage.

Tromp fought his last and indecisive actions of 1653 against other English commanders, Blake being too sick to go to sea. But he could not break the English fleets, and sustained heavier losses than the enemy in attempting to do so.

At last, on 31 July 1653, in action off Scheveningen, Maarten Tromp was killed on his quarter-deck by a musket ball in the chest, just as Nelson was to die at Trafalgar, but with the sombre difference that Tromp's death signalled defeat.

General-at-Sea Robert Blake
1598–1657

Thy name was heard in thunder through th'affrighted shores of pale
Iberia, of submissive Gaul, and Tagus trembling to his utmost source,
O ever faithful, vigilant, and brave, thou bold asserter of Britannia's
fame, unconquerable Blake
Legend printed beneath the contemporary portrait opposite

Arise or decline in maritime power has always reflected the spirit
and prosperity of European nations. Spain ran through the full
cycle in the sixteenth and early seventeenth centuries, from the
great voyages and great conquests to the failure of the Enterprise,
the surrender of the Netherlands and the loss of Portugal. England's decline
and Dutch growth in power coincided at the beginning of the 1600s. During
Robert Blake's childhood, James I allowed Elizabeth's proud navy to rot, and
with the Spanish treaty of 1604 in effect gave way all that 'the sea-dogs of
the Golden Age' had striven and died for. But by the time of Blake's death,
59 years later, a modern permanent navy had been created, and England's
maritime influence was greater than ever. Robert Blake, more than any
other single officer, was responsible for this renaissance.

Like Drake, Blake was of West Country stock, and was the first born of
12 children. Apart from their courage and skill and qualities of leadership,
the two admirals had nothing else in common. Blake was a paragon of
sobriety, self-discipline and modesty in all things – the very incarnation of
the Puritan. He came from more affluent and elevated stock than Drake. His
father inherited a prosperous shipping business in Bridgwater, Somerset,
and married a well-off widow. Robert grew up close to the sea and within
sound of shipwrights at work and of the loading and unloading of merchantmen. He was educated at a good grammar school and at Wadham College,
Oxford, taking his BA in 1618. He had grown into an impressive looking
young man, rather short in stature, with a broad brow, clever dark eyes and
a firm mouth. His features were described as heavy.

With the death of his father in 1625, Blake took over the family responsibilities and business. Little is known of him at this time; nor was he the sort
of man about whom legends flourished. He certainly would have gone to
sea in his own ships, and no doubt travelled widely and met many people –
including Maarten Tromp.

Like so many of his generation, Blake was brought into heroic promin-
ence by the Civil War of 1642. There had been early evidence in him of
anti-monarchism and now, in middle age, he threw himself enthusiastically behind the parliamentary cause. His most notable skill, which
improved with experience, was at withstanding siege: first at Bristol, where

Although he lacked Nelson's fire and flamboyance, many people regard Robert Blake as 'the Hero's' equal. He had no greater admirer than Nelson himself.

Typical close
engagement in the
Anglo–Dutch wars.

he served under Popham, then at Lyme against Prince Maurice, and finally at Taunton, where he held out for nearly a year against fearsome odds. Blake became Cromwell's most besieged officer, as well as one of his most notable colonels.

In 1649 Blake, Edward Popham and Richard Deane were appointed jointly by the Council of State as commissioners to lead a naval administration, and 'to oppose and suppress whoever maintains the title of Charles Stuart, eldest son of the late King, or any of his issue claiming a title to the Crown'. Their first problem was to renovate, repair and make ready for sea a naval squadron, to victual it and man it with reliable officers and seamen. Then they were to hunt down and destroy Prince Rupert's powerful naval force.

Typically, Blake was surprised and flattered by the appointment, which was, he said, 'extremely beyond my expectations as well as my merits'. However, his merits proved equal to his new responsibilities, and during the summer of 1649 he proved himself as successful a blockader at sea as he had shown himself capable of withstanding blockades on land. Blockade work demanded qualities as important as those required by an admiral in combat. They included patience, the power to instil and sustain enthusiasm in his officers and men, and seamanship at a high level.

Prince Rupert was in Kinsale harbour, in Ireland, with his force, and while Cromwell went about his ugly work on land, Blake frustrated all Rupert's efforts to escape. It was not until November storms made the waters off Kinsale untenable that Blake withdrew under orders, and Rupert got away at last, holing up 800 miles to the south, in the Tagus off Lisbon.

The Council of State countered this move by ordering Blake to prepare another squadron for sea to renew the blockade. He was on his station by late February 1650, 'to pursue, seize, scatter or destroy all ships of the revolted fleet, and all other adhering to them'. One year later, on Blake's return to England, Rupert was still at large, but the squadron he had commanded had been pursued and scattered, and largely destroyed, in a series of minor actions following blind-man's-bluff pursuits from the mouth of the Tagus to far into the Mediterranean. There had been no stirring, annihilating fleet action; but guile, anticipation, patience and tact in dealing with Spanish, French and Portuguese weaknesses and susceptibilities had reduced Rupert to a naval vagabond wandering purposelessly about the Mediterranean.

On 13 February 1651, parliament voted Blake a testimony of gratitude, and £1000, 'upon a relation made by General Blake of the safe arrival of that part of the Parliament fleet which is under his command, and of the wonderful appearance of the powerful hand of God with him in his services at sea'.

After further successful action in the Scilly Isles and the island of Jersey, Blake was done with fighting his fellow countrymen. Within a few weeks of his contests with the Stuarts, he had to face more formidable antagonists in the Dutch admirals.

Blake and his men in
close combat at Tunis,
making 'them feel us as
enemies'. He succeeded
in releasing the Dey's
English prisoners.

Blake has always been most noted for his actions against Tromp and the
attack on Santa Cruz, Tenerife, in the year of his death. Although not always
successful in the Dutch war at sea, he certainly had the advantage over his
friend and antagonist. The wound he received in the Three Days' Battle
never seriously threatened his life; the fever it brought on certainly did. He
was fifty-four and had always enjoyed excellent health. But the illness, which
kept him an invalid until May 1653, weakened him and may have
accelerated his end.

However, Blake very nearly had a last crack at Tromp. Early in June he
was fitting out a squadron of 18 men-of-war in the Thames when he heard
that Tromp was at sea again and likely to be engaged by Deane and Monk.

By the time he joined the main fleet, Deane had been killed, but Tromp had got the worst of the engagement and was in full retreat. Blake joined the pursuit, but failed to exchange shots again with his old antagonist, who died in action eight weeks later.

After this, Blake was given shore appointments until his health had improved enough for him to go to sea again. His work was varied and important during the critical last months of the First Dutch War. Although there were many officers who had longer experience of the sea, none had fought so hard and successfully, and he was regarded as an unsurpassed organizer and administrator. He was widely accepted as the leader of the navy at a time when there was no formal post to denote supreme rank. He was made a commissioner of the navy and a commissioner 'for purging the Church of ignorant, scandalous, and inefficient ministers',[1] though he probably gave most of his attention to the first and treated his cleansing work, and also his membership of the Little Parliament, as nominal only.

For the next three years, with only brief breaks, Blake was continuously at sea, at first in the Channel, where he was engaged on enforcement of the Navigation Act which had precipitated the Dutch War, and destroying the privateers from Dunkerque and St Malo who made life such a misery for English merchant sailors.

At the end of September 1654 he sailed to the Mediterranean with a powerful force of 20 fighting ships. His instructions were of a general nature. Negatively, he was not to act in an unfriendly manner towards Spain, not yet – not until another and totally aggressive expedition despatched to the West Indies had completed their operations satisfactorily. He was to take whatever reprisals he considered suitable against the French, deal with the African pirates, protect English trade, and generally show the flag.

The expedition was conducted with complete success. In military terms, Blake showed himself as firm, dexterous and courageous a leader as he had in the Channel. One of his tasks was to secure the release of the numerous English slaves held in Tunis by the Dey of Algiers, and ensure that the corsairs ceased their piratical practices. When Blake's considerable diplomatic prowess failed, he resorted to violence, or, as he put it in a letter to Cromwell, 'Their barbarous provocations did so work upon our spirits that we judged it necessary for the honour of the fleet, our nation, and religion, seeing they would not deal with us as friends, to make them feel us as enemies.'

On 4 April 1655 the squadron sailed into the strongly defended harbour and engaged the forts at musket range, shattering them and toppling the guns. Then boarding parties dealt with the Dey's nine men-of-war in the harbour, driving off the crews in fierce hand-to-hand fighting and setting fire to the lot. After that, Blake went back to diplomacy, from a stronger stance, and secured the release of the Englishmen without difficulty.

Blake had broken all the rules. It was everywhere accepted that it was suicidal for warships to attack strongly manned fortifications. Tunis proved this to be false. But Blake's Mediterranean cruising in those early months of 1655 proved more and has been judged one of the most important operations in English naval history, for this reason: as a result of the show of strength before the Mediterranean nations, following the defeat of the Dutch fleet in home waters, the English navy gave warning to the world that English trade was not to be interfered with. As one historian has put it,

In 1655 the navy came to its majority. It passed from being the protector of the shores of England, and the force which could carry out an isolated enterprise, into the permanent armed chivalry of the sea always at hand to protect all those who go upon the sea on their lawful occasions, and the untiring enemy of the enemies of mankind.[2]

Blake's expedition did more than that. It established his country's naval presence and paramountcy in the Mediterranean, which, while often in danger and sometimes briefly broken, endured until the massive new naval strength of the United States and Soviet Russia superseded it in 1945.

The complexity of Blake's duties, which extended to delicate negotiations with the Vatican, with the French and Spanish, the Sardinians, Italian princes, and others, to attacks on pirates and on shore fortifications – all this is wonderful enough. But, unlike the spoon-fed, telegraph-and-radio-guided, and finally computerized commanders of the twentieth century, Blake was acting entirely *on his own initiative*.

From these operations in the Mediterranean, Blake was despatched directly to blockade Cadiz – work which lasted with scarcely a break for more than two years and required cruising, summer and winter, in all weathers. It was as original and prodigious an accomplishment as the more violent duties he had performed in the Mediterranean, requiring constant vigilance, constant attention to the victuals, morale and fighting fitness of his officers and men.

For a man who, in seventeenth-century terms, was in late middle age, whose wound and sickness had so weakened him in the Dutch War, and who had suffered the rigours of command at sea for so long, the strain of shipboard life as admiral commanding this force was immense. The diet could not have helped either. There was no understanding of scurvy – nor was there to be for a century or more – and many of his men succumbed to it. In the early spring of 1657, when news reached him that 16 Spanish treasure ships were off Santa Cruz, Tenerife, in the Canary Islands, Blake was in much worse physical shape than he had been on his appointment to his command. But his vigour and resolution had not lessened by one iota.

The governor of Tenerife was Don Diego Diagues. He was conscious of his responsibility for the Spanish treasure in his temporary charge, knew well of the hovering presence off Cadiz of Blake with his force; but he was not much concerned when intelligence reached him that Blake was on his way. Besides the powerful force of fighting ships he had in Santa Cruz, the fortifications into the narrow-mouthed bay were powerful and were generally considered to have made the port invulnerable.

A party of Dutch traders who knew better (and knew the English), replenishing supplies at the port, is said to have warned Diagues that Blake would attack, and received only a confident laugh in reply. The Dutchmen departed hastily. Diagues put the finishing touches to his defences, and awaited the sight of English sail from the north-east.

With the experience and confidence inspired by Tunis behind him, Blake sailed in with the wind and tide on 20 April. God, he knew, would have to be on his side. The high mountains covering the approach could becalm his squadron beneath the forts. Or, if the wind got up from the sea, he might never get out again on the tide.

Fortune did not favour the antichrists, as Blake's men regarded them. The breeze took the English ships steadily in, and they demolished the main fort at the entrance as they did so. Blake's vice-admiral tackled the six Spanish galleons, and after a brisk fight took all of them; meanwhile Blake himself steered for the treasure ships. These, too, were all taken with few casualties, assisted by the fact that the on-shore wind blew the smoke of battle on to the fortifications.

It was found impossible to work the treasure ships out of the harbour; and after a while the prize crews found it dangerous to remain on board. So orders were given to fire everything afloat. It was a tremendous Catholic conflagration, made more glorious to the eyes of the attackers by the new direction taken by the smoke. Neatly, as the tide had turned, so the wind changed with it, taking Blake's squadron out of Santa Cruz, past the battered forts, and into the open Atlantic. It had been the cheekiest blow against Spanish maritime power since Drake's attack on Cadiz in 1587.

Blake was exultant. But he knew that he was dying. He longed to see his beloved Somerset and his home at Bridgwater once more. He was not to be given this reward. Within sight of the coast off Plymouth, Robert Blake died in his flagship the *George* on 7 August 1657. He was buried with full honours in Westminster Abbey, but he was not to lie for long at peace. His country's internal dissension was not yet at an end, and with the restoration of the monarchy the body of the man who had fought so gallantly against it was removed from his honoured grave.

3
David and Goliath

King Gustavus III of Sweden
1746–92

It dismays me to see my poor nation so sunk in corruption as to have to rely upon anarchy.
King Gustavus on succeeding to the Swedish throne, 1771

Remote from the great struggles for maritime power in the Atlantic and Mediterranean, the English Channel and the North Sea, naval wars broke out intermittently in the Baltic Sea and its gulfs, mainly between Sweden and Russia, in the eighteenth century. They were wars conducted with special ferocity under distinctive conditions, like the Lake Campaign of the American War of Independence. Even galleys took a notable part in the fighting, 200 years after Lepanto had shown the hopeless weakness of the oared fighting ship in face of artillery fire. But the comparatively calm seas of the Baltic allowed the galley to exploit to the full its advantage of acceleration, speed and manoeuvrability, like the torpedo boat and torpedo bomber of the twentieth century.

The backbones of the Baltic fleets in the Swedish–Russian wars were, however, the three-masted ship-of-the-line and the frigate, and these fighting ships in no way lagged behind western design and constructional standards, for the good reason that they stemmed mainly from British inspiration. On the Swedish side, a Yorkshire family was largely responsible for shaping the Swedish navy which won the country's greatest naval battle at Svensksund in 1790.

Early in the eighteenth century, a shipwright named Chapman settled in Gothenburg, bringing with him many years of experience in his craft, which he gladly passed on to others in the shipbuilding business. His son and grandson pursued the same craft, greatly encouraged by the Swedish naval authorities. The grandson, Fredrik Henrik af Chapman, in order to keep abreast of western trends, sailed to England and openly toured the shipyards, taking notes and copying drawings, until he was at length arrested as a spy. On his release, he returned to Sweden in 1744, started a shipyard of his own, became chief naval architect and shipbuilder to the Swedish admiralty, and a member of its board. The fleet that King Gustavus III led into battle – he was the last sovereign to do so – was largely the work of the Chapman family.

The nature of Empress Catherine II's (the Great) battle fleet was also much influenced by another Englishman, Sir Samuel Bentham, who accepted Catherine's offer of a post as shipbuilding adviser, and remained in Russia for many years. Both fleets possessed ships in the line of battle commanded by English officers.

Gustavus III's comment on his accession to the throne, quoted at the head of this chapter, was fully justified. Sweden was rife with corruption, ruled

Fredrik af Chapman,
the British creator of
the eighteenth-century
Swedish navy.

for years by two mafia-like parties while the crown was the powerless symbol it is today. The nation, in its isolation from the rest of Europe, was under the thrall of the Russian empire.

Gustavus possessed exceptional qualities as a politician and manipulator, as well as determination to revive his country's quality and strength. He succeeded in toppling both factions of the nobility in August 1772, and set about the process of regeneration and reform. In a remarkably short time Sweden's commerce, agriculture and financial standing were all radically improved, along with the arts, of which he was an enthusiastic patron.

During these years, however, the powerful and corrupt nobility was seething with unrest and resentment. Gustavus countered the danger by taking upon himself stronger dictatorial powers. The war with Russia was entirely his own doing, provoked by him in the belief that Sweden was otherwise doomed to be swallowed up by Catherine's massive empire.

The Swedish armada sailed from Karlskrona at the end of April, determined to seek out Catherine's fleet and bring it to action. The engagement, when it occurred two weeks later, was inconclusive, but Gustavus succeeded in fighting his way into the harbour of Fredrikshamm where he captured a great number of Russian merchantmen and blew up the arsenal.

The next confrontation occurred in Viborg Bay four weeks later where Prince Carl, the king's brother, lay with his fleet off the port, which was now occupied by the Russians whose own fleet was stationed out to sea just beyond cannon range, an ever-threatening presence. On 3 July Prince Carl determined to escape from this trap and break out to the open sea. The battle at first went well for the Swede until one of his own fireships broke loose and collided with a ship-of-the-line, which in turn struck a frigate. By a stroke of bad luck, one of the ships caught fire and blew up, and the other two exploded almost instantly. The Russians took advantage of the confusion to press home their attack, which resulted in worse Swedish losses before Prince Carl got his survivors away to safety.

Gustavus had no reason to be pleased with the performance of his navy up to this time. But like so many commanders before and since, the king was to benefit by the folly of the enemy rather than by any clever manoeuvring of his own.

On 9 July 1790 Gustavus had his combined force of galleys and sailing ships in Svensksund Fjord, anchored behind a long line of low rocks, almost invulnerable to attack and advantageously positioned to counter-attack. There had been heavy fighting over the past days, during which the Swedes suffered greater losses than the enemy.

Gustavus had succeeded in reinforcing his fleet with new ships, so that the total Swedish strength was of some 300 men-of-war, including many small gunboats and transports. Command of a force consisting mainly of sailing ships was given to Prince Carl, while the king's own force was made up of the galleys and smaller vessels.

July 9 happened to be Empress Catherine's birthday. The Russian admiral was determined that she should have a present of a victory, and he should have the hoped-for benefits accruing from it. Ignoring the superior tactical position of the king, the Russians sailed in to the fjord.

Gustavus watched the advancing ships from his flagship with relish. In their eagerness to get at the foe, and with more than half an eye on the honours list at the end of this historic day, individual commanders struggled for the most advantageous position, creating a shambles. Instructing his commanders to hold their fire, the Russian ships-of-the-line and the frigates were in point-blank range when the Swedish ships opened fire. The destruction was fearful. Amid the 'cannon's opening roar' hundreds of Russians fell, and at the end of the bloodiest sea battle the Baltic has ever known nearly 10,000 of Catherine's sailors were dead or wounded, at the cost of some 300 Swedes.

Peace was declared at Varala on 14 August. In spite of the overwhelming Swedish victory at sea, the terms in no way specially favoured King Gustavus. All he had succeeded in doing was to postpone the loss of more of his territory.

To the end, Gustavus failed to winkle out completely the corrupting influence of the Swedish nobility. After his war with Russia, which had been so negative in its results, opposition to his autocracy was strengthened. Like Lincoln, he was assassinated at the opera.

King Gustavus's memorable achievement as an admiral, besides leading his men personally into battle, lay less in the victory at Svensksund than in the strength and high status which he gave to his country's navy.

The Battle of Svensksund, with King Gustavus's frigate in action in the foreground.

81

4
The Classic Years

Le Comte de Grasse
1722–88

The admiral who turned the tide at Yorktown

No doubt one reason why that Yorkshire shipwright, Chapman, had been glad to offer his services to the Swedish authorities was the reactionary attitude of the British towards ship design in the early years of the eighteenth century. What a contrast with the enterprise and exciting experiment of the first Elizabethan era!

The French navy was in little better shape at this time; in fact, looking back over French naval history, the periods when it has not been in decline are comparatively rare. One of them occurred at the same time as the struggle for independence of the American colonists, an historical coincidence which had profound consequences.

Cardinal Richelieu laid the foundations of the French sailing navy in the early seventeenth century. Then there was a long period of decline until Jean-Baptiste Colbert (1619–83) pulled it together again, benefiting from the fighting experience of the Dutch and English in their three wars (1652–4, 1665–7 and 1672–4). Decay set in once again after his regime, until a new renaissance was instigated by the great Duc de Choiseul, who was responsible for the admirable fleet that fought first for Louis XVI and then Napoleon Bonaparte. He was sacked in 1770, but by then his work was virtually complete: France had new fortifications, new bases, new ships and a new spirit of confidence to fight with. The French fought alongside the American revolutionaries and Spain, and against the British Royal Navy, from 1778 to 1805 with only brief lulls.

By contrast, the British navy was in one of its less frequent periods of decline. The splendid work of George Anson (1697–1762) had been dissipated by 1778, a year when – at least on paper – France could have dominated the seas about Britain and cut her vital trade routes. She did neither. But in the next three years her naval presence in the West Indies and on the American Atlantic seaboard was materially to influence the course of the American War of Independence and directly lead to the British surrender at Yorktown.

The Comte de Grasse did not have as high a reputation as a fighting admiral as some of his contemporaries. But he was the man who brought about the repulse of the British at Chesapeake Bay on 5 September 1781, one of the most decisive naval actions, and for this reason alone deserves his place in history.

Thanks largely to Colbert and de Choiseul, the French had the best fighting ships in the world. When the British captured a French ship they copied it. When the French captured a British ship they modified it. The French achieved a degree of quality in their frigates and ships-of-the-line – the

PREVIOUS PAGES Close action: the Battle of the Saints.

84

battleships – which was not to be improved upon until steam and steel took over. The logical French applied science to ship design and were blessed by a number of brilliant designers – Coulomb and Groignard among them – who had no equal anywhere. They sailed faster, were more manoeuvrable and were better balanced than their British counterparts. (By the middle of the eighteenth century, the for'ard castle was a feature of the past and had been replaced by a curving forecastle-deck. The aftercastle had gone, too, and only the slightly raised curving quarter-deck was left as a reminder of the huge, wooden, castellated castles that once sat upon the sterns of Spanish galleons of 200 years ago.)

British gunnery and guns were marginally superior to the French. The British had the advantage, too, in personnel, partly because there was a greater maritime population to draw upon, the French being a predominantly agrarian nation. The British sense of superiority at sea, which went back to before Hawkins and Drake and endured into the twentieth century, was a great strength. The British, like the Dutch, and later the Americans, felt at ease at sea. The Latin and Slav races have tended to regard it as an enemy.

Relations between the men and the officers were better in the British navy than in the French or Spanish navies. Latin naval tradition was marked by the clear division between those who made the ship go (the galley slaves and seamen) and those who fought, members of an exclusive aristocracy who regarded the others as a cross between an animal and a machine.

The English and Dutch had no galley-slave past, the seas they sailed being unsuitable for those precarious vessels. Although life was hard and discipline and punishment severe, there was a greater sense of common purpose on board the fighting ships of the northern nations. The officer's sense of responsibility for his men reflected the more flexible social system on land, where it was possible (just) to rise a few rungs, as Drake did, and only too easy to slip down many.

Finally, there was the difference in strategic attitude between the French and the British. The French, like the Germans in the First World War, were not looking for a showdown. It was not that they were cowards – far from it – but their political strategy was to *preserve* their fleet as a threat and only to do battle when the odds were overwhelmingly in their favour.

The British spirit was always more strategically aggressive, although tactical initiative was becoming stultified by the notorious *Fighting Instructions*. The French had the same problems with their chairbound hierarchy, and fighting at sea had deteriorated into a slogging match between two parallel lines.

The French decision to come to the aid of the American colonists in 1778 stemmed more from a thirst for revenge for the terms of the Treaty of Paris, which brought an end to the Seven Years War, than concern for the brave colonists. The first actions of the French fleet in the Caribbean, under the

The Comte de Grasse, an unsympathetic engraving published in the *London Magazine* when he was a prisoner in England.

Admiral Thomas Graves, who showed few of the qualities of his young contemporary, Horatio Nelson.

command of the Comte d'Estaing who had greatly superior strength, were timorous and hesitant. The same spirit, and the same odds, prevailed in European waters where the Comte d'Orvilliers lost a marvellous opportunity of severely defeating the English Channel fleet at the Battle of Ushant.

If the French fleet had been commanded by the American John Paul Jones, who caused widespread dismay along the British coastline with one small ship, there would have been little of the Royal Navy left by the end of 1779. But even with the reinforcement by the Spanish navy from June 1779, the French could not bring themselves to face a fleet action.

Vitality was introduced into the war by new appointments of more impressive officers. On the British side, Sir Charles Middleton (later Lord Barham) was made controller of the Royal Navy, and Sir George Rodney – choleric, elderly but aggressive and experienced – was appointed to command in the West Indies. Rodney reached Barbados on 17 March 1780. Just a year later the Comte de Grasse sailed from Brest with no fewer than 26 ships-of-the-line protecting a massive convoy of reinforcements for the French forces in the West Indies.

The Comte de Grasse was a typical product of the Duc de Choiseul's renaissance. Born in 1722, he entered the French navy as a young man and served in the Mediterranean and in the Indian Ocean, where he fought courageously and successfully against the British commander, Sir Edward Hughes.

De Grasse brought his convoy safely to within sight of the French-held island of Martinique on 28 April, when he was confronted by a powerful force of British ships-of-the-line under the command of Rodney's subordinate, Sir Samuel Hood. By shrewd manoeuvring, and with the luck of the wind favouring him, de Grasse succeeded in getting his convoy safely to its destination while he held off Hood and, in an indecisive action, committed more damage than he received.

After this encouraging start to his command, de Grasse took his main force to Tobago which he captured on 2 June in spite of all Rodney's efforts to foil him. De Grasse then returned to Martinique to prepare the expedition which was to reinforce Washington's campaign against their mutual enemy. The speed and industry de Grasse applied to this crucially important work resulted in the sailing of his armada to Chesapeake Bay, with 3300 French troops, on 5 August.

On 30 August, the day before the British commander sailed from New York for the same destination, de Grasse anchored inside the ten-mile-wide entrance to the Chesapeake. Without delay he landed his troops on the south side of the James River and they soon provided vital reinforcement to La Fayette's army facing the British commander on shore, Lord Cornwallis. At the same time, French men-of-war sealed off the James River to prevent Cornwallis crossing south into Carolina – an excellent example of the influence of seapower on a land campaign, and of the effectiveness of well conducted combined operations.

At 8 am on 5 September 1781, de Grasse's look-out frigate reported sails to the north-east. De Grasse believed them to be his expected reinforcements, and he decided to sail out and meet them to give cover. Shortly after this it became apparent that the numbers were too great for the ships to be his additional squadron. They were in fact the full British West Indies fleet of 19 ships-of-the-line with accompanying frigates.

The British fleet was under the command of Admiral Thomas Graves, with Hood as second-in-command. Rodney had returned to England on

Contemporary illustrations and 'a Representation' of the Battle of Chesapeake Bay; and OPPOSITE BELOW a simplified map showing the confusion of the British line, with de Grasse setting about the van of Graves's line.

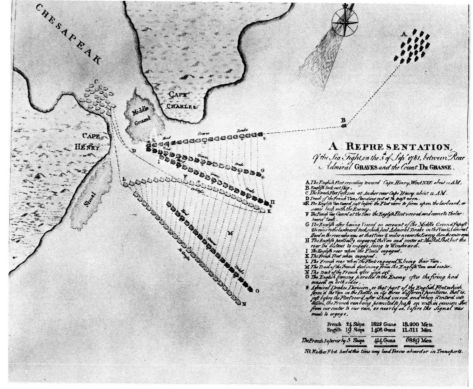

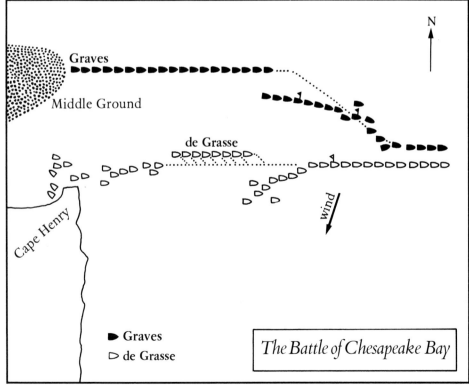

The Battle of Chesapeake Bay

89

sick leave, but had warned his replacement that the French force from
Martinique was almost certainly destined for Chesapeake Bay to reinforce
the Franco–American army attacking Cornwallis. Graves, however, slow
on the uptake and slow to act, had arrived too late.

De Grasse found himself in a seriously disadvantageous position, with tide
and wind against him, and with a powerful fleet waiting outside the bay,
ready to pick off the French van as soon as it emerged.

It was not until midday that de Grasse could get under way on the ebb
tide. At the same time, Graves hoisted the signal to form the inevitable single
line. But he also ordered a course which put his ships on a converging line
with the French, thus sacrificing his advantage and handing it to de Grasse,
who at once set about the British van, giving it a severe drubbing while
taking little punishment himself.

De Grasse was already superior in numbers. But because of his enemy's
mismanagement, the British rear was not even in touch with him. With the
Terrible and the other leading British ships half obscured by smoke and
continuing to sustain serious damage, two signals in quick succession were
seen to be hoisted on the flagship, the ninth ship in the British line. The first
was to close the enemy by one cable (one tenth of a nautical mile), the second
to bear down and engage the enemy. Contradictorily, the signal for the line
was preserved, and when brought down later, quickly restored, to the total
confusion of every commander in the fleet because the line signal was considered to be paramount to all others, according to *Fighting Instructions*. De
Grasse made off in search of his reinforcements, having no difficulty in
evading his pursuers.

Graves was forced to burn one of his 74s, which had been too damaged to
remain safely afloat, and he had suffered considerable damage to the masts
and rigging of some of his other big ships. But he was still in good enough
fighting trim to face de Grasse a second time, and could have done so if he
had not again become paralysed by indecision. When at last he probed
Chesapeake Bay again on 13 September, *eight days* later, it was hardly surprising that he found it contained not only de Grasse but his reinforcements,
too, which had also slipped through – a force double the strength of his own.

Hood, who had been unable to get at de Grasse at all with his rearguard
during the Battle of Chesapeake Bay, felt entitled to say, 'I told you so,' or
words with that meaning. He also regretted, in writing, that 'the commander-in-chief had not set the example of close action'.

Graves departed for New York, leaving Cornwallis to his fate – which
occurred a month later when he surrendered to Washington at Yorktown.
Eighteen days later, de Grasse sailed out of Chesapeake Bay with his intact
and virtually undamaged fleet and headed for the West Indies, well satisfied
with his performance.

Although deprived of almost all of a reinforcement and supply convoy
which came to grief, de Grasse kept up his offensive in the Caribbean,

capturing St Kitts from the British and preparing plans for a joint Franco–Spanish assault on Jamaica. He had one brush with the enemy at sea during the winter. Hood was now in command, and there was no clear victor as a result of the action off St Kitts on 26 January.

Both sides received reinforcements during February and March, Rodney rejoining as British C-in-C with 12 more ships-of-the-line, and de Grasse welcoming two more big ships as well as a great volume of supplies, arms and soldiers for the forthcoming invasion. A head-on collision became likely as soon as de Grasse began to form up his armada of 150 merchantmen, with 35 ships-of-the-line and supporting fighting ships to escort them, the biggest and most complicated operation in his long career at sea.

De Grasse proposed a circuitous route to Jamaica that kept him as close as possible to friendly ports. In accordance with usual French thinking, the last thing he wanted was a fight *en route* – or at all if it could be avoided. He left his base with this massive armada on 8 April 1782, watched by a distant British frigate.

Rodney and Hood, his second-in-command, had between them inspired a new spirit of self-confidence and aggression since the belated departure of Graves, and there was no loss of time or lack of determination in the pursuit. If de Grasse, with his faster fighting ships, had not been saddled with his lumbering mass of merchantmen, he could have shown a clean fleet of sterns to any British force. All that he could do when the British hove into sight off Dominica was to install his convoy, with two of his precious ships-of-the-line, under the French shore batteries in Basseterre Bay, Guadeloupe, and then sail out to meet the enemy.

De Grasse was not looking for a direct confrontation. In accordance with traditional French practice, he contrived to 'tease' Rodney and Hood with his superior speed and sailing qualities, attempting to bring a proportion of the British fleet to battle with overwhelming superiority – to nibble at it piecemeal in the hope that it would all go away.

It looked at first as if he might succeed, too, when his second-in-command, the Marquis de Vaudreuil, with 14 sail faced Hood with only eight. But superior British gunnery, especially with the short-range but devastating carronades, the 'mashers', caused de Grasse to recall him before he sustained too great damage.

Three days later, on 12 April 1782, de Grasse found himself, by ill chance, in a position from which he could no longer avoid a full-scale confrontation with Rodney and Hood. It happened in the same area as the earlier brush, in the channel separating Dominica and the group of islands off Guadeloupe called Les Saintes. The French sailed south, with the wind on their port quarter, the British north, both fleets in orthodox line ahead.

The meeting between the two van ships was like the igniting of a long fuse, which ran down the length of both lines as they passed each other by, firing their full broadsides at point-blank range. As usual, the British suffered

Rodney receiving de
Grasse's sword on the
quarterdeck of his
flagship. The crew
celebrate while
surviving ships of the
French fleet escape.

most in their masts and rigging, the French in their hulls, which were easily pierced by the mashers, causing grievous casualties.

But while the two fleets were still passing one another, starboard to starboard, the wind settled the issue by veering, allowing the British ships to luff. Rodney gave the order to break through the French line, and this time there was no misunderstanding. A number of the French ships, which had been forced suddenly to close haul, found themselves isolated and each surrounded by three or four British ships-of-the-line, all firing their mashers straight into their hulls at musket range. The effect was so terrible that those who could, fled from the scene of carnage. Nor would they return in response to de Grasse's signal.

De Grasse in his flagship *Ville de Paris*, the largest warship in the world, fought gallantly against the hopeless odds before at last surrendering, with 300 dead and not a round of shot on board. It was a great moment for Rodney when he received the sword of his gallant French foe.

But Hood was not pleased about this time-wasting ceremony. Again he blamed his superior officer, this time for failing to follow up the defeat by pursuing the rest of the French fleet. 'I am very confident we should have had twenty sail of the enemy's ships before dark,' he grumbled – perhaps with good reason; Nelson, who was not present, agreed with him.

The Battle of the Saints was decisive only in that it temporarily saved Jamaica from a French invasion. A powerful French force remained intact in the Caribbean, a source of great British anxiety until the peace treaty of 1783 was signed. However, but for the capture of the French flagship and c-in-c, and four other big ships, the terms of the peace treaty would not have been so strongly favourable to Britain. And the morale effect of the French defeat, confirming once again British paramountcy at sea, was to have a great influence in every battle in the wars with France that still lay ahead.

De Grasse was taken to England on board the *Sandwich*. His ship failed to complete the journey. The magnificent *Ville de Paris* was too badly knocked about to survive Atlantic gales, and went down *en route*.

De Grasse never went to sea again, after his repatriation. He could reasonably claim to have altered the course of history off Chesapeake Bay. But he died a disappointed man.

Vice-Admiral Viscount Nelson
of Burnham Thorpe
1758–1805

I will be a hero.
Nelson (aged seventeen)

Horatio Nelson lived in an age of violent conflict. His country experienced only brief periods of peace during all his forty-seven years. For the rest of the time, it was fighting, fighting, fighting – against the French both as royalists and revolutionaries, the American colonists, the Spaniards, the Dutch, the Danes. At one time virtually the whole of the continent of Europe was at war with Britain, and the country was more alone and friendless than in 1940.

Nelson grew up in a period of patriotic euphoria occasioned by the victories of the Seven Years War, when the nation was still ringing with the names of those great admirals Edward Hawke, Augustus Keppel and Edward Boscawen. Any attempt to portray 'the Hero', as he was known in his own country, must be made against these turbulent, competitive and often dangerous times in which he lived, when the industrial revolution and the opening of new markets made trading and commercial competition more fierce than ever.

Nelson devoted his life to the practice of the art of war at sea. He was fortunate, and his country was fortunate, that he had such an abundance of opportunity for exercising his art, and for proving that he was unsurpassed at it.

His family etched their mark on Horatio Nelson as sharply as the times in which he lived. His father was a clergyman, a learned man with a rich character, an uncompromising will and a spritely sense of humour. Less is known of Mrs Nelson. Her portrait shows kind, clever eyes and the full, sensuous lips her son inherited. She bore 11 children, none of whom revealed special qualities except her Horatio. She died when he was nine, and he mourned her all his life.

No fewer than 15 of his family and immediate forbears were clergymen, and his deeply held religious convictions sustained and guided him all through his life, until that most famous of all the prayers he composed before his final battle:

May the Great God whom I worship Grant to my Country and for the benefit of Europe in General a great and Glorious Victory, and may no misconduct in anyone tarnish it, and may humanity after Victory be the predominant feature in the British Fleet. For myself individually I commit my life to Him Who made me, and may his Blessing light upon my endeavours for serving my Country faithfully. To

Him I resign myself and the just cause which is entrusted me to Defend. Amen, Amen, Amen.

Nelson's adultery with Emma Hamilton and the subsequent sufferings of his wife caused him special guilt. It was the one great sin he committed in an unusually blameless personal life. He himself confessed frequently to the sin of pride: but more of that later. He was, fundamentally, a good man. This can be seen in so many of his letters. Above all, he was a compassionate as well as a passionate man.

His father had very little money. Both he and his wife enjoyed aristocratic connections that were close enough for them to be a consideration, and a help. The son grew up to be generous with money, almost profligate, and, even in that flamboyant and class-conscious age, to be regarded as snobbish in matters of rank, title and decoration.

The Revd Edmund Wilson's parish was Burnham Thorpe in north-west Norfolk, a mile or two inland from the sea and from the thriving little port of Burnham Overy Staithe. Horatio Nelson was born in Parsonage House – long since pulled down – on 29 September 1758. Twelve years later he was sent away to sea in order to lighten his widowed father's burden. Having already attended boarding schools, Nelson was accustomed to separation from his family. He was in good hands, and was enthusiastic at the idea of becoming a sailor.

Mrs Nelson had a brother, Maurice, who looked very like her, and was a kind, stalwart and honourable man. Maurice Suckling was a captain in the Royal Navy with the record and reputation of a hero. Nelson's romantic nature was aroused by this masterly figure who had made brief but memorable visits to his sister during Nelson's early boyhood.

Entry and advancement in the Royal Navy were governed by a highly developed system of patronage and preferment, and was to be for many years to come. Maurice Suckling gladly agreed to become Horatio's patron, and Horatio joined his ship, the *Raisonable*, at Chatham in March 1771. For the next seven months, Horatio learned the fundamentals of seamanship in all its branches, from navigation to gunnery, from the handling of small boats to helping to shorten sail in a high wind. He showed himself to be intelligent, eager and enterprising.

The world into which this small, frail-looking boy entered was a harsh and exclusive one. For the lower deck – 'the people' as they were then called – life was crude, with periods of hardship on long passages when the food was unpalatable and discipline was maintained by fear of the lash. This was the period in the navy's history when the service, according to Winston Churchill's immortal description, was governed by 'rum, sodomy and the lash'. The rum (very powerful and half a pint a day in quantity, but later watered down) was a solace and made drunks of most sailors; sodomy was widely practised and nodded at; and the lash was an accepted disagreeable fact of life at sea, like weevils in the ship's biscuits: sometimes there were more weevils, just as there were more lashes with a 'taut-handed' captain.

The attractions of life at sea were comradeship, steady victuals and pay, adventure, and the lure of prize money.

When required, the volunteers were joined by men forcibly 'impressed', and these were more often than not the sweepings off the streets and the prisons, a low discontented and dangerous lot. But a good captain could shape a mixed body of men into a good fighting and sailing team, and not only by the lash, as many captains proved.

The eighteenth-century Royal Navy attracted an excellent quality of officer. There were exceptions, like the uneven Bligh and that arch-flogger Pigot who was in the end – and rightly – murdered by his men at sea; and Admirals Byng and Hotham, who were less eager to engage the enemy than some of their contemporaries. But there were many more like Suckling, well-educated, God-fearing, fair-minded and aggressive patriots. The officers' world was separated by a wide gulf from that of the people, but this was a fact of life which everyone accepted, on land as well as at sea. To be a Royal Navy officer was to belong to a club, with unwritten rules of conduct and behaviour, a strong sense of loyalty, and a style of living and even a language that was exclusive.

Although most officers experienced setbacks and defeats at some time in their career – and Nelson was no exception to this – the factor that made the Georgian navy as near-invincible at sea as Bonaparte's army was on land, was its self-confidence, and its tradition and habit of winning battles, frequently against heavy odds, in ships that were often inferior in sailing qualities. In spite of periods of poor administration and neglect, the conviction of superiority deriving from Elizabethan days still lived. Suckling himself, for example, with two other captains, once attacked without hesitation a vastly superior force of seven Frenchmen and routed them.

Like all young midshipmen, Nelson had some rough times during the early part of his career. He accepted them stoically, never referring to them complainingly. But it was noted that even when he was a very grand admiral, he would go out of his way to show kindness to young men in the service.

The boy learned fast. Suckling had him sent in a merchantman to the West Indies to give him experience of a long ocean voyage, and then charged him with new responsibilities in his own ship, HMS *Triumph*. As Nelson himself wrote later, 'I attended well to my navigation'; and his reward, at the age of fourteen, was to be given the command of the ship's tender on its trips in the Thames estuary; and 'by degrees I became a good pilot'. As Drake had learned before him, these tidal waters with their deceptive shoals and currents, provided a good training-area for young navigators.

Suckling took up a shore command, and got a berth for Nelson in one of two ships setting out on an Arctic expedition. The belief that there must be

The Parsonage House, Burnham Thorpe, Nelson's birthplace.

Widely believed to be a portrait of Horatio (or Horace as he preferred to be called at the time) as a midshipman of fifteen.

a short, northern passage to the East was to endure for many more years yet. Captain Cook would shortly but fruitlessly be attempting a passage home from the Pacific by way of the Bering Strait. This Arctic expedition of 1773 was to search for a north-east passage. It failed, like all the others, and the ships were nearly crushed in the ice. Nelson also had an experience, which was lovingly cited by the Victorians as an early example of his boldness in the face of insuperable odds, when he tackled a polar bear with the butt of a musket.

From the frozen wastes of the Arctic, Nelson was hustled out East by a warmer and more agreeable route around the Cape. Suckling had this time decided to vary the boy's experiences with service in a fighting ship under a hard captain. Before he was at length laid low with fever, from which so many Englishmen died in the East, Nelson had learned what life was like on board a well-ordered ship on a long commission. He was once briefly in action, he witnessed more than 200 floggings of offenders, he saw much of the coastline of India and Ceylon, and admired Trincomalee harbour. A varied diet.

He was shipped home to recover from the fever. The passage, he later claimed, marked a turning-point in his life, and at the same time revealed, it has been said, some of the elements of the mystic in him – or was it just his mercurial temperament? The slow convalescence from the fever had left him weak and listless, depressed in spirit, and without hope for his future career as a naval officer. Then 'a sudden glow of patriotism was kindled within me', he later claimed, 'and presented my King and country as my patron; my mind exulted in the idea. "Well, then," I exclaimed, "I will be a hero, and confiding in providence, I will brave every danger."'

Whatever visions of his future Nelson may have witnessed on board the ship bringing him home, the first opportunity of so many in his life to demonstrate his gallantry quickly presented itself. Suckling was now comptroller of the navy. The American colonists had declared their independence. Nelson passed out as a lieutenant at the age of eighteen, and, after a brief period on Gibraltar convoy work, was appointed to the frigate *Lowestoffe* for duty in the West Indies.

Nowhere in the world was the competition for possessions and trade fiercer than in the Caribbean, with its scattering of rich islands, spread over a wide expanse of sea. The days when Spain regarded this area as her own exclusively were long since past. In the late eighteenth century the flags of Britain and France, Denmark and Sweden, Holland and Spain all flew on the islands. Great fortunes and some of the greatest estates ever established in England were founded on the rich products, and especially sugar, from Jamaica, Barbados and other islands. As evidence of the Caribbean's importance, we have already seen how Britain and France despatched massive fleets and convoys to the West Indies when war broke out, and how the most decisive naval battles took place on that side of the Atlantic.

Suckling's final act on behalf of Nelson was to ensure that his captain on his new commission was a good man. He was more than that. Captain William Locker possessed, among many qualities, the zeal of a great fighter, and he, more than any other single person, stimulated in his pupil the natural resolution and fighting prowess that made 'the Hero'. When Nelson was the most famous admiral in the world, he wrote to his old master, 'I have been your scholar; it is you who taught me to board a Frenchman.'

In fact, it was an American privateer, not a Frenchman, that was Nelson's first boarding victim. It was blowing a gale and his ship's first lieutenant had failed to put a prize crew on board. 'Have I no officer in the ship who can board the prize?' Locker is supposed to have cried out in exasperation. Nelson's success, and his comment on it, are in character. 'Difficulties and dangers do but increase my desire in attempting them.'

For his part, Locker speedily recognized that he had a young man of exceptional potential as a lieutenant, and encouraged him by giving him command of a small schooner in which to cruise among the islands. It was, in effect, an advanced hydrographic exercise for the young lieutenant. 'In this vessel I made myself a complete pilot of all the passages through the islands situated on the north side of Hispaniola,' wrote Nelson – knowledge that was later to prove invaluable.

In 1778 there occurred several events that were to be of long-term importance to Britain and the Royal Navy. France informed the British government that she had signed an alliance with the rebellious colonists in North America. That great reformer and administrator, Sir Charles Middleton (later Lord Barham), was appointed controller of the navy. Admiral Sir Peter Parker was appointed c-in-c the West Indies. And, far down the scale of responsibility and command, Nelson was appointed third lieutenant in Parker's flagship, *Bristol*.

A keen judgement of character is one of a senior officer's most valuable assets. The Royal Navy was fortunate in possessing so many keen judges, including Nelson himself later. Within a month or two, Parker had promoted Nelson to be first lieutenant, and in December 1779 commander, when he was given the brig *Badger*.

Almost as important as this dramatic rise in Nelson's responsibilities and rank was his meeting with Cuthbert Collingwood, who succeeded him as commander of the *Badger*. Collingwood was ten years older than Nelson. The gulf in age made no difference. This solid, shrewd, dogged and courageous Northumbrian became Nelson's closest naval friend. He made a marvellous foil for Nelson, and they worked and fought together in productive and destructive harmony until the very end, off Cape Trafalgar. Collingwood was the first of the 'band of brothers',[1] the most potent outside force in Nelson's armoury.

It was typical of Collingwood's generous nature that he was among the first and most enthusiastic to congratulate Nelson when, after only six months as a commander, Parker promoted him again, to post-captain. And he was not yet twenty-one.

By one of the ironic chances of war, Captain Nelson's first real fighting was on land and not at sea. But it was an appropriate chance that it was against the Spaniards – the 'Dons' – and, as with that other little captain, Francis Drake, the fighting took place in central America.

Now that Spain had joined France against the British, Parker mounted an offensive operation against the Spanish positions in Nicaragua, including the forcing of a passage with boats up the River St Juan, and eventually down-river into the Pacific, there to attack Spanish settlements. It was very Elizabethan in its bold conception, but it was the rainy time of the year and the ill-equipped British were racked by yellow fever. Collingwood, who fought in the same area as Nelson for the first time, lost 180 of his 200 men, all to the dreaded 'yellow jack'. The fort of San Juan was captured, and Nelson revelled in the adventure until he was struck down – not with fever, mercifully, for that would have killed him. Dysentery was bad enough.

It was five years since he had been invalided home from the fevers of the East. And now the West Indies had defeated him, too. He was well cared for, first by Parker's wife, and then by Captain William Cornwallis, whose older brother was fighting the American revolutionaries on land. Cornwallis took Nelson home in his ship, the *Lion*, and they became friends. Cornwallis was a powerful and influential man in naval circles, where Nelson had lost his closest contact and patron with the death of Suckling.

It was Nelson's misfortune that his illness led to his eventually missing the fighting at sea in the closing stages of the war, and above all Rodney's victory at The Saints in 1782. No fame. No prize money. 'It would almost be supposed to try my constitution,' he commented. His recovery was slow. He had almost lost the use of his limbs for some time, and even in January 1791 he was writing that they had not fully recovered, although his 'inside was a new man'.

Nelson convalesced mostly at Bath. His father spent as much time there as he could, thankful to escape from the east winds of Burnham Thorpe; and Nelson was able to get to know his sisters and brothers again after his long absence. Edmund Nelson has left no record of his reaction to his son, whom he must now have recognized was destined at least for distinction if not fame in his profession. The best picture of him at this time – or shortly after – has been provided by the future King William IV, Prince William Henry, who became a friend and admirer. He was, wrote the prince, 'the merest boy of a captain I ever beheld'.

His dress was worthy of attention. He had on a full laced uniform; his lank un-powdered hair was tied in a stiff Hessian tail of an extraordinary length; the old-fashioned flaps of his waistcoat added to the general quaintness of his figure. . . . I had never seen anything like it before. . . . There was something irresistibly pleasing in his address and conversation, and an enthusiasm when speaking on professional subjects, that showed he was no common being.

It was not until August 1781 that Nelson felt fit enough to ask the admiralty for a new command. He was offered, without hesitation, an excellent French prize, the frigate *Albemarle*. He was eager to be off to the fighting now. Instead, to his chagrin, he was employed for the whole winter in the North Sea – and that was no billet for this recently recovered, frail-looking, little captain – and then on convoy work in the North Atlantic. The only times he saw the French was when he was sighted and pursued by such an overwhelming force that even he was compelled to evade it, and in an abortive attack on a French-held island. The *Albemarle* was attached to Hood's squadron at New York. But by then the victory over de Grasse at The Saints had already been celebrated.

About the only record he had to show for his two years in the *Albemarle* was that of his first love-affair – or the first recorded love-affair, for it is unlikely that such a passionate and hot-blooded young man had not had a few women by the time he was twenty-four. The woman was a Canadian 'beauty', and nothing came of it. His next love-affair came with the peace, and in France of all places. With the end of his commission, and of the war, Nelson travelled to northern France with the intention of learning the language, no doubt so that he could upstage surrendered French commanders he might graciously invite to dine in his cabin.

There is no record of what he thought of the language, only that he learned a smattering and did not like France. At St Omer he was entertained by an English clergyman's family, and fell in love with one of the daughters. This time he appears to have been in earnest, for we see him writing to William Suckling, who worked at the navy office and was as well-off as his late brother, begging for an allowance so that he could offer his hand in marriage to the girl: 'Either I am to be happy or miserable: – it depends on you.' But no, it depended on the girl; and it was unrequited love again. Nelson returned to London, to be granted within weeks the only peacetime commission in his life.

Peacetime commissions were few and far between in the Royal Navy, and they normally went to officers of special merit or special influence, usually both. In the Georgian navy, at the end of a war the great majority of the fighting ships were laid up, their masts and yards and armament put into store, the people dismissed, the officers placed on half-pay, which was not enough to live on – less than £50 a year for Nelson as a captain.

Nelson was deservedly fortunate in being granted this commission. It lasted some three years. But it brought him little professional benefit or pleasure, and much frustration. His ship was the frigate *Boreas*, his station the West Indies again, his C-in-C Rear-Admiral Hughes, a weak and feebly corrupt nonentity, his work policing.

The American colonists had possessed a near-monopoly of the American trade with the West Indies. When they won their independence, they expected to be treated as privileged exceptions to the Navigation Act – still in force since the Dutch wars – prohibiting all but British ships from trading with British possessions. The various British governors, the commercial, plantation, and trading men and customs house officials (in many cases there were overlaps) all recognized profit in disregarding the act. Hughes was not prepared to enforce it, and far from merely ingratiating himself with the merchants was no doubt making something on the side. Nelson would have none of this and interpreted the letter of the law, seizing American ships and making himself highly unpopular. He was supported only by Collingwood, who joined him on the station and exercised his north-country high principles as strongly as his friend.

But at least, and at last, Nelson found his love returned in the West Indies.

The woman was Frances (Fanny) Nisbet, a young widow with a boy of five called Josiah. She was staying with her uncle, the President of Nevis, when Nelson came into her life. They were married at St Kitts on 11 March 1787. Prince William was best man. At the end of the year, the *Boreas* was paid off in the Medway, and Nelson found himself without a ship, or the prospect of another ship or another war. Even leaner professional years lay ahead. They were made tolerable only by the company of his comely, kindly wife and his young stepson.

No one will know what effect on Nelson's highly volatile and sensitive character five years of neglect by the admiralty had upon him. This period of enforced naval inactivity may on the one hand have offered him the opportunity of self-assessment, and of planning both his future style and attitude as a commander of men, and his strategy and tactics when he would be a fleet admiral and war with France would be renewed – both of which he knew must happen.

On the other hand, this period from December 1787 to January 1793 may have been one of such frustration and bitterness that it led to a further hardening in his character. Certainly there is plenty of evidence that Nelson became more ruthless and in some ways more insensitive in his later years of command. The Nelson of 1781 could not have behaved so cruelly towards the harmless and defenceless Fanny as he behaved in 1801. Nor would he have condoned the unnecessary harshness of some of his captains.

But, for the present, we see in 1788 a man of thirty years, vigorous, ambitious and self-confident, content for the present with the life of a country gentleman of slender means, delighting in the company of his new wife, and glad of what he thought must be a brief rest in his professional life.

As a matter of course, he concerned himself with the lot of the under-privileged in the farming area of north-west Norfolk (he and Fanny were living happily with his father), and is known to have written to Prince William about the restlessness of the labourers and the real risk of a spread of revolution from France. But not very much is known about these land-bound years. He read a great deal, travelled about the country to stay with relatives and friends, and to London to meet his fellow officers at one or other of the naval clubs to which he belonged.

Later on, his time was increasingly given up to trying to get a new appointment. Collingwood and other of his friends were given commands. Nelson became convinced that he was being deliberately ignored. He had been an object of envy in the past, and had made enemies by his strict enforcement of the Navigation Act during his last commission. 'I made every use of every interest to get a Ship . . .', he wrote, 'but in vain: there was a prejudice at the Admiralty evidently against me.'

At last he was granted his wish. On the threshold of one of the most prolonged, bitter and critical wars in his country's history, Nelson was given command of a ship-of-the-line, HMS *Agamemnon*, a twelve-year-old 64. He was to serve in the Mediterranean under his old friend, Lord Hood.

Nelson made the journey to London in a state of exultation, bringing with him his stepson Josiah who was to serve in his ship as a midshipman. He was delighted with the *Agamemnon*. 'My ship sails very well indeed. We think better than any ship in the fleet,' he wrote to Fanny. The same would soon be said of the ship's fighting prowess: of that he was convinced.

As Europe was convulsed by revolution and war, as Britain was threatened with the loss of her trade by which she lived – from India and the East, from the Americas, from the Baltic – and threatened with the loss of her colonies abroad and by invasion at home, the pattern of Nelson's last 12 years of command can be followed through triumph and failure to its sublime conclusion.

Nelson's first mission for Hood was portentous. It took him to the kingdom of Naples, where Hood hoped to raise troops hostile to the revolutionary cause in France for the defence of loyalist, but threatened, Toulon. There Nelson met for the first time that busty, seductive mother-figure of questionable morals, Emma Hart, by then married to the elderly British Minister there, Sir William Hamilton. 'She is a woman of amiable manners,' Nelson wrote to his wife, who in later years had reason to doubt it.

Toulon was lost while Nelson was away. He enjoyed his first engagement with the enemy at sea in October 1793, when he fought single-handed five Frenchmen, odds that he considered perfectly acceptable, although he did in fact withdraw in the end without making a prize, as his masts and rigging were threatened with total destruction.

Another land campaign followed soon after. The British now desperately needed new Mediterranean bases, and Hood fixed on Corsica and Minorca as two islands from which he could continue operations. Nelson and his men were mainly responsible for capturing Calvi in the north-west of Corsica. The price was heavy, though. The *Agamemnon* lost many of her men, by disease and in battle. And here Nelson received his first disabling wound. 'I got a little hurt this morning,' he wrote to his c-in-c.

In fact, a ball that had nearly taken off his head had struck the earthworks in which he was sheltering, and filled his face with sand and rock fragments. His right eye was permanently damaged. 'I can distinguish light from dark, but no object.' Contrary to tradition, Nelson never wore a black patch over it. The shade he sometimes wore was over his good eye as protection from the sun's glare.

Although, largely thanks to his patron, Nelson had been blessed with good captains, his commanders-in-chief were of a more uneven quality. Hughes had been a disaster. Hood was without fault in Nelson's eyes. But he was soon replaced by William Hotham, a man of slender determination, who allowed 'a glorious victory' to elude him the first time he met the enemy in force.

Hood had done great damage to the French fleet before the evacuation of Toulon. But a powerful force survived, and it was these 17 ships-of-the-line which Hotham intercepted with a force of 14 on 13 March 1795. Nelson and Thomas Fremantle, a frigate commander, managed to cut off two of the big French ships, and after suffering some damage, forced their surrender. It was a sharp, savage but entirely successful action as far as it went, but Hotham refused to take it any further and pursue the enemy. 'We have done very well. We must be contented,' was his timorous comment.

The fighting was going badly on land, and Nelson and his fellow captains knew that there could be no offsetting these setbacks by success at sea under this admiral. The state of affairs was soon recognized by Lord Spencer and his board back in London, and Hotham was replaced by Sir John Jervis, an officer as different in calibre as a culverin from a pistol.

Jervis arrived when the heat of war, and French successes, were both intensifying. Spain had switched sides, the British were soon without a naval base in the Mediterranean, everywhere the French were triumphant.

For Britain, 1796 was a year of fear and alarm, as doom-laden as the summer of 1940 was to be. Still there was no great fleet action. But Nelson participated in several sharp minor actions, always at a handicap in numbers, always the victor.

Nelson's first opportunity to demonstrate to the world his genius as a tactician and his personal fearlessness came on St Valentine's Day, 14 February 1797, off Cape St Vincent on the Atlantic coast and the extreme south-west tip of the Iberian peninsula. A Spanish fleet of 27 ships-of-the-line, attempting to rendezvous with powerful French and Dutch fleets

preparatory to an invasion of England, was sighted at dawn. Its interception was vital for Britain's security, even though Jervis could muster only 15 ships.

Jervis determined to split the Spanish fleet, which looked immensely impressive on the horizon, but were sailing loosely, and attempted to destroy them piecemeal by superior gunfire in a close mêlée. It was a good idea, but Nelson, last but two in the line, was the first to recognize that Jervis had acted too slowly and that the Spanish groups were in danger of uniting into one line and escaping altogether. Against all the rules in the book, and without informing Jervis, Nelson wore his ship, the *Captain*, 74, out of line and sailed on his own straight into the centre of one of the Spanish divisions, which included the 130-gun *Santissima Trinidad*, *Salvador del Mundo*, 112, and *San Josef*, 112. Seven Spanish sail were soon thundering away at the much smaller British ship.

To the eternal credit of Jervis, he not only commended Nelson for his initiative after the battle, but despatched support the moment he recognized his subordinate's intentions. It was as well that he did. The *Captain* was soon without foremast or any sail, shroud or rope, and was therefore completely unmanoeuvrable.

In order to regain mobility, Nelson decided to board the nearest Spaniard – and, moreover, to lead the boarders personally, to the astonishment of the enemy when they saw the English commodore himself, armed with pistol and cutlass, fighting his way on board. No one can tell the tale better than Nelson himself:

A soldier of the 69th regiment having broken the upper quarter-gallery window, I jumped in myself, and was followed by others as fast as possible. I found the cabin doors fastened, and some Spanish officers fired their pistols: but having broke open the doors, the soldiers fired. . . . I pushed immediately onwards for the quarter-deck, where I found Captain Berry in possession of the poop, and the Spanish ensign hauling down. I passed with my people, and Lieutenant Pearson, on the larboard gangway, to the forecastle, where I met two or three Spanish officers, prisoners to my seamen: they delivered me their swords. A fire of pistols or muskets, opening from the admiral's stern gallery of the *San Josef*, I directed the soldiers to fire into her stern. . . .

Undeterred, Nelson and his men boarded a second large Spanish ship from the first, taking possession of the upper deck while the Spanish gunners below were still working the guns. As the smoke slowly cleared and the sounds of battle faded, it became evident that, besides the *San Josef* and *San Nicholas*, the 'personal' spoils of Nelson, two more Spanish ships of the line had been taken, and the remainder of the fleet was in full flight.

And from this same gunsmoke off Cape St Vincent, there emerged at last the popular figure of 'the Hero' himself, one-eyed from previous combat, now bruised in the groin and with part of his hat shot away, his face and uniform grey with the dust of close action; audacious and scornful of

OPPOSITE 'There was a service hand to hand with swords,' wrote Nelson of this action of 3 July 1797 off Cadiz, 'in which my Cockswain, John Sykes, now no more, twice saved my life.'

tradition and regulation when there was profit in doing so. The Nelson legend had been born with that first broadside from the gun decks of the *Captain*.

Nelson savoured his success and the fame it brought him – together with a KB and promotion: Rear-Admiral Sir Horatio Nelson – and was not afraid to show it. He loved the style in which his unique feat of boarding one prize from the first was referred to as 'Nelson's Patent Bridge for boarding first-rates'. He frankly (and truthfully) claimed that it had been 'his' battle, even though Jervis was granted the title of Earl of St Vincent. This sort of talk was not approved of by some of his fellow officers. Those closest to him, like Troubridge and Collingwood, merely chuckled indulgently, and enjoyed his enjoyment in his fame and success.

There was something engagingly boyish and frank about Nelson's immodesty. He would not hesitate to write, after one gallant episode, 'Perhaps my personal courage was more conspicuous than at any other period of my life.' Equally, he gave credit to others when it was due, and before his abortive and expensive attack on Santa Cruz, Tenerife, in emulation of Blake's feat, he told St Vincent that he in no way regarded himself as Blake's equal.

Nelson's love of his medals and decorations was equally engaging. An eyewitness later described him as 'covered with stars, ribbons and medals, more like a Prince in an opera'. Yet, beneath all this panoply and talk of his own courage and tactical genius, there was genuine modesty and humility. After one misfortune, he wrote to his wife, 'I believe firmly that it was the Almighty's goodness to check my consummate vanity. I hope it has made me a better officer, as I feel confident it has made me a better man. I kiss with all humility the rod.'

The public disregarded the failure at Tenerife which followed hot upon the triumph at St Vincent. In fact, Nelson's loss of his right arm in the bloody Santa Cruz engagement only further embellished his heroic image as he stepped ashore in September 1797 after four years' absence. The common figure of an admiral was a fierce, arrogant, elderly tyrant, fat with good living from prize money. Now, here was an admiral who really *fought* – look at that one eye, that one arm, that pale complexion, that weary youthfulness! Yes, here was a real admiral, a real hero, a people's hero.

Not long after St Vincent, Nelson and his captain, Ralph Willet Miller, were paid this tribute by the people in a paper found on the quarter-deck: 'Success attend Admiral Nelson God bless Captain Miller we thank them for the officers they have placed over us. We are happy and comfortable and will shed every drop of blood in our veins to support them. ...'

Considering that this was written at the time of the mutiny at the Nore, the biggest and most desperate in British naval history, it is an exceptional tribute and confirmation of Nelson's special affinity with the unprivileged.

The victory of St Vincent was more of a moral than a material blow to

Britain's enemies. The failure of the Spanish commander to face up to an inferior force and the supreme self-confidence of the British attack reminded the French and Spaniards of British dominance at sea – a reminder that was also rammed home to the Dutch when Adam Duncan defeated them at Camperdown. (Nelson was absent and remarked that he would have given his other arm to have been there.)

Nelson's next three great victories were much more materially decisive. On 29 March he hoisted his flag as rear-admiral on the 74-gun *Vanguard* and sailed out to take command of a powerful squadron in the Mediterranean under the overall command of Jervis, now Lord St Vincent. The first concern of the British in those early months of 1798 was a great armada Napoleon Bonaparte had assembled at Toulon. Was it intended eventually for the invasion of England? Or would it first sail east for the invasion of Egypt, then deal with Britain later? Nelson and his captains surmised that Alexandria would be its destination.

Foiled by filthy weather and a dearth of scouting ships from observing the emergence of Bonaparte's armada and of shadowing it later, Nelson took his squadron of 14 ships to Alexandria, found the port empty, returned to Sicily for news, missing the French ships on the way in the dark and by a few miles; and then on an inspired hunch, sailed for Egypt a second time.

Bonaparte never did have much luck at sea, and Aboukir Bay was the setting of one of his worst drubbings at the hands of the British Navy. After landing his army, his powerful fleet (much more powerful on paper than Nelson's) was anchored in a line across the mouth of the bay, protected additionally by well-sited shore batteries. It was an almost secure position, but before the British masts appeared over the horizon, Bonaparte had despatched an order to the French c-in-c Vice-Admiral F. P. Brueys, to bring his ships into the old harbour. The order, which might have saved the fleet, did not reach the flagship in time, and the reason for this was simple: Nelson's decisiveness.

To the dismay of Brueys, the British squadron sailed straight into the attack, seemingly without taking counsel or making preparation of any kind, as if they had predicted just this situation. Indeed they had, and every one of Nelson's captains knew exactly what to do. Yet the essential ingredient of flexibility remained, and as a blood-red sun set behind the advancing British ships-of-the-line, decks cleared and sanded against blood, guns run out with powder and shot at the ready and nets spread against boarders, five of the leading British ships slipped round the bows of the anchored Frenchmen, risking the notorious shoals of the bay, and began to engage the enemy on his port side.

It was a totally unexpected manoeuvre which led to the first five French ships being engaged on both quarters simultaneously by eight British sail. The French fought with great gallantry, but, dismasted and with decks running with blood, they could not for long stand up to this double pound-

ing by the fastest and most accurate gunners in the world. The first surrender occurred at 9 pm. Others followed. With both sides anchored, the battle developed into a night slogging match in which the French stood no chance of prevailing.

After seriously damaging her first assailant, the huge French flagship *Orient* was set on fire by two more British ships. Brueys was already mortally wounded, bravely crying out, '*Un amiral français doit mourir sur son banc de quart,*' when threatened with being taken below. As the conflagration grew, consuming masts and sails and illuminating in her death pyre the fearful fighting all about her, the nearest ships closed their ports and flinched away from the inevitable climax.

The *Orient*'s magazines exploded at 10 pm, stunning every gunner into silence for, some said, as long as three minutes, and signalling her fate to Bonaparte and the French army 15 miles away. The gunners continued their bloody work through the night with increasing weariness and decreasing pace as one French ship after another struck her colours.

Dawn revealed a scene of fearsome carnage. The French had lost some 3500, the British less than 1000, although Nelson was once again among the wounded, suffering from a deep gash above his blind eye. Only two of the French ships-of-the-line escaped being sunk, burned-out or captured, and the British were too tired, or too disabled, to pursue them. On board one was Rear-Admiral Villeneuve, who was to suffer the misfortune of facing Nelson again seven years later.

When Nelson sailed away with his battered squadron from Egypt, he left

ABOVE LEFT A famous explosion in naval history was the blowing-up of *L'Orient* at the Nile, commemorated here in a snuff box.

a stranded French army and a frustrated Bonaparte astern, while the bows of his ships cleaved waters that were now indisputably British. Thoroughly aware of the strategical and diplomatic importance of his victory, he had despatched a reassuring message to the headquarters of the East India Company which had feared the implacable march of Bonaparte's army, and to Naples for onward despatch to London.

After the Nile victory: a romantic rendering of Nelson and some of the crew of the *Vanguard* at prayers of thankfulness, published after his death.

The news had an electrifying effect on everyone in Britain, and a stunning effect on the first lord of the admiralty who fainted. There were illuminations and dancing in the streets of towns and villages.

'Joy, joy, joy, to you, brave, gallant, immortalized Nelson!' wrote Fanny, by contrast to her stern appeal after St Vincent to be more careful. Emma Hamilton, the woman who was to steal the Hero from her, exclaimed, 'Good God what a victory! Never, never, has there been anything half so glorious, so complete!'

Nelson did not go home to enjoy the acclaim of the British people. It is a pity he did not. Several times in his brief life of fame he would have done better to quit after victory. The attack on Santa Cruz, following St Vincent, had been a military disaster. Now he was to bring upon himself personal disaster and disgrace after the glory of his Nile victory.

There were sound political reasons for Nelson's taking his squadron to Naples, the one Mediterranean land ally the British could rely upon. There was no justification for going ashore and settling in with the Hamilton household, and to the despair of his captains and friends, making a fool of himself with the seductive Emma.

The tenacious hold that Emma Hamilton had on Nelson never relaxed for the rest of his life. That she was vulgar and coarse, was a climber and courtesan, in no way diminished Nelson's passion for her, and he was blind to the follies and damage he committed as a result of his relationship with her. She aroused in his passionate heart the mother love of which he had been early deprived, at once stimulated his vanity and made him laugh, and she doubtless met his sexual needs with abandonment and variety. 'What must be my sensations at the idea of sleeping with you!' he once wrote to her. 'It sets me on fire.' For the last seven years of his life Nelson was totally consumed by this woman, and with her must rest the chief responsibility for his unfortunate behaviour from The Nile until his return to England in November 1800.

Nelson became deeply and ill-advisedly involved in Neapolitan politics, acting high-handedly, and at one point dealing out very rough justice. This also and inevitably caused him to become entangled with the irresolute and second-rate King Ferdinand, from whom Nelson accepted the Gilbertian dukedom of Brontë, and, less laughably, a substantial income.

Worse still, Nelson acted high-handedly and insubordinately with his new c-in-c, Lord Keith, who became very vexed with him. His only success – and no mean one at that – was the defeat and capture of a French force which included the last ship-of-the-line unaccounted for at The Nile and subsequently.

Nelson returned to England overland with Emma, who was now carrying his child, and the ever-tolerant Sir William Hamilton, their progress marked by adulatory receptions at Vienna, Prague and Hamburg among other cities.

There was adulation in London, too, on the grandest scale; but it did not extend to royal circles. Nelson vainly hoped that Emma would be received at court, and scarcely expected to be publicly snubbed by George III, as he was at a levee which he stupidly attended covered in foreign decorations and orders, for the wearing of which royal permission had not then been granted.

Fanny behaved with great dignity. Once she wrote to Nelson, 'Do, my dear husband, let us live together. I can never be happy till such an event takes place. I assure you again I have but one wish in the world, to please you. Let everything be buried in oblivion, it will pass away like a dream ...'

But the dream endured remorselessly; and Nelson had this letter returned unread. Worse still for Fanny, the rest of the Nelson family, including even the father, all of whom had been close, turned against her so that it seemed as if she had no friend in the world. From 1800, Fanny becomes a grey, sad little figure who, for another 30 years, continues her unacknowledged blameless life on her husband's pension.

However strongly many people deplored Nelson's liaison with Emma and his apparent indifference to his wife's grief, his priceless professional skill could not be ignored. And it was, once again, desperately needed. Tsar Paul of Russia, in liaison with Bonaparte, had created a pact against Britain with Prussia and the Scandinavian nations. The Baltic trade was vital to Britain's security and prosperity, and the government decided to take firms steps to destroy the pact before it could become damaging.

A powerful naval force was therefore despatched to Copenhagen with instructions to deliver an ultimatum to Denmark: quit the alliance or face the consequences. The Danes rejected the ultimatum and warned their fleet and the shore defences of imminent attack.

Nelson led the attack against the 18 anchored Danish ships with only nine sail of his own, and for a time it looked as if British grit and gunnery would not be sufficient to offset this disparity. It was in the thick of the engagement that Nelson's most famous and waggish remark was made, 'I really do not see the signal,' as he held his telescope to his blind eye. The signal was from his C-in-C, Admiral Sir Hyde Parker, a supine officer who, from a safe distance, had querulously ordered Nelson to withdraw before all his ships were sunk. But the Nelson habit of victory prevailed. Only one Danish ship escaped, and some 6000 Danes became casualties, while British losses were about 1000.

Nelson was made a viscount. But it had been a sorry business. The Danes were not traditional enemies of Britain as the French were, and a pre-emptive strike in an undeclared war could not attract the same acclaim as The Nile. The northern alliance dissolved eventually as a result of the Battle of Copenhagen; and peace at last was re-established with France by the Treaty of Amiens in March 1802.

Nelson settled down to a cosy and sentimental suburban *ménage à trois* existence in a fancy house called Merton, south-west of London, complete with hen-coops and pigsties and a stretch of ornamental canal called 'the Nile'. He doted on his daughter Horatia, who was never told – though surely she guessed – the real identity of her father. The three – husband, wife and Nelson – were socially unacknowledged by the 'best' people, which caused Nelson much bitterness. But in the political and defence establishment his position was now unassailable, the highest in the land consulted him, and to the common people the grey-haired, scarred, one-armed figure was the very personification of patriotic heroism.

Across the Channel, Bonaparte's lust for battle grew stronger with every passing month of abstention. In May 1803 he declared war on Britain again. Immediately, and inevitably, Nelson was given an appointment. It was to be the Mediterranean again for him, and he hoisted his flag as c-in-c in the *Victory*.

After this bucolic and mainly happy interlude, the remainder of Nelson's life was to be dedicated to the preservation of his country's freedom and independence at a time when all Europe was under the heel of the ruthless conqueror, soon to crown himself Emperor Napoleon I. Bonaparte was now hell-bent on the invasion of Britain, and built up a powerful army in northern France. The invasion depended for its success on France's seizure of control of the sea. The defiant and waggish claim, 'I do not say they cannot come. I only say they cannot come by sea,' was attributed to St Vincent, now first lord; but it was upon Nelson in the Mediterranean and his old friend Cornwallis in the western approaches that the reality of these words depended.

Bonaparte's strategy was to concentrate his fleets, including the Spanish fleet when that nation once again allied itself with him, drive for the Channel and hold it for long enough for his invincible army to cross and march to London. It was the British fleets' task to watch the enemy, prevent this concentration, and destroy any fleet that emerged from its base. Blockading was hard, monotonous, dangerous work demanding seamanship, and patience of the first order. To keep thousands of men, many serving against their will and many from the criminal classes, engaged and fit and fed and disciplined for month after month within the confines of crowded, unhygienic and pitching wooden men-of-war demanded inspired leadership. Cornwallis, Collingwood and Nelson were past-masters at blockading.

Nelson's first preoccupation was with the Toulon fleet under the command of Admiral Pierre Villeneuve, who had also been appointed supreme commander of the combined fleets when and if they ever succeeded in combining. Operating from his base in Sardinia, Nelson kept Toulon covered by relays of frigates. But more than once the French succeeded in getting out undetected. The second time, they escaped through the Straits of Gibraltar, got as far as the West Indies and then doubled back with Nelson in hot pursuit. Villeneuve was intercepted by another British force, was

Emma Hamilton at
Merton. A pencil
sketch by Thomas
Baxter.

HMS *Victory* at sea
before Trafalgar.
Today you can pace
her decks at
Portsmouth.

slightly damaged, but made it safely to Cadiz, where he joined up with the main Spanish fleet.

Nelson had already returned to England for the last time when the news of Villeneuve's escape and juncture with the Spaniards reached him. He had been at sea almost continuously for two years, and this was a very different man from the slack and self-indulgent Nelson of Naples. However Bonaparte might dispose his Grand Army, however distant Villeneuve might be, the threat of invasion and defeat of his beloved homeland would remain while the powerful combined fleets of Spain and France remained intact. 'I think I shall yet have to beat them,' he is reported as remarking as he gazed out upon the peace and beauty of Merton with his mistress and his child at his side.

Nelson was 25 days in England, for much of the time in Whitehall discussing policy and plans with the statesmen and leading naval figures of the time. He embarked in the *Victory* at Portsmouth on 15 September, seen off by a crowd of cheering admirers. His flagship was off Cadiz by the 28th, and on the following day, his forty-seventh birthday, his 'band of brothers' dined on board. To them he outlined his plan for dealing with the combined fleet when it came out, as it must eventually. In characteristic style he called it 'the Nelson touch', and its effect on his listeners was – as he described it – 'like an electric shock. Some shed tears, all approved – "It was new – it was singular – it was simple!"'

Orders were given for Collingwood's close blockade to be changed to an open blockade, with the main force of ships-of-the-line withdrawn while frigates kept watch as they had off Toulon for so many months. They did not have long to wait. Unknown to Nelson, Bonaparte had given orders for Villeneuve to withdraw to the Mediterranean. Reassured by the seeming disappearance of the main British battle fleet, Villeneuve sailed his massive fleet of 33 ships-of-the-line out of Cadiz on 20 October, hoping to steal south, through the straits, and make his way unmolested to Toulon. He was renowned for his good luck – had he not escaped from the Nile bloodbath? – and that was one reason why Bonaparte had selected him as c-in-c.

But by the following dawn, Villeneuve saw that his luck was out. There, far to the west and just visible in the grey light, was the British battle fleet, 27 ships-of-the-line, the most potent naval fighting force the world had ever known. Slowly, laboriously in the light breeze, Villeneuve reversed the course of his ships, and headed north back towards Cadiz. The British fleet had the benefit of the wind, but it was a long pursuit during which every man had plenty of time to put his affairs in order. For his part, Nelson prepared a document bequeathing, as he put it, Emma as a legacy to his king and country, and wrote the prayer on pages 94–5. Then, as his fleet slowly closed on the combined enemy, he came out on deck, his chest embellished with the sparkling orders, decorations and stars of chivalry he had earned, each one a glinting target for enemy sharpshooters. His old

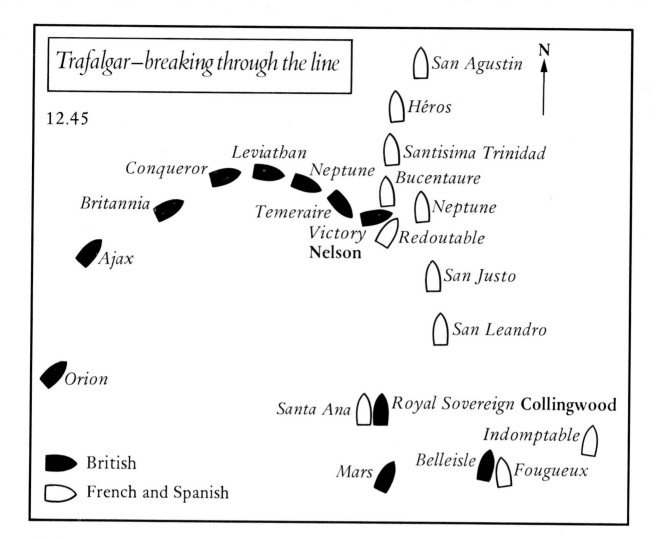

Trafalgar—breaking through the line

12.45

N

San Agustin

Héros

Santisima Trinidad

Leviathan

Conqueror

Neptune

Bucentaure

Britannia

Temeraire

Neptune

Victory
Nelson

Redoutable

Ajax

San Justo

San Leandro

Orion

Santa Ana

Royal Sovereign **Collingwood**

Indomptable

Belleisle

Mars

Fougueux

British

French and Spanish

friend and flag-captain, Thomas Hardy, suggested a plain coat instead, and although Nelson agreed, he said there was no time. It was a curious remark which can be interpreted in many ways.

From the flagship's halyards there fluttered the signal to all the fleet that was to become famous in the English language: 'England expects that every man will do his duty'.

The plan of battle was as simple as Nelson had claimed. Having, as he believed, drawn the enemy from his base, and the enemy having formed into the traditional single line of battle, Nelson now split his fleet into two parallel columns led respectively by Collingwood in the *Royal Sovereign* and himself in the *Victory*, and sailed straight at the enemy line, like twin lines of cavalry against the long wall of a fortress.

It was also as new as Nelson claimed, reversing every basic rule because it allowed the enemy to concentrate his fire on the leading ships in turn as they

OVERLEAF The *Victory* breaking the line at Trafalgar. The French *Redoutable* is on the *Victory*'s starboard, with the *Temeraire* alongside her.

came within range. The two flagships would inevitably receive a fearful drubbing, but the weight of metal would diminish ship by ship as they broke through and engaged in close gunnery duel an increasing number of the enemy. It was the quickest and most decisive means of bringing about a mêlée, a close action in which British gunnery and fighting skill would be best exercised: and Nelson was a fanatic for pace and decision.

Collingwood's ship was faster than the *Victory*, and Nelson on his quarter-deck watched with satisfaction as the three-decker stormed in towards the enemy guns – 'See how that noble fellow, Collingwood, carries his ship into action,' he exclaimed.

Soon the *Victory* was as hotly engaged as the *Royal Sovereign*, each taking and giving fearful punishment. Minute by minute the support grew until by one o'clock almost every British ship-of-the-line was hard alongside a Frenchman or a Spaniard, and the din of cannon and muskets and grenades and crashing masts and yards and shouts and screams filled the air about the 60 great fighting ships – many a survivor lost his hearing for good on that day of the greatest battle in sailing ship history.

It was at this time that Nelson was struck through his epaulette, hard above his decorations, by a sharp-shooter's musket ball. It penetrated his body and lodged in his spine. He was carried below, crying out, 'They have done for me at last'; and, with the thunder of battle still raging, but with the knowledge that his fleet had won an overwhelming victory, he died there some three hours later.

It was indeed a crushing victory, justifying all Nelson's inspired confidence and tactics. The trust he had placed in his captains, allowing them full initiative; the trust he placed in the people to fight as they had always fought for him, paid off in full.

Two in three of the enemy were captured or destroyed. Not one British ship was lost. It was the overture to Bonaparte's final defeat on land ten years later. On 21 October 1805 Nelson had confirmed the boast that the French would not come by water, the French and Spanish navies were crushed, and Britain became the maritime master of the world for more than a century.

'Thank God I have done my duty,' muttered Nelson on his deathbed. And so he had. And, this time there was no opportunity to tarnish the brilliance of his victory. This time he came straight home, to a grief-stricken nation, and the funeral of a hero.

> Admirals all, for England's sake,
>   Honour be yours and fame!
> And honour, as long as waves shall break,
>   To Nelson's peerless name.
>
> *Henry Newbolt*

OPPOSITE 'The Hero' is dead, Trafalgar has been won, Britain is safe. The *Victory* off the Isle of Wight in November 1805.

5
Steel, Steam and Cordite

Admiral Heihachiro Togo
1848–1934

*The rise or fall of the Empire depends upon the result of this
engagement. Do your utmost, every one of you*
Togo's signal before the Battle of Tsu-Shima

The remainder of this book is concerned with the rise of three new naval powers, the consequences of their rivalries and conflicts, and the great admirals of this pre-nuclear age of steam and steel.

The naval supremacy of Britain endured from 1805 until the end of the First World War, when the gunpower of the Royal Navy was so immense that it could have taken on and sunk all the world's navies together. Britain's period of supremacy included many struggles and challenges. The naval power of France and Spain was not destroyed at Trafalgar. Later, the new American navy was an embarrassment in 1812–14. Then the French again gave cause for alarm which led to political crises and 'naval scares' in Britain. But in spite of *matériel* weaknesses and ultra-conservative practices, the British navy remained supreme; or the rest of the world believed it to be so, which was the same thing.

The new naval powers were the USA, Germany and Japan. The creation of these navies led to the end of isolation and independence for Britain. A century after Trafalgar, Britain was obliged to seek naval allies in the Pacific and the Mediterranean in order to secure her home waters against the most dangerous threat to her supremacy since Nelson's time.

In the twentieth century, Germany twice challenged Britain and was twice defeated; Japan challenged the USA and was defeated; then Russia challenged the USA, and the outcome of that has yet to be seen. But the first and most unexpected challenge of all was that of Japan against Russia.

The commander who was one of the chief architects of the rapid rise of the Japanese navy, and who led this navy into battle against 'the mighty bear', was Heihachiro Togo. Japan's greatest sailor admired and sought to emulate Horatio Nelson. He began his naval career when the memory of Trafalgar was still green, learned gunnery on board the *Victory*, shaped the twentieth-century Japanese navy, and – such was the span of his life – when he died the day of the gun was almost over.

As British boys were once brought up on the legends of Nelson's fighting career, so generations of young Japanese learned of the heroism of Admiral Togo. This usually began with the story of his behaviour as a boy of fifteen when his home town of Kagoshima was bombarded by British men-of-war following the murder of a British merchant and the Japanese rejection of an ultimatum demanding compensation. Young Togo, with two of his brothers

PREVIOUS PAGES The age of steel, of smoke, of long-ranging guns and the creation of new maritime powers. The German High Seas Fleet at sea.

and his father, is said to have donned ceremonial warrior costume, with two swords at the sash, and defied the Western guns from the beach, acting with cool courage under fire.

Five years later, as a cadet in the Imperial Japanese Navy, Togo was one of several of his countrymen on board a British ship passing west through the Straits of Gibraltar. Dawn was breaking, and the Japanese youths had asked to be awoken early in order that they might identify Cape Trafalgar as they steamed past. Soon they would be learning more of that battle as well as the rudiments of naval gunnery and tactics, seamanship and navigation. Japan had determined to build a great navy, and this newly opened-up country naturally turned to Britain for ships and inspiration, as well as for the training of her future admirals. Seven years were to pass before Togo returned to his homeland, there to begin the long, hard climb up the promotion ladder.

Unlike his hero, Togo made no early notable impression on his seniors. Nor did he experience any early active service, as Nelson did, in which he could show his courage and initiative. He was regarded as an adequate, painstaking, conscientious but in no way exceptional officer. For a time he served as first lieutenant in the royal yacht *Jingei*, but there is no record of his attracting the attention of the mikado. In 1881 he married – by family arrangement – the nineteen-year-old daughter of a noble samurai.

Togo, hero of the new steel age at sea.

Togo was given his first ship in 1884, a year that marked the beginning of a long period of conflict along the seaboard of China and Korea as the European powers and Japan squabbled with one another and with China over concessions and trading ports and bases. Ultimatums were delivered and rejected, protocol was flouted, punitive expeditions mounted, towns bombarded.

More critical trouble developed between Japan and China in 1894, and it was Togo's ship that fired the first shots which led to the Sino–Japanese war. Unlike Nelson, Togo never lost a fight. He badly damaged two Chinese men-of-war, and then, controversially, proceeded to shell and sink (after due warning) a troopship carrying more than 1000 Chinese soldiers to Korea. It was awkward that the ship and her captain happened to be British.

After war was officially declared between the two Eastern nations, the main fleets were soon in action. The Battle of the Yellow Sea on 17 September 1894 was the first major action between the new 'steel' fighting ships, and the results were studied with interest by every naval power to see what lessons might be learned from it.

Fire was opened at 6000 yards, an inconceivable range to the gunners at Trafalgar, and a single high explosive shell could cripple a big warship – as one 8-inch shell demonstrated by almost sinking the Japanese flagship. But the Chinese suffered far worse losses, especially from the well directed Japanese quick-firers, and at the end of the day five of the Chinese ships had been destroyed. It was an inspiring experience for Togo, whose own ship had been hit nine times.

Togo's flagship, the British-built *Mikasa*.

OPPOSITE A formal portrait of the Comte de Grasse.

OVERLEAF
LEFT The Battle of Chesapeake Bay.

RIGHT The action at Cape St Vincent, 1797. The *Victory* raking the *Salvador del Mundo*.

FOLLOWING PAGES Some of the ships in which Nelson served: *Agamemnon, Vanguard, Elephant* and *Victory*

Although the Japanese gained control of the Yellow Sea in this action, Togo was to see a lot more action before peace was signed on 17 April 1895. His handling of his ship had been exceptional, and now for the first time he was becoming recognized as a future great leader. In January he had been promoted rear-admiral.

During the years that followed the successful Sino–Japanese War, Togo served mainly ashore on staff appointments, becoming commander of the important naval base at Sasebo. He did not get to sea again until the outbreak of the Boxer Rebellion in 1900. The experience of fighting alongside Russian, British, French and German troops, and of observing the performance of their men-of-war at close hand, was invaluable to Japan, and helped to create a deep measure of national self-confidence. Togo watched the Russian navy with special care, and came to the conclusion that it was 'by no means so formidable as many think.... Their discipline can hardly be called strict,' he wrote in his report, 'and I have noticed gaps in the training of their ships' companies....'

Already deep suspicion and hostility were growing between Japan and Russia. Russia was determined to become a major power in the Pacific. She was building a railway clear across Siberia, had secured a lease on Port Arthur in Korea, and in 1900 absorbed Amur province. In Manchuria she

"Dewey? We Do!!!"

had taken over a major railway from China, and had occupied Mukden and great stretches of Chinese territory.

Moreover, Russian diplomatic pressure in Europe had led to Japan's being forced to yield up the territorial gains she had made at the expense of China. Japan realized that she could not stand alone any longer, and that if she was aspiring to major power status she must find an ally. This led to the Anglo–Japanese Alliance of January 1902. Preparations for war went ahead rapidly in 1903, and on the night of 8–9 February 1904, the Japanese navy made a surprise attack against the Russian naval base at Port Arthur. The order was given by Admiral of the Fleet Heihachiro Togo, now c-in-c of the Imperial Japanese Navy.

At the age of fifty-five, Togo gave an impression of solid worth, an admiral in the Collingwood rather than the Nelson style. He was short in stature even for a Japanese officer, standing just 5 feet 3 inches, wore a grey moustache and short beard. Contemporary photographs show him with sloping shoulders and a slight stoop. Those who knew him at the time of the Russian war – the British naval attachés with his fleet, and Western newspaper correspondents – described him as severe in his manner, painstakingly conscientious, clear in his thinking; and then the surprise: with a suppressed but caustic sense of humour. One of the attachés, who saw him through all his triumphs and anxieties, commented that 'Never at any time, have his limits appeared to be in sight. He is indeed a noble man.' His modesty struck others. But everyone's first and most lasting impression was of the quality of his eyes, dark, missing nothing, 'piercing men even to the bottom of their hearts'.

Like most commanders of small navies at the time, Togo possessed a mixed bag of ships, some built in foreign yards, others at home. His own flagship, the *Mikasa* of 15,000 tons and carrying a main armament of four 12-inch guns, had been built by Vickers in England and was as formidable as any fighting ship in the world.

The Russo–Japanese War marked the steel battleship's finest hour. For half a century the battleship had been going through a series of painful and sometimes hilarious metamorphoses without the benefit of a single fleet action to guide the architects and builders. Ships were built that were little more than floating steel batteries with an enormous gun set into a barbette fore and aft. The Russians even built completely circular fighting ships. Some had armour plating nearly 2 feet thick over the vitals and none elsewhere; others sprouted a mass of guns of different calibres and with hulls evenly protected all over. Large numbers of battleships were built with engines to supplement the sails, or sails to supplement the engines, with an arrangement whereby the funnel collapsed to the deck and the screw was hauled in when there was sufficient wind – 'up-funnel, down-screw' ships these were called. The British built a notable battleship which turned turtle

PREVIOUS PAGES
ABOVE LEFT The Russian fleet at Tsu-Shima.

BELOW LEFT 'Dewey? We Do!' Patriotic zeal at the time of the Spanish–American War.

ABOVE RIGHT HMS *Agincourt* at Jutland.

BELOW RIGHT Admiral Sir David Beatty, a formal portrait painted by Sir Arthur Stockdale Cope.

OPPOSITE The sinking of the *Scharnhorst*, painted by C. E. Turner.

on its trials, drowning the designer and all on board. Everyone was groping in the dark, and forty years after the battle of Lissa, rams were still being built into the stems of battleships whose guns possessed a range of ten miles.

By the 1890s designers had settled down to a safe formula, with ships of around the *Mikasa*'s size, a speed of around 15 knots, and with four heavy and numerous smaller calibre guns. This was the class of ship that formed the backbone of the Russian and the Japanese navies.

The Russian navy had a mixed fighting tradition. But the Russian is basically a land animal, and although as brave in combat as any in the world, he was poorly led in these operations and the victim of revolutionary propaganda. The Japanese navy had no fighting tradition at sea in the modern sense. But the Japanese are a maritime people and the modern navy had been developed with remarkable co-ordinated skill and speed. The spirit, courage and discipline of the lower deck were beyond question, and the officers were well-trained and dedicated.

As in 1941, the Japanese surprise strike was intended to cripple the Russian Far East Fleet at Port Arthur. The moral effect of the torpedo boat attack was greater than the material result, as it was at Pearl Harbor. Although greatly feared as a weapon of sea warfare, the torpedo had not then been developed into the deadly missile of the First World War. Nor did either side exploit its full potential. If they had done so, the fleets of 1914 might have been of a very different composition.

Togo's responsibilities were even heavier than those of the generals. He had to keep the seas open in order that the Japanese armies might be landed in Korea, and then supplied and reinforced for as long as the war might last. His fleet was of about the same strength as Russia's. But whereas the Russians could call in reinforcements from Europe, all Japanese naval strength was committed from the outset.

Togo acted cautiously and skilfully, and had luck on his side. The Russians rarely ventured from their bases at Port Arthur, Vladivostok and Chemulpo. On one occasion when the big ships came out, the admiral was killed by a one-in-a-thousand chance hit on the conning tower: he was a good man, too, the best Russia had. On another occasion, the flagship struck a mine, drowning the crew and their admiral. Other ships were picked off when opportunity occurred, or forced into neutral ports to be interned.

The blockading and patrolling caused a great strain on the Japanese ships and men, and by the time news was received by Togo that the Russians were preparing a great fleet in the Baltic intended to destroy his own, many of his ships were the worse for wear and in need of a complete refit.

Once again, fortune was on his side. The Russians took their time, and the quality of the fleet was not all that it was cracked up to be.

By the end of 1904, Port Arthur had fallen to the Japanese army, the Russian Far East Fleet had virtually ceased to exist, and within another month Togo had completed the refitting of his ships and his plans for the reception

The tragic figure of the Russo–Japanese War, Admiral Rozhestvensky, depicted against the setting of his only victory, over British trawlers in the North Sea.

Rozhestvensky's
battered flagship after
Tsu-Shima.

and destruction of the Baltic Fleet which was still *en route* from European waters.

The commander of what was optimistically called 'a reinforcing fleet', or 'the Second Pacific Squadron', was Admiral Zinoviev Rozhestvensky, a brave and tragic figure in naval history, who was given a task quite beyond his abilities.

The departure of the Russian fleet from the Baltic was governed by the completion date of four new battleships, and it was not until October 1904 that Rozhestvensky's armada of 42 men-of-war and auxiliary and supply ships was ready to depart. The ships varied from the new and untested battle-

ships and some sound and modern cruisers to ancient 10–knot vessels which had once been rigged for sail and another which one officer described as 'half cruiser, half yacht, a caprice of our luckless naval designers'.

The supply problems were mountainous, and about the only things that did not run out were champagne in the wardrooms and revolutionary literature on the lower decks. The fleet faced an 18,000-mile voyage without a single Russian base *en route*, a variation of temperature from below zero Fahrenheit to 120 degrees, and the nightmare of having to coal at sea or in neutral ports with all the legal problems this must involve.

His Imperial Majesty Tsar Nicholas II came to see them off, boarded the leading ships and wished them all 'a victorious campaign and a happy return to your native land'. But at a banquet given by the admiralty on the last night one of the battleship captains arose from his seat in answer to the toast to success. '... You wish us victory,' he concluded, 'but there will be no victory.'

The voyage to meet Togo in battle was a seven-months'-long nightmare marked by mutiny, prostration from heat, insanity, international protests and conflicting and mainly lunatic instructions from home. On 8 April 1905 Rozhestvensky, at the end of his tether and now certain of his fleet's destruction, passed Raffles Light off Singapore, and thousands turned out to see his rusting, heterogeneous fleet steam by. Black smoke scored the tropical sky, and it could be seen that the vessels were low in the water from the coal piled upon their decks.

Seven weeks later, after receiving more unwanted decrepit reinforcements from home, Rozhestvensky steamed into the Straits of Tsu-Shima between Korea and the Japanese island of Kiu-Siu. At 1.30 in the morning, in moonlight and broken mist, a look-out in one of Rozhestvensky's ships spotted a strange vessel. Minutes later, the ether which had been broken previously only by occasional mysterious messages, was suddenly alive with urgent information. One of Togo's reconnaissance armed merchantmen had found the foe at last....

Togo had long before calculated that the shortest route to the last remaining base of Vladivostok was the most likely one to be followed by Rozhestvensky. Almost certain confirmation came with the news that the Russians had dispensed with their six supply ships and sent them to Shanghai. But with the meticulous care he always exercised, Togo kept his reconnaissance ships on their stations to avoid any possibility of Rozhestvensky slipping round the east side of the Japanese islands.

When Togo with the main Japanese battle fleet first sighted his adversary, Rozhestvensky was steaming on a north-easterly course at some 10 knots, his maximum speed, in twin columns line ahead, the first column consisting of the four modern battleships to starboard and ahead of the second column, which was made up of the rest of his fighting ships. The hospital ships and auxiliaries were far to the rear.

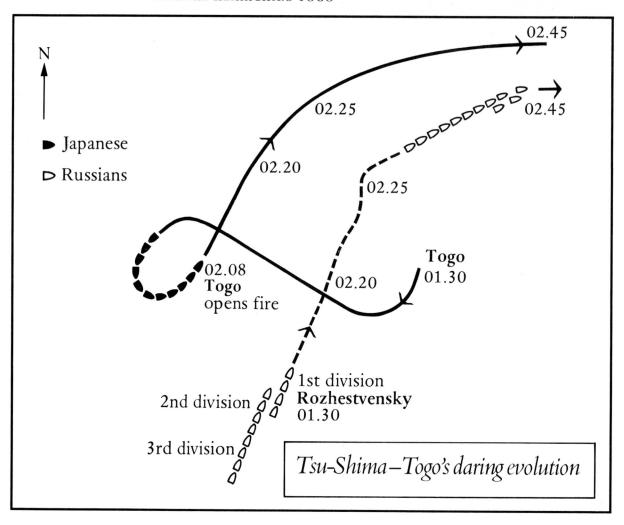

N

● Japanese
▷ Russians

02.45

02.25

02.20

02.08
Togo
opens fire

02.25

02.20

Togo
01.30

02.45

1st division
Rozhestvensky
01.30

2nd division

3rd division

Tsu-Shima — Togo's daring evolution

The firepower of the two fleets was slightly to the Russian advantage. But there were many factors favouring Togo: his ships were faster, he had a fresh, eager fleet, sailing in its own waters and led by men of high morale and skill. These alone were sufficient to tip the balance over far in the favour of the Japanese.

Togo led his fleet into its greatest engagement with all the flair and self-confidence of his English mentor. From the bridge of the *Mikasa*, to the north-east of Rozhestvensky, he directed his ships to follow across the bows of the Russian columns, and then, when well to the north-west, ordered a 270-degree turn. This would bring the Japanese single column on a course parallel to that of the Russians, and, with their superior speed, in a tactical position to 'cross the T' of the enemy at leisure.

It was an evolution which, like Nelson's plan at Trafalgar, carried with it great risks because, during the long, complicated turn, which only well-trained commanders could follow, Togo would be exposing his ships in succession to the full broadside weight of the Russian fleet.

To Togo's amazement, few shots were aimed at the crucial turning-point, and afterwards as he closed the range, Rozhestvensky made no effort to turn in and slip astern of his column, where he could have done terrible execution to the Japanese rear. His antagonist appeared incapable of making a decision as if paralysed by the rigours of his Odyssey from the Baltic – as indeed he was.

Once formed into two roughly parallel lines, with both fleets blazing away with their heavy and medium calibre guns at a range of some 6500 yards, the early Russian fire was surprisingly accurate, better than any Togo had witnessed at his earlier battles. But it deteriorated rapidly as the Japanese closed the range and caught up the rhythm of rapid fire with instantaneously fused shells.

The Russian flagship suffered badly, and Rozhestvensky was first injured in his conning tower and then smoked out of it. But it was the big, slab-sided Russian battleship *Oslyabya* that was the first to go down. The days of wooden ships, of boarding and few sinkings were long ago over, and soon others had followed her to the bottom. Rozhestvensky was driven off his flagship and, sorely wounded, sought refuge in one of his destroyers.

By nightfall, the Japanese victory was almost complete. Togo called off his heavy ships and sent in his torpedo craft. By dawn, several of the Russian cruisers had escaped to the south, to be interned by the Americans. Of those that remained afloat, one or two fought gallantly against hopeless odds while others raised the white flag. Admiral Nebogatoff, who had succeeded Rozhestvensky as C-in-C, surrendered the remainder of the ironclads on the morning of 28 May without firing a shot; and Japan had achieved her victory.

Tsu-Shima was as near an annihilation as circumstances could reasonably demand. Togo had sunk, captured or disabled 8 battleships, 9 cruisers, 3 coast defence ships and 9 destroyers. Some 8000 Russian sailors were dead or had been captured. In 24 hours, Russia had ceased to be a major power not only in the Pacific but in the world. Fifty years were to pass before she regained status at sea.

Tsu-Shima was also the only major, decisive fleet action in the history of the steel battleship. Only the gun had counted. In future, underwater or aerial weapons would at first be a tactical consideration and then the dominant influence.

Togo's victory at Tsu-Shima led to Russian capitulation on land. At the Treaty of Portsmouth, signed on 29 August 1905, Russia gained comparatively generous terms. American and European treatment of Japan in the aftermath of her great triumph had consequences beyond the calculation of those who sought to destroy the pride of the newly emerged, energetic and ambitious Japanese people.

Admiral of the Navy George Dewey
1837–1917

A fine set of fellows, but unhappily we shall never see them again.
British comment in Hong Kong on the departure of the American
Asiatic Squadron for Manila, April 1898

George Dewey, folk hero of the infant United States Navy, was born in Vermont on 26 December 1837, of Pilgrim Fathers' stock. His great-grandfather had fought at Lexington; his father, a doctor, brought up the family alone after the death of his wife, when George was five. According to George Dewey himself, describing his childhood, the strict religious influence and severe discipline at home in no way suppressed his high spirits; to the extent that when he was fourteen his father despatched him to a military academy. From here, young Dewey was sent to Annapolis.

In 1854 the Naval Academy was not long established, and was little known to the general public. Only a year earlier, Commodore Matthew Perry had arrived off Tokyo Bay with a letter from the American president making known his desire to trade; and it was in Perry's flagship, the *Mississippi*, that Dewey first saw action: 'It was the wonder of her funnels, spouting smoke to make her wheels move, and the sight of her guns that so impressed the Japanese.'[1]

But Dewey first went to sea after graduation in the 4000-ton *Wabash*, one of the same class of steam frigates as the famous *Merrimac* which fought the *Monitor* in 'the first ironclad duel'. In 1858 the United States Navy had a Mediterranean Squadron which was a very small token force by comparison with the French and British fleets. For the young midshipman, service in the Mediterranean, and later the Caribbean, broadened his concept of the world and swept away any dusty remnants of childhood parochialism.

With the opening of the Civil War, the Federal Navy found itself so short of officers that Dewey was at once promoted to the senior responsibility of executive officer of the *Mississippi* at the age of twenty-four. As one of the ships of the Gulf Squadron, it was the task of the *Mississippi* first to carry out blockade duties, and then – more interestingly – to work its way up the river for which she was named, beating past the Confederate forts 'and laying New Orleans under our guns'.

During this, the *Mississippi*'s most active period, her commander was Captain Melancton Smith, a fearless, cigar-smoking, temperance-fanatic fighter, who threatened to put in double irons any man he heard swearing. It was a time and an occasion that was rich in fire-eating eccentrics.

The attack on the forts and the forcing of the passage through to New Orleans took place on the night of 23–24 April 1862. The squadron's commander was the legendary and veteran fighter, David Glasgow Farragut.

Folk hero of the infant
United States Navy.
George Dewey, a
modest man, thrust on
to the stage of the
patriotic Spanish–
American conflict.

Everything was hurled at the squadron's ships as they proceeded up river, from shell and mortar fire to rams and fireships. 'Don't flinch from the fire, boys!' Farragut was at one moment heard to shout when the flames threatened to fry his men at the gun ports. 'There's a hotter fire waiting for those who don't do their duty!'

Dewey took up his post on the hurricane deck of the *Mississippi*. Captain Smith had told him, 'I cannot see in the night. I'm going to leave that to you, Dewey. You have younger eyes.' At one moment Dewey's young eyes spotted 'what appeared to be the back of an enormous turtle painted lead color'.[2] He recognized it as the Confederate ram *Manassas*, and was able to give the order to the helmsman in time to avoid a beam attack. Even so, the effect of the ram's glancing blow was like the shock of running aground. It was one of the most memorable events in Dewey's life when, on the following morning, the battered *Mississippi*, along with the other survivors of the night's fighting, anchored off New Orleans, her guns covering the streets of the panic-stricken city.

At the Battle of Fort Hudson later, the fighting was even hotter, and the sorely damaged *Mississippi* had to be abandoned. By contrast with New Orleans, it was a wretched moment for the young lieutenant when he had to admit defeat and take to the boats with his captain, and then row clear under heavy enemy fire, leaving the dead behind in the blazing wreck. But, as he wrote later in his memoirs:

In that disaster, as in every action, I myself had gained experience in the midst of danger and confusion when I was still young enough to profit by the lesson. No word of commendation I have received is more precious to me than that of Captain Smith's report, in which he said: 'I consider that I should be neglecting a most important duty should I omit to mention the coolness of my executive officer, Mr George Dewey, and the steady, fearless, and gallant manner in which the officers and men of the *Mississippi* defended her, and the orderly and quiet manner in which she was abandoned.'[3]

Dewey served out the rest of the Civil War as a prize commissioner. More than 30 years were to pass before he again saw action. This was an uneventful and uninspiring time, with long periods of shore duty broken by brief sea appointments. Dewey several times contemplated retiring from the service. But his loyalty paid off. He was a sound administrator, and when he was appointed chief of the Bureau of Equipment in 1889 there was promise of more interest. A new restlessness was abroad in the land. 'In common with every other ambitious officer in the navy', Dewey recalled, 'I was feeling the pulse of the new spirit and problems.'[4]

Like the Germans and the Japanese, and strongly influenced by the writings of Dewey's contemporary, Alfred Thayer Mahan, the meaning and value of seapower, for so long understood by the British, French, Dutch and others, was becoming more widely appreciated. America had determined to transform her navy from what had for so long been little more than a coastal defence force into a major fleet.

At the same time, Dewey recognized the waste and futility in scattering so widely and thinly about the world what small strength the US Navy already possessed. As early as 1890, over lunch with the secretary of the navy, he recommended closing down the European, South Atlantic and South Pacific stations, bringing home all the ships and dividing them between the North Atlantic and the Pacific. As Dewey admitted, the advice was a little ahead of the secretary's time; but not by long. And it was an identical policy to that advocated by Jackie Fisher for the British navy a decade later.

No one was more deeply involved in this naval renaissance than George Dewey. As president of the Board of Inspection and Survey from 1895, he was responsible for checking in the minutest detail the standard of the new generation of fighting ships. Then in 1897, with his appointment to the American Asiatic Squadron, he commanded some of these same ships. Within a few months, he was leading them into their first action.

Spain's first naval war for almost a century brought about results as disastrous for her as those which stemmed from Trafalgar. In the context of the 1970s, it is difficult to regard the Spanish–American War of 1898 as a politically or morally inspiring affair. Nor, in the purely naval sense, did it offer any of the lessons for the future that were so eagerly seized upon by the world's admiralties following the Russo–Japanese War.

'Though the Spaniards had months of warning, nothing except the hearts of the seamen were ready for the fight,' ran one contemporary comment. 'The mismanagement, or the corruption, or the ineptitude among her governing men must have been so awful.'[5] Spain's pathetic and ill-led forces were destroyed in their bases or after putting up only token resistance; and this sort of annihilation gave no guidance to ship designers, gunsmiths or tacticians who had for so long been working without guidelines.

The American Asiatic Squadron had no base of its own; and precious little ammunition. Dewey was aware of the shell shortage before he arrived in Japan to take over the command, and had already arranged the acceleration in the delivery of supplies. But in the event of war with Spain, which already seemed imminent, by contrast with his enemy who had a strongly fortified base at Manila, he would be fighting with one hand tied behind his back.

With the arrival of reinforcements, Dewey's squadron consisted of four modern but unarmoured cruisers, and a few smaller vessels. On 25 February 1898, Commodore Dewey received telegraphed orders from 'Teddy' Roosevelt, assistant secretary of the navy, 'In the event of declaration of war Spain, your duty will be to see that the Spanish squadron does not leave the Asiatic coast, and then offensive operations in Philippine Islands.'

Dewey overhauled his ships at Hong Kong, and with exercises and gunnery drill brought his small fighting force to a peak of perfection. He did not have to wait for long for action. On 25 April, more than two months

The last sad remains of once-paramount Spanish naval power: Manila Bay after Dewey's victory.

after the battleship *Maine* blew up in Havana harbour, Dewey received a cable informing him that America was at war with Spain. 'Proceed at once to Philippine Islands,' began the most banal fighting orders ever received by a commander. 'Commence operations particularly against the Spanish fleet. You must capture or destroy. Use every endeavour.'

'We proceeded in two columns, the fighting ships in one column,' wrote Dewey, 'and the auxiliary vessels another twelve hundred yards in the rear; and with a smooth sea and favouring sky we set our course for the entrance to Manila Bay, six hundred miles away.'[6]

Dewey's assault on the Spanish fleet in Manila Bay can be compared with Blake's descent upon the Spaniards in Santa Cruz, Tenerife. Dewey's knowledge of the defences of the bay was sketchy, but he had every reason to believe that the fortifications were powerful, and that the Spanish fleet, even if it was marginally inferior in gunfire to his own, possessed the inestimable advantage of being able to shelter inside those fixed defences. Dewey had also received information that the approaches were heavily mined.

Outside Manila Bay, Dewey ordered his squadron to heave to. His commanders came on board the flagship *Olympia* and Dewey addressed them: 'We shall enter Manila Bay tonight and you will follow the motions and movements of the flagship, which will lead.' That was all. Every detail, every contingency, had already been discussed, and Dewey and his commanders understood one another as well as Blake and his captains back in 1657.

It was 36 years since Dewey had lost his ship to the Fort Hudson shore batteries. Separated by the Pacific Ocean from his nearest base, even the smallest damage to his ships here could be a serious problem. Shortly after midnight, as the cruisers steamed at full speed between Corregidor and El Fraile, an 8-inch gun battery opened fire. A heavy shell passed between two of Dewey's ships, and as he ordered the fire to be returned, he awaited more flashes from the shore batteries.

To his astonishment, none came. The next battery was as silent. What had happened? The only evidence that they were steaming fast into Spain's most important and heavily fortified base was the absence of lights.

With the coming of daylight, Dewey could search for the Spanish squadron with greater promise of success. A few more shells passed harmlessly overhead at dawn. Minutes later, look-outs identified the Spanish ships – seven in all – formed up in a crescent before the township of Cavite, on the southern side of the bay. With intermittent and poorly aimed fire dropping about them, Dewey's ships proceeded in line ahead, like Nelson's at Copenhagen, awaiting the order.

At 5.40 am, Dewey turned to his flag-captain and uttered one of the best remembered statements in American naval history: 'You may fire when you are ready, Gridley.'

The range was 5000 yards; and at once the fore 8-inch gun of the *Olympia* opened fire. The action quickly developed into a deadly target practice for Dewey's cruisers. The Spanish gunners were soon demoralized, and it was left to the individual initiative of the Spanish ships' commanders to get under way and attempt to ram the enemy, and the crews of little torpedo boats to make gallant but ineffective attempts to attack the American warships.

Uncertain of the amount of damage he had caused, and disturbed by false reports of shell shortage on board his vessel, Dewey gave the order for the withdrawal of his ships, and for the men to take breakfast. (This move was wrongly ascribed to Dewey's theatrical nonchalance: the creators of folk-lore were prolific in '98!)

In fact, the action was already over, which became clear as soon as the smoke of battle had cleared. That night, Dewey wrote in his diary: 'Reached Manila at daylight. Immediately engaged the Spanish ships and batteries at Cavite. Destroyed eight of the former, including the *Reina Cristina* and *Castilla*. Anchored at noon off Manila.'[7] The day ended as dramatically as it had begun:

As the sun set on the evening of May 1, crowds of people gathered along the water-front, gazing at the American squadron. They climbed on the ramparts of the very battery that had fired on us in the morning. The *Olympia*'s band, for their benefit, played 'La Paloma' and other Spanish airs, and while the sea breeze wafted the strains to their ears, the poor colonel of artillery who had commanded the battery, feeling himself dishonored by his disgraceful failure, shot himself through the head.[8]

In this Alice-in-Wonderland war, no provision had been made for the occupation of the Philippines in the event of the destruction of the Spanish fleet, even though the failure to destroy it might have been fatal. It was not until three weeks after Dewey's annihilating victory that troopships sailed from San Francisco, and the naval base and city were not occupied until mid-August.

As a young midshipman in the Mediterranean, Dewey had observed the favourable consequences of Western colonial rule, and had noted that the tidy state of affairs in Egypt was 'an unanswerable argument in favour of British occupation'.[9] He therefore regarded the transfer of colonial responsibility for the Philippines, that 'rich prize for an ambitious power', from the decadent Spaniards to the United States government as a benign act. 'By a morning's battle we had secured a base in the Far East,' he boasted.

And it would remain so until the successors of his contemporary, Heiha-chiro Togo, deprived the United States of the base of Manila, and all the Philippines, 43 years later.

The occupation was not a peaceful one. The Philippinos violently objected to the American presence because they thought originally that the Americans had come to liberate them. The fighting continued while Dewey returned

THE PRIZE BRAND.

Cousin Jonathan. "THESE LOOK VERY NICE! WONDER IF THEY'LL BE THE BETTER FOR *KEEPING!*"

home to a heroic reception that was remarkable, even by American standards, with the construction in New York City of a triumphal arch like Paris's Arc de Triomphe.

Recognition for Dewey from the navy was equally notable. A special rank was created for him, that of admiral of the navy, equal to the rank of admiral of the fleet in the Royal Navy, which the US Navy would soon rival in power and fighting prowess.

It was not until 5 October 1899 that Dewey was able to haul down his flag in the *Olympia* after the completion of the most exhausting and feverish celebrations of victory over the pathetic remnants of the once-great Spanish empire.

George Dewey's life spanned an eventful period in naval history. He was born in the year Queen Victoria came to the British throne. He witnessed the naval emergence of Japan and Germany as well as the American renaissance which he had done so much to bring about. Steam power and the high explosive shell were hardly considered when he was a boy. He grew up with the ironclad, saw the rise of the Dreadnought and the first assertions of power of the submarine and the fighting plane.

Dewey died on 16 January 1917, three months before his country embarked on a war that made the events at Manila and Santiago seem trivial. In terms of the size of the squadrons involved and the destruction they wrought, Manila Bay was no more than a skirmish. But the important thing was that the American people did not think so at the time, and the pride that this successful foreign involvement engendered in 1898 was only matched by the loss of pride caused by a subsequent American foreign involvement 75 years later.

The crash of guns in Manila Bay awoke America to the importance of seapower. The United States' twentieth-century maritime supremacy stemmed from the pathetic smoking wrecks of Spanish men-of-war at Manila and Santiago as surely as English pride and self-confidence emerged from the scattered wrecks of Spanish galleons in 1588.

OPPOSITE British comment on the victory of the developing American navy in 1898.

Grand Admiral Alfred von Tirpitz
1849–1930

We require a certain measure of sea power as a political factor against England.
Tirpitz to the German Emperor

The father figure of the German Navy was a man who originally evinced no interest in the sea and never saw a gun fired in anger. His work began in earnest in 1897 when he became the leader of a navy of insignificant size and power.

On 26 June of that year the British navy assembled at Spithead for review by the queen-empress to celebrate her diamond jubilee. The ships were drawn up in five columns, 30 miles of fighting power. They had names like *Revenge*, *Victorious* and *Magnificent*. It was the most impressive display of maritime strength the world had ever seen.

Among the other monarchs and members of royalty present was the Queen's grandson Willie, Emperor Wilhelm II of Germany, a man of boundless ambition whose complex and fractured personality was to be one of the first causes of the worst war in history.

The Kaiser suffered from a great jealousy of many of Britain's qualities and achievements; and above all he envied his grandmother her navy, its style and grandeur, its assumption of superiority, its fighting history and traditions, its sheer size. Never mind that he already commanded the largest and most efficient army in the world. Willie wanted a navy, too, to match up to his country's new-born wealth, industrial strength, trading status and wide-flung empire.

In that same month Tirpitz took up his appointment in Berlin. His ambitions for a massive navy were as powerful as those of the emperor, who was his closest ally.

Tirpitz's introduction to the navy at the age of sixteen had not been propitious. A corvette which had on board almost every cadet being trained for the new service was sunk and no one survived. It was rumoured that the Prussian Junker party, hostile to a new upstart service, had bribed a Danish skipper to ram the cadets' vessel – an indication of the navy's status at that time.

From the outset, the navy carried the stigma, in Prussian eyes, of being bourgeois and intellectual. In fact, these foundations gave the service its great strength. Its intellectualism, by contrast with the army's philistinism, was to prove invaluable. So were its versatility and flexibility of mind. But as Tirpitz himself accepted, the new navy was 'not in keeping with the Prussian tradition'. The Franco–Prussian War of 1870–1 only served to enhance the reputation of the all-conquering army while the small and ineffectual navy could do nothing against the French.

'. . . a certain measure of sea power'. The words of Tirpitz (LEFT) in 1896 were no more than an echo of Kaiser Wilhelm II's (ABOVE) aspirations.

Tirpitz rose progressively through the ranks of the service during the 1870s and 1880s, just as Togo was gaining promotion with similar lack of exceptional recognition in the similarly small Japanese navy on the other side of the world. Eleven of what Tirpitz declared to be 'the best years of my life' were spent with the experimental torpedo branch, an omen of the future role of the German navy in two world wars. Like the submarine service and, later still, the air arm, in most of the world's navies, Tirpitz's torpedo branch 'constituted a corps within a corps, the united spirit of which was everywhere recognised, but also envied and opposed'.

With the accession of Kaiser Wilhelm II in 1888 following the scramble for new colonies which had begun four years earlier, a new spirit swept through the German navy. In the early days, the sentiment in the service had been pro-British, the old comradeship of anti-Bonapartism and a deep respect for British naval achievement still prevailing. As German trade and imperial ambition increased, feeling amongst all classes in Germany became more and more anglophobic. Britain, as the richest and most successful trading nation in the world, had the largest navy. The correlation of success with number of battleships was further nurtured by the writings of the American admiral, Alfred Thayer Mahan.[10]

No one read Mahan with more enthusiasm and trusting belief than Tirpitz, and he was soon acquiring the reputation of a strategist as well as a specialist in *matériel*. Soon after the 'Kruger telegram' incident, which had further worsened relations between Britain and Germany, the German minister of marine, Admiral Albrecht von Stosch, wrote to Tirpitz to enquire 'how we could conduct a naval war with England with any success'.[11]

Tirpitz replied (13 February 1896) by pointing out the alliance-value of a navy. 'Up to the present our policy has failed completely to grasp the political importance of sea power,' he wrote, underlining this sentence.

If we intend to expand and strengthen ourselves commercially by means of the sea, then, if we do not provide ourselves simultaneously with a certain measure of sea power, we shall be erecting a hollow structure. When we expand we shall run against interests everywhere that are either already established or will be soon. This means conflict of interests.[12]

The idea that a nation could not expand its trade without a head-on conflict was typical of German belligerence and paranoia at this time. We must, was Tirpitz's cry, 'arouse our nation to build a fleet'.

Tirpitz had come to know the Kaiser when Wilhelm was still only the son of the heir to the throne. In 1887 his torpedo boat flotilla escorted the prince across the North Sea for the golden jubilee celebrations of his grandmother. Neither prince nor naval officer was to forget their cold reception.

Prince Wilhelm had long before evinced a keen interest in naval affairs. The moment he became emperor, he threw himself into the cause of naval expansionism and even acquired for himself a special permanent naval committee. He became extremely well informed on naval affairs, especially on matters relating to *matériel*. The British director of naval construction once declared that there was probably no admiral in all the Royal Navy so knowledgeable about warship detail as the German emperor.

Unfortunately for the German navalist cause, the divided command structure, with all its petty competition and jealousies, added to political opposition from pacifist and liberal elements, resulted in only slow progress. Tirpitz found himself temporarily out of favour and accepted a seagoing command in the Far East. In 1897, when he returned to take up the supreme command, the burning topic – the *only* naval topic – was the imminent and unprecedented increase in the size of the navy.

'The Kaiser wants a fleet like that of England,' wrote a foreign office official in Berlin to the German ambassador in London. 'With 28 first-class battleships – and wanted to direct his whole domestic policy to that end, i.e., to a fight.'[13]

'When I arrived in Potsdam', wrote Tirpitz, 'the Emperor told me that everything was ready for the navy campaign.' For his part, Tirpitz presented the emperor with a long paper on the constitution of the new fleet. It was as uncompromising and specific in its theme as the kaiser's. 'The military situation against England demands battleships in as great a number as possible. . . .'

Tirpitz turned out to be a consummate diplomat. He needed all his powers of persuasion, wiliness and forceful attack to get his first Navy Law through the German parliament, the Reichstag. His methods included ingratiating himself with the politically outcast but still popular Prince Bismarck by asking him to launch a battleship named after him. A Navy League was set up for the arousing of popular support for a great fleet to challenge the Royal Navy. This meant public meetings, lectures, the printing of thousands of pamphlets, and even the special publication of a translated edition of Mahan's *The Influence of Sea Power on History*.

Politically, Tirpitz sought to show that this greatly expanded navy was a force for peace, its object being merely to give Germany 'a chance against a superior enemy', 'a sea force which will compel even a sea power of the first rank to think twice before attacking our coasts'.

In March 1898, after a prolonged political battle, Tirpitz, and his emperor, got their way. The 1898 Navy Law fixed the strength of the fleet at 19 battleships, 8 armoured coast defence ships, 12 large and no fewer than 30 light cruisers, with proportionate torpedo and auxiliary craft. Almost overnight, a new navy had been conceived. As one authority has expressed it: 'The Navy Law of 1898 ... began a new era. The emphasis in German military affairs shifted dramatically from the land to the sea. From April 1898 to August 1914, the fleet ... dominated Germany's international relations.'[14]

The 1898 law was only the beginning. With the acceleration of a battle-ship sliding down its launching slip, new and larger programmes followed

Hipper's flagship *Lützow*, the near-unsinkable battle cruiser at Jutland. But she sank.

the first. Even before the law had passed through the Reichstag, informed opinion in Britain perceived the dangers. 'The British public are being daily taught to regard the Kaiser as the implacable and vigilant foe of their country,' wrote the *National Review* '... We clearly cannot afford to allow the German Emperor to hold the balance of sea power in Europe in the early years of the twentieth century.'

Tirpitz remained one of the two key navalist figures in the Anglo–German battleship race of 1898–1914. His chief opponent, the captain (so to speak) of the other team, was the British admiral, John Arbuthnot Fisher, a dynamic, extravagant, single-minded administrator whose favourite description of himself – self-termed at that – was 'ruthless, relentless and remorseless'.

John Fisher's rise through the ranks of the Royal Navy was in parallel with Tirpitz's but very different in style. He regarded himself as a messiah of reform, an exterminator of lassitude and supineness, a promoter of all that was revolutionary, from training to deployment, from ship design and armament to tactics. He was nine-tenths right in all that he did, and his reforms were indeed sorely needed. What will always remain in doubt is whether he could have carried out these reforms by less divisive and less destructive methods within the short time allowed him.

Fisher became first sea lord in 1904, and, like one of his favourite giant battle cruisers, survived the political and naval broadsides fired at him with-

The British
Dreadnought, apotheosis
of imperial sea power
in 1906. She upset all
Tirpitz's calculations.

out respite until 1910 by outpacing his enemies and by the support of King Edward VII and a handful of powerful politicians and newspapermen.

Where Tirpitz was steady, successfully concealing his highly strung temperament, Fisher was unpredictable in his style. Tirpitz avoided publicity, Fisher sought it – but he sought it like a flamboyant theatrical *entrepreneur* who wants to tell the world of his great show. Tirpitz's one concession to unorthodoxy was his twin-spiked beard. Fisher remained clean-shaven all his life, but like Nelson (his God), he loved his chest to flash with orders and decorations, and would flirt outrageously and dance the night through with pretty women when most men were long past such high jinks.

In accordance with medical and social custom, Fisher and Tirpitz took the waters at Marienbad and Carlsbad. They were sometimes neighbours, or even stayed at the same hotel. But there is no record that these two men, who were guiding their mighty navies and their fatherlands towards inevitable collision, ever met.

The German Navy Law of 1898 was followed by a second in 1900 which replaced the earlier one and provided for a battle fleet, a foreign fleet and a reserve, amounting to 38 battleships and 52 cruisers. This was a force which would make Germany the world's second naval power and would even more seriously threaten Britain's supremacy.

Britain's treaties with Japan and France, in 1902 and 1904, secured the Pacific and the Mediterranean, but Britannia could no longer claim to rule the waves alone. She had to re-deploy many of her overseas squadrons and close down foreign stations, in order to concentrate her main strength against this new threat across the North Sea.

Fisher's answer to Tirpitz's massive proposed increase in battleship strength was the *Dreadnought*, the first all-big-gun, turbine-powered fast battleship, which revolutionized fighting-ship design and made every other battleship in the world (including British) obsolete.

The lessons of Tsu-Shima had confirmed the belief of many experts that mixed battery ships-of-the-line were less efficient than those with a single-calibre broadside. Germany was bound to follow suit. Britain relied on surprise and her greater ship-building resources to keep herself ahead.

Tirpitz ordered the widening of the Kiel Canal to allow the new and bigger ships to proceed swiftly between the Baltic and North Sea. He signed contracts for dreadnoughts that were less heavily gunned but much tougher than the British ships. (They proved to be almost unsinkable.)

Fisher introduced the battle cruiser, an ultra-fast cruiser with the gun-power of a battleship. Tirpitz increased the number of shipyards and gun factories, and laid down more and better battle cruisers. Fisher introduced the 13.5-inch gun while Tirpitz was engaged in raising the German heavy gun calibre from 11 to 12 inches. Tirpitz ordered long-range submarines, and as early as 1912 he wrote to the Kaiser: 'Forgive my disturbing your holiday; but it is a question of an urgent and important matter – the improve-

A German Zeppelin in 1915, h

...he German fleet, is a precursor of new naval power.

The final arbiter of naval power in 1917, until new counter-weapons and tactics defeated them. This is the German U25 at sea.

ment of our airship construction. The new naval airship will represent an enormous advance. To me the time seems to have come when we should proceed to the systematic building of an aerial fleet . . .'[15]

The formidable increase in the size of Fisher's navy, and creation of Tirpitz's battle fleet, were carried out in a climate of conflicting jingoism and pacifism on both sides. Political capital was made out of the race in Germany and Britain, ministers fell, prime ministers and parties were threatened, admirals were sacked. Internal acrimony often exceeded the conflict in interests between the two nations themselves.

The proportion of the national resources of both countries given up to the construction of fighting ships, their dockyards and bases, their armament and supplies, the recruiting, training and equipping of their crews, increased year by year. In August 1914, when the long expected armageddon exploded upon Europe (Fisher had predicted the date within a month in 1910), Britain had in commission some 65 battleships and battle cruisers, and Germany almost as many.

Just as (so it was said) Germans used to cross themselves at the sight of Fisher in Marienbad, so Tirpitz was reviled in Britain, and his great size, his bald head, ferocious frown and singular beard were featured in hundreds of critical cartoons.

At the outbreak of war, Tirpitz had complete confidence in the magnificent fleet he had created; and it was with anguish that he bowed to the political pressures which forced on his beloved service a passive role, with survival as a fleet in being rather than as an aggressive fighting fleet. 'It only needed the right command to bring out all its qualities,' he wrote after the war, 'and to lead the fleet to victory.'

Later, when the long-range submarine had proved its effectiveness beyond even Tirpitz's wildest dreams, he was among those who most strongly supported unconditional warfare on allied shipping. This had been conducted on a limited scale and for a limited period from 18 February to 30 August 1915, when it was abandoned for political reasons and in the face of American protests. Its success stirred the German war leaders to propose its re-introduction early in 1916. But the new campaign, announced on 11 February 1916, was hedged about with so many limitations intended to placate American opinion, that Tirpitz did not believe it could be effective.

Tirpitz always believed, and with good reason, that German naval policy was conducted with insufficient defiance and determination, and on 12 February he resigned as secretary of state for the navy after eighteen tumultous years.

Later, when his battleships at last came to grips with Fisher's dreadnoughts, they showed their overall quality. Then, when Germany resorted again to unrestricted submarine warfare, a few comparatively inexpensive u-boats came nearer to destroying British maritime power than all the dreadnoughts together that Tirpitz had laid down.

Tirpitz died, a bitter and disappointed man, eleven years after the surrender to the Royal Navy, and five years before a new German navy was to rise from the wrecks of his High Seas Fleet which had scuttled itself in Scapa Flow.

Admiral of the Fleet
Earl Jellicoe of Scapa
1859–1935

We cannot rely on much if any superiority in gunnery in my opinion. The German Fleet has shown itself to be highly efficient and their gunnery in any action in which they have not been hopelessly inferior has been markedly excellent.
Jellicoe to the Admiralty, 19 November 1914

John Rushworth Jellicoe, groomed for the role of the twentieth century's Horatio Nelson, failed to live up to expectations.

The two navies which confronted one another across the North Sea in August 1914, and upon which Germany and Britain had lavished so much of their wealth and resources, had been built by many men with many skills. For Britain, Fisher had been the leader of reform and rebuilding; and Tirpitz had been more responsible than anyone else for the creation of the High Seas Fleet. Both men might have failed without the support of their sovereigns.

But from this decade and a half of hectic rivalry there stand out other great figures. Ironically, one of the best on the British side was German-born, and a 'highness' at that. Prince Louis of Battenberg combined German intellectualism and exceptional powers of organization and diligence with British self-confidence. He took over the admiralty soon after Fisher retired and worked in harmony with Winston Churchill as first lord in the critical period leading to war, and during the first dangerous months. Admiral Sir Percy Scott, the contentious gunnery expert, was another; and among the politicians were Lords Selborne and Lee, and that *éminence grise*, Lord Esher.

Tirpitz, too, had selected some first-class talent to lead the German navy. The officers were a highly professional body, but rather careful. They were like high-grade schoolmasters from good upper-middle class homes who did not much care for the sea, and regarded their ships as a soldier regards his tank – something to climb into and operate dutifully and efficiently when the need arises, but not a home in itself. The German officers had the highest regard for their ships, judged them as embodiments of the German industrial and scientific miracle to be the best in the world, and therefore not to be thrown away lightly.

Like the German airmen in the First World War, the Germans tended to retire unless certain of victory, not because they lacked courage (far from it) but for the rational reason that victory must be certain and overwhelming with minimum damage to themselves. The only time the Germans stayed to fight (at Coronel in December 1914), they had every advantage overwhelmingly on their side. In all other major actions, the German commanders either withdrew or remained only long enough for the arrival of support. This policy led the German Admiral von Spee to miss a great opportunity at the Falkland Islands when he could have committed crushing damage on a superior British squadron which he surprised coaling in its base.

The Germans had reason to be proud of their ships. They were at least the equal of their British opposite numbers, they were less easily damaged or sunk, and had superb guns. German mines and torpedoes were markedly superior to British underwater weapons. So were the shells. The British took risks in shipbuilding, as they took risks in combat. They were experimental. They risked inferior protection for bigger guns just as they risked defeat in the romantic tradition.

The spirit of the British navy was more extrovert than that of the German. Officers and men possessed an absolute conviction of superiority, and were supported by a tradition of maritime superiority and the consciousness of being the senior service. British naval officers were like members of a good club, decent, convivial, loyal, and regarding intellectualism as bad form. But they had also been inspired by the aggressive spirit since the harshly competitive rough and tumble of public school life. Most of them had also spend a great deal of time on tough and dangerous sports like hunting, steeplechasing and polo.

It is, therefore, a paradox of history that when the breast-beating finally ceased and live ammunition was slipped into the breeches of the 12-inch guns, both sides assumed a cautious stance. Like the Spanish and French before them, when faced with a British blockade, the Germans remained behind the protection of their fixed defences. More surprisingly, the British commander, complaining of inadequate superiority in heavy ships, retreated to ever more distant bases, until the Grand Fleet ended up for a while in a lough on the north coast of Ireland, the c-in-c complaining that in his previous base 'if a submarine did get in, she practically has the British Dreadnought fleet at her mercy'.

The c-in-c had been groomed by Fisher for many years to lead the Grand Fleet when war came. He was in appearance and manner neither what one would have expected that firebrand Fisher to select, nor was he the British idea of a gallant salt, in the Nelsonian tradition. He was small – though actually 2 inches taller than Nelson at 5 feet 6 inches – but he had an unimpressive demeanour, and to anyone who did not know him well, an inadequate style and manner.

John Rushworth Jellicoe was born at Southampton on 5 December 1859. The navy was traceable in his ancestry on both sides, on his father's side not very creditably, as his great-great-grandfather had been imprisoned for embezzlement while working as pay clerk to the navy at Portsmouth.

But there could have been no more upright and worthy citizens than Jellicoe's parents. His father was commodore of the Royal Mail Steam Packet Company; his mother full of good works.

Jellicoe joined the navy at the age of twelve, and after doing two years of elementary training on board the *Britannia*, went to sea in 1874 in a sailing frigate. Not much had changed since Nelson's day. The frigate possessed steam power but rarely used it, engines being considered as products of the devil, and engineers as a dirty and lowly tribe who must mess separately.

He was early recognized as an able young officer, with a keen enquiring mind. He forgot nothing and did everything well, including all the usual sports for which he was less well endowed than many. Nor did he ever get into a flap. It was the precision of his brain and his cool calm and control in a crisis which recommended him most strongly to his superiors. Jellicoe specialized in gunnery at a time when it was a very neglected branch, and, with men like Percy Scott and Frederic Dreyer, improved gunnery from a condition deserving of mockery to something approaching German standards by 1914.

Above all, Jellicoe was a just man, a nice man with a happy disposition and a happy home life. Of his few faults, only one was widely known before his appointment as C-in-C, and it was thought that it would not be revealed under the stress of war. This was his difficulty in delegating anything. Like many men with brilliant brains, he could not bear the idea of anyone else doing what he could do better. So he tried to do everything, and could not. But the stress of war emphasized rather than reduced this weakness, and revealed others. He proved to be a complainer. He complained frequently of the weakness of his fleet and the dangers in which he was placed. And he showed almost as strong a disinclination as the German C-in-C to take risks.

The result was that the great armageddon in the North Sea, the twentieth-century Trafalgar so longed for by the British people, did not take place. Instead, the news was of intermittent British ship losses, and barely credible insults, like the defeat of a British squadron in the Pacific and the bombardment without German loss of British east coast towns.

It was typical of John Jellicoe's character that he had taken over the supreme command of the British battle fleet reluctantly at the outbreak of war because the post was the most coveted in the service, and it was held by a gallant friend.

Soon Jellicoe had more material problems on his hands. He discovered that his bases were inadequately protected against submarine penetration, and that the German U-boats possessed far greater range and sea-keeping qualities than had been predicted, even by the Germans themselves. As the U-boats continued to pick off British cruisers in the North Sea, the fleet began to suffer from periscope nerves. Jellicoe wanted to exercise his great armada but felt more and more reluctant to do so at the risk of losing some of his big ships. His margin of superiority of dreadnoughts was very narrow during the early weeks of the war. He was deprived of three battle cruisers for the search for Admiral von Spee in the Pacific, and had a battleship sunk by a single mine, which only increased his feverish anxiety about the German undersea offensive and the quality of his dreadnoughts.

Prince Louis of Battenberg and Winston Churchill, running the naval war in London, became concerned about the tone of Jellicoe's communications. In a memorandum about minelaying by enemy destroyers, Jellicoe wrote: '... caution is especially necessary in following round the enemy's rear, and the flag officer leading the line must exercise great discretion....'[16] Was this the language of the new Nelson? And would John Jervis or Cuthbert Collingwood have fretted at the news (false as it turned out) that new German ships joining the fleet had bigger guns than had previously been thought? Now, complained Robert Blake's twentieth-century successor, 'We cannot rely on much if any superiority in gunnery in my opinion.'[17]

The months passed while the army crossed the Channel and engaged the German army in ever greater numbers and with ever greater gallantry and casualties. For almost two years the main battle fleet failed to sight the enemy or fire its guns in anger, while Jellicoe worried about his inadequate strength and the growing menace of the U-boats. He demanded, and received, constant reassurance from the admiralty. '*The great thing is not to be downhearted!*'[18] wrote Fisher, who had been recalled to the first sea lord's office on the tragic resignation of Battenberg after the expression of hysterical anti-German feeling. Downhearted, indeed! How would Drake, off Panama, have reacted to a message suggesting that he should not allow himself to become depressed?

In this case, Jellicoe's disappointment had offensive origins. His battle cruisers had just failed to contact units of the German fleet which had made a brief excursion into the North Sea. The cruisers were doing what fighting there was, and it was not until the end of May 1916 that there occurred the opportunity for a gun duel with the High Seas Fleet. Jutland was at once the dreadnought battleship's apex and nadir, and the greatest gun duel in the history of sea warfare.

Since January 1916, under its new C-in-C, Admiral Reinhard Scheer, the Germans had demonstrated a more aggressive attitude. It was soon clear that this might bring about the long awaited clash of arms, and from February on there were several sightings and 'near misses' between the big ships. This new German stance was welcomed by all ranks in the British fleet, whose patience had been sorely tested through two inactive northern winters. Both fleets had felt the prick of guilt at their own inaction when so many were dying in the squalor of trench warfare.

On 15 May 1916 Scheer laid a trap in the North Sea, into which he hoped to lure the British battle cruisers. U-boats were withdrawn from preying on merchantmen and ordered to patrol offensively in a long line south-west of Norway. The German battle cruisers were then ordered out in order to make an ostentatious demonstration off the Norwegian coast in the hope of

Battle Orders by printed instructions, more detailed than ever before, and a distant cry from the spontaneity and courageous flair of the Napoleonic Wars. No wonder commanders flinched from taking the initiative!

tempting the British battle cruiser force across the line of U-boats. When it was committed to battle, the Germans would attempt to draw their enemy on to the main German force of battleships hovering over the horizon.

That, at any rate, was the basic outline of intention. It could take no account of the fact that British Intelligence had acquired the German code, and was in any case a most skilfully conducted department which knew more about German day-to-day operations and long-term plans than the Germans themselves could have dreamed possible.

Jellicoe, with the main British Grand Fleet of 24 battleships and 3 battle cruisers, was anchored at his base in Scapa Flow in the Orkney Islands north of Scotland and in Cromarty on the afternoon of 30 May. Admiral Beatty

with 4 very fast battleships and 6 battle cruisers was farther south in the Firth of Forth.

At 5.40 pm Jellicoe was informed by the admiralty that there was unusual German activity and that 'the Germans intend some operations commencing tomorrow'. By eleven o'clock that evening the whole British Grand Fleet was at sea, some 150 fighting ships, from 28,000-ton battleships capable of firing 15,800 pounds of high explosive shells 20 miles every thirty seconds, down to nippy little destroyers of barely 1000 tons but carrying just as deadly a load of destruction.

Jellicoe had ordered Beatty to a rendezvous with his own main battle fleet at a point 90 miles west of the entrance to the Skagerrak.

Jellicoe's flagship *Iron Duke* – too precious to be hazarded in combat.

169

In Jellicoe's flagship, the *Iron Duke*, as in all the other ships of the fleet, there was little expectation of battle. They had been out on sweeps too often with only abortive results. 'It takes two to make a fight,' they would say. 'And the Hun's always on the run.'

By the early afternoon of 31 May, a calm, faintly misty day in the North Sea, it seemed as unlikely as ever that there would be any action. A message from the admiralty – false as it turned out – related that the German flagship was still in its base.

Then, soon after two o'clock, one of Beatty's light screening cruisers sighted a small merchantman, stationary and blowing off steam. It was a Danish vessel which had been ordered to heave to for inspection by a pair of German destroyers acting as distant screen for the German battle cruisers. The light forces of both sides opened fire. An innocent neutral was to be responsible for bringing together the two greatest fighting fleets in the world. The heavier ships of both sides were drawn progressively into the gun duel until, at 3.20 pm, the two battle cruiser forces were in touch and at 3.47 Beatty opened fire at a range of 15,000 yards.

Jellicoe was still far to the west when he picked up the first signal from Beatty's light cruisers indicating that units of the enemy had been sighted. He did not draw the conclusion that the German battle cruisers, let alone the main High Seas Fleet, was in the vicinity; but he did order an increase in speed, and a change of course to the south-east.

News of the action remained sparse. It was almost four o'clock before Jellicoe was informed by Beatty that he had sighted enemy battle cruisers and was engaging them, and for another forty minutes he was left in ignorance of what was going on.

During this first phase of the battle, neither the German nor the British battle cruiser forces knew that their respective enemy main battle fleets were out and in close proximity. The Germans were successfully drawing Beatty's force into the jaws of the High Seas Fleet, in accordance with their tactical plan. But the Germans did not know that the battleships of the Grand Fleet, in their turn, were hastening to the support of its battle cruisers.

Never was sea fighting as confused as it was in the First World War when speeds had risen from some 5 knots in Nelson's time to over 30 knots, when every ship marked its passage with a trail of black smoke – blacker than ever at high speed – and the smoke from gunfire and shell strikes added further to the fog of uncertainty. Radio signalling remained unreliable, and garbled messages could confuse worse than silence. Moreover, visibility is rarely clear in the North Sea even at the best of times.

The first small sign of emergence from the fog of uncertainty occurred at Jutland when a British seaplane carrier hoisted out a machine which took off and at 3.33 pm reported that the enemy had turned south. That was all. But its signal was an omen of the future of naval warfare.

At 4.38 Jellicoe intercepted a signal from a British light cruiser indicating that something more than German battle cruisers were at sea. A few minutes after this, the C-in-C issued the general signal: 'Enemy's battle fleet is coming north'. And now, at last, it seemed as if the great clash of arms might after all take place, and men made private and spiritual as well as public and practical preparations for combat, as they had since Salamis.

Jellicoe's main force was disposed in six parallel columns of four battle-ships each, all racing south-east at 20 knots, like a fork plunging towards its victim. Unlike the days of sailing warships proceeding to battle, of the 105,000 British and German sailors at sea, only a handful could observe anything beyond their gun breeches and dials, their torpedo tubes or the heaped shovel of coal they were about to thrust into the roaring furnace. And not even Jellicoe himself knew where the enemy would appear, if he appeared at all. The only further message from his subordinate, fighting somewhere out of sight to the south, was received soon after five, and all it said was '26–30 Battleships, probably hostile, bearing S.S.E., steering S.E.'

It was not until six o'clock that any hard and authoritative news was received, and this came from one of Jellicoe's own ships, the *Marlborough*, leading his extreme starboard column, which reported sighting gun flashes on her starboard bow, and then battle cruisers – their own battle cruisers, firing at an unseen enemy.

Jellicoe had to make up his mind how best to respond to this surprising information. Clearly, the moment had come when he might cripple the German fleet with all the profound consequences this would have for the Allied cause – the end of the U-boat peril, the final destruction of German commerce in the Baltic, the establishment of communications with the hard-pressed Russians. At the very worst, the end of the war would be brought nearer.

Many had been the critical situations which British admirals in the past had been called upon suddenly to solve, but never had there been one which demanded higher qualities of leadership, ripe judgement and quick decision, than that which confronted Admiral Jellicoe in this supreme moment of the naval war. There was not an instant to lose. . . .

Thus wrote Sir Julian S. Corbett in his official account of Jutland. Deployment into single line-ahead battle formation had to be carried out instantly. But in which direction? To port, or starboard? The enemy was both closer and farther to the west than Jellicoe had expected.

At 6.15 Jellicoe ordered the Grand Fleet battleships to deploy to the east, away from the enemy. Only his own battle cruisers, sent ahead to support Beatty in his contest, continued their course, doing fearful damage to several German cruisers on the way, and then receiving the full broadside fire of the German battle cruisers at close range. The flagship *Invincible* was almost at once struck by heavy shells and blown up, to join at the bottom of the

The British battle cruiser *Invincible*, first of her breed, blowing up at Jutland. A German shell ignited her magazine.

North Sea two of Beatty's own battle cruisers which had succumbed to the devastatingly accurate German fire earlier.

The battleships of the German High Seas fleet were proceeding north in line ahead and with the imminent expectation of destroying all Beatty's ships, when they suddenly sighted through the mist and gunsmoke the unmistakable and awesome picture of the Grand Fleet in one long line of steel and guns stretching from one uncertain horizon to the other. The trap the Germans had thought they had sprung on the British had suddenly turned inside out, and there seemed to be no escape for them.

Those who were close to Jellicoe on the *Iron Duke*'s upper bridge remarked on his coolness and confidence. He was wearing an old blue Burberry, a white scarf round his throat, and an old tarnished admiral's cap. Could any figure contrast more strongly with that of Nelson at the summit of his own career and in action as a fighting admiral?

The air was heavy with gunfire, and flashes from time to time lit up the swirling mist and smoke. Visibility was getting worse all the time, and the sun would set in another two hours. The exact position of the German vanguard was still unknown, the British scouting, with one or two honourable exceptions, being lamentable.

Then at 6.30 pm, before the deployment was completed, the head of the German line came into view, and the British ships opened fire. Instantly, the German fleet responded with a conjuring trick, demonstrating to Jellicoe that the impossible was possible. In spite of their tight-packed line, the German battleships turned individually on their own sterns like pirouetting ballet dancers, reversing their direction through 180 degrees, and disappeared into the haze and smoke, at the same time despatching their destroyers to fire torpedoes and lay a smokescreen to confuse Jellicoe's gunlayers even further.

It was a brilliant manoeuvre which left Jellicoe bewildered and perplexed, just as the advancing destroyers created alarm. Sensing danger from an imminent torpedo attack, and the risk of isolated units or divisions being cut off and massacred in the mist, smoke and ever-increasing confusion, Jellicoe now ordered the battle fleet to turn away in order to 'comb' the tracks of any torpedoes and keep his ships together.

The Jutland action now resolved itself into three separate endeavours. The first was that of the Germans to escape undamaged from the trap into which the High Seas Fleet had fallen through weak Intelligence, inadequate scouting and the arrogant assumption that theirs was the only trap that could be sprung. The second was the British endeavour to cut off the German fleet before it could regain the safety of its own minefields and bases. The third was shared between the light craft on both sides, and this was simply to remain as far as possible in touch with both sides, reporting on the movements of the enemy and committing and avoiding as much damage as possible.

By a singular chance which will become clear later, the van of the British battle line suddenly re-sighted the German battle fleet at 7.10 pm. It was approaching from the west and was some 10,000 yards distant. At once fire was re-opened, this time with devastating effect as more and more units of the High Seas Fleet came within sight and range, each silhouetted against the evening light, while only the muzzle flashes of Jellicoe's ships were visible to the German gunlayers.

The position was even more desperate for the Germans, especially as the leading ships slowed down in face of the daunting barrage of heavy shells, causing bunching farther down the line.

'The fire of our battleships was very effective at this period,'[19] wrote Jellicoe; and it suddenly and unexpectedly and undeservedly seemed possible that a great victory was at hand. But as quickly and apparently magically as before, the German fleet turned about through 180 degrees and was lost in the smoke and mist, leaving only a few already sorely battered battle cruisers and 13 destroyers to continue on course, seemingly to self-immolation.

Once again, Jellicoe ordered the Grand Fleet battleships to turn away from

The British Grand Fleet at sea. This photograph was taken from the battleship *Marlborough*, torpedoed at Jutland. She survived, little damaged.

the threatened torpedo attack, thus throwing away all hope of engaging the enemy by gunfire in daylight. He had already decided not to attempt to fight in the dark: it was too risky, he calculated, as the fleet had not been trained for night fighting.

The remainder of the Jutland battle, during the last hours of daylight and through the night, resolved itself into a series of mainly individual actions between the light craft. All of it was confused, and much of it alarming and bloody.

The following extracts from an unpublished letter from Lieutenant Irvine Glennie in the flotilla leader *Broke* to Prince Louis of Battenberg's brother, written immediately after the battle, give some idea of the speed and unpredictability of events and the terror of night fighting at sea:

We hadn't the smallest idea of what was going on beyond what we actually saw.... Everything was a hopeless jumble and we saw our battleships which should have been 5 miles ahead and we also saw many ships in the dark but couldn't make them out. About 10.00 there was another and prolonged burst of firing away to s.w. followed by a tremendous explosion which must have been somebody touching off a magazine ...

Later in the night the ship came within point-blank range of a German battleship which illuminated it by searchlight and opened fire with 5.9-inch guns. 'They did a lot of damage, killing or wounding all the guns' crews – the quartermaster – and all the fore supply and fire parties – 50 killed and 30 wounded all told[20] – not bad work for 1 to 2 minutes. ... Directly after this we were in collision with the Sparrowhawk.'[21]

With the loss of only one battleship, the German battle fleet succeeded in breaking through the British flotillas and making their escape. At dawn on 1 June (and it could so well have been another Glorious First of June, like Howe's victory of 1794 off Ushant), Jellicoe found himself with 14 fewer ships than he had commanded the day before, but in possession of a North Sea empty of the enemy.

Once again the Germans had succeeded in slipping out of sight. But Jellicoe himself had, by his own evasive action, permitted them to do so, twice shying away from the threat of torpedoes, the second time (as it turned out) from a mere 21, all of which were comfortably evaded.

Any member of Jellicoe's staff who had read the admiral's summary of strategy and tactics formulated seven weeks before the battle, might have known that there was unlikely to be any decisive result. 'It is not, in my opinion', Jellicoe had written, 'wise to risk unduly the heavy ships of the Grand Fleet in an attempt to hasten the end of the High Sea Fleet, particularly if the risks come, not from the High Sea Fleet itself, but from such attributes as mines and submarines.' The memorandum continued in the same negative tone of not running risks and not courting disaster.

There was no braver body of men than those who formed the appropriately named Grand Fleet. Six thousand of them gave their lives at Jutland, more than the Spanish and French lost at Trafalgar, simply to retain the *status quo* in the naval war.

At Jutland the art of sea warfare had been trivialized by two fleets that were more deeply concerned with survival than victory. The only undisputed victor was the torpedo, which in the event did little more damage than at Tsu-Shima. The advent of the steel, two-million-pound super-battleship had turned commanders' minds away from victory and towards survival.

On the British side, Jutland aroused deep disappointment and ferocious controversy, which lasted for decades. Statistically, the Grand Fleet had had a comfortable advantage over the High Seas Fleet and had suffered considerably greater losses in men and in tonnage sunk. It had allowed this priceless opportunity for victory to slip away into the Wagnerian night. It could be argued that it was a negative victory because the Germans had not stayed to fight, Britain still controlled the seas on which (except for the Baltic) no German ship traded, and the blockade remained intact. But so did the High Seas Fleet; and the war on land continued its bloody progress, with the Allies opening a new offensive on the Somme a month later – 57,540 British casualties alone on the first day.

After a decent lapse of time, Jellicoe was relieved of his command and made first sea lord. It was not a happy appointment. He was not at home in a desk job. His period at the admiralty coincided with ever-increasing losses of merchantmen from U-boat attack. He was slow and reluctant to institute convoys, the salvation of so many merchantmen since the beginning of commerce attrition, and disagreed more and more with his first lord, who finally dismissed him at the end of 1917.

Although retaining his dignity and calm in public, Jellicoe was deeply affronted by the treatment he suffered. So were many of his fellow officers. His leadership at the Battle of Jutland was hotly debated for the rest of his life, and he published his own version in his memoirs 16 years before his death in 1935. Churchill criticized his tactics in detail, but accepted that caution was justified as Jellicoe was 'the one man who could lose the war in an afternoon'. He did not. But he could have won it in an afternoon, too.

Admiral Reinhard Scheer
1863–1928

Scheer showed enterprise and daring, unlike his predecessor. But when his High Seas Fleet met the enemy in strength, he scurried for safety.

His only concern [at Jutland] was to get out of range and out of sight as soon as he could.
Professor Arthur J. Marder

Reinhard Scheer, who commanded the German fleet in its greatest battle, was a typical product of Tirpitz's navy, middle class by birth and brought up strictly in a domestic environment notable for its industry and preoccupation with efficiency. He joined the navy in 1872 when it was still only a token coast defence force, and in the next 25 years watched it grow into the second most powerful in the world.

Fate rather than any failing in his character caused Scheer to be late for the important events in his life. He was late in joining the navy as a cadet, late in achieving recognition. He was thirty-nine before he was even appointed second-in-command of a ship, and he was middle-aged before he was singled out for future possible greatness.

In 1907 Scheer was appointed commander of a destroyer flotilla. Like Tirpitz, he had specialized in the torpedo branch, and his confidence in the power of the torpedo in war was much higher than that of most of his fellow officers. He wrote and published a book on the tactical use of the torpedo, described as 'the earnest address of a hard worker to men of his own spirit'.

However, Scheer left destroyers for the battleship fleet two years later, and was promoted chief of staff to the C-in-C in 1912. On the outbreak of war Tirpitz was fully aware of the exceptional qualities of this captain, who certainly showed no signs of dilatoriness in handling ships and possessed a brilliant tactical mind. In Scheer, there was none of the emotional fervour of the great commanders on both sides during the Napoleonic Wars. His effectiveness, like that of most of his contemporaries and of his service, rested in order and efficiency and a sense of duty and team spirit.

In 1914 the High Seas Fleet was commanded by Admiral von Ingenohl, an officer of considerable ability who found his aggressive spirit and will to win frustrated by the high command and – of all people – the Kaiser, the monarch who had boasted of his navy's destructive power to all the crowned heads of Europe. After two early cruiser actions, in which the Germans came off worse, Ingenohl was relieved of his command for risk-taking. A safe, solid commander, von Pohl, replaced him, and further restrictions were placed on the activities of the High Seas Fleet.

Scheer was among the many senior officers who fretted at the lack of enterprise and the lost chances of aggressive action against the British Grand Fleet while it was still in a state of near-parity with the High Seas Fleet and before the new 15-inch-gunned super-dreadnoughts reinforced it. During

these early months of the war Scheer was, in turn, commander of the second (pre-dreadnought) and third (dreadnought) squadrons.

Scheer's flagship,
Friedrich der Grosse.

Then, by a stroke of fate that was to have profound consequences, Pohl was struck down by a fatal illness, and Scheer was appointed in his place in January 1916. It was 'the almost universal lament' in the German navy that he had not been given this command earlier.

The raising of Scheer's flag in the battleship *Friedrich der Grosse* led to an immediate change of policy and attitude. The fast waning morale of officers and men was raised at the prospect of raids and offensive sorties in the spirit of the first months of the war. Everyone suddenly realized that their pride in their ships, their weapons and skill were about to be put to the test.

Scheer might be late again; but not too late. In fact, the timing of his appointment could be described as fortuitous. The German high command was beginning to recognize that the large and expensive land offensives, like

179

Verdun, were not going to bring about speedy victory. The British civilian army was taking the field, the war machines of France and Britain were becoming fully mobilized, the British blockade was beginning to bite.

Success at sea for the Germans could bring about a radical adjustment in the balance of power to continue to wage war. Not outright victory, but success. There was an important distinction between the two. Dominance at sea could lead to the severance of the Allied sea routes by unrestricted U-boat warfare, and to the whittling down of the strength of the Grand Fleet as Ingenohl had planned and to some extent implemented in 1914.

Scheer knew, and the high command knew, that no degree of superior gunnery and tactics and good luck could grant the High Seas Fleet victory in a straight gunnery duel with Jellicoe's Grand Fleet. By 1916 the odds at around four to seven were too great to overcome.

The plan was, therefore, to engage in raids which would utilize the two new branches of the fleet, the Zeppelin for reconnaissance, the U-boat for unseen attack, thus bringing into play a new dimension in sea warfare. With the advantage of superior knowledge of the enemy's movements, it was also planned to pounce on isolated British squadrons or units with the concentrated superior power of surface ships.

Scheer had to wait until late May before putting into effect his major plan. This was because he needed the better weather and longer daylight of early summer, and time for the repair of one of his most powerful ships. He mustered in all 18 U-boats for the submarine trap, a few for mine laying off British bases, the rest for patrolling off them, no fewer than seven being assigned to the Firth of Forth entrance, the base of the enemy battle cruisers which were Scheer's first target.

Scheer's own battle cruiser force was commanded by Admiral Franz von Hipper, an officer with all the dash and flair of Beatty, the ideal commander of a powerful scouting force. Hipper's five battle cruisers sailed from the River Jade at 1 am on 31 May with orders to make their presence known off Norway, hoping to entice out Beatty's battle cruiser force and then draw it towards Scheer's squadrons, which had sailed from their bases later and were to cruise 60 miles to the rear. Ahead of these two forces, five Zeppelins were to reconnoitre, signalling by radio any sighting of enemy vessels.

Scheer kept his main fleet at economic cruising speed for the long haul north. He was not, in fact, capable of more than 18 knots, as he had, in an uncharacteristically sentimental act, and in answer to the pleas of its commander, included his old squadron of pre-dreadnought battleships in his battle fleet. By this tactically unsound decision he had committed himself to an inferiority of at least three knots compared with Jellicoe's battle fleet – an inferiority which had sealed Rozhestvensky's fate at Tsu-Shima, and was all the more serious because the first principle of his policy was to avoid direct confrontation. (These old battleships were dubbed 'five-minute ships' – the time they were expected to survive a gun duel.)

It was a calm, clear night in the North Sea, and the expectations of battle were higher amongst the Germans than the British as they had so rarely embarked on such an aggressive operation.

At 3.20 the next afternoon, the electrifying news was received from Hipper – 'Enemy battle fleet in sight' – and Scheer at once ordered his 22 battleships to increase speed to the fleet's maximum of 18 knots. Then, half an hour later, Scheer received the signal from Hipper that he was engaging British battle cruisers. After that, as the gun duel over the northern horizon warmed up, Scheer got only spasmodic reports; but he knew that his heavy scouting forces were drawing a vulnerable and inferior enemy towards his guns at a closing speed of some 40 knots, and that he had success almost within his grasp.

The German battle fleet's first sighting of the enemy occurred soon after 4.30 when a four-funnel light cruiser far to the north-west was seen to turn, exposing its silhouette, and make off into the haze at a range of some eight miles. At once the heavy guns of the leading German battleships started to open fire, sending up high fountains about the fleeing, zig-zagging British ship.

Minutes later, Scheer sighted the leading enemy heavy ships pounding down from the north-west with shell splashes from Hipper's fire bursting about them. The visibility was poor, and getting worse, but it was possible to make out the British three-funnel battle cruisers turning through 180 degrees and hauling away to the north-west.

At the same time that they began to disappear, pursued by the first shells from his battleships, four more British dreadnoughts steamed out of the smoke and haze. They were identified as battleships, with two funnels, steaming fast as if on a suicide course straight towards them. They were thought to be *Queen Elizabeth* class battleships. As alarming confirmation, well-directed 15-inch shellfire began falling among the German battleships in the van, scoring many near misses and hitting the *Markgraf* and *Grosser Kurfürst*.

Scheer did not believe that he had chanced on anything more dangerous than an isolated squadron of enemy battleships, and although their heavy shells – twice the broadside weight of his own flagship – were discomfiting, he soon saw the British ships inevitably reverse course in the face of the fire of so many more German battleships, suffering hits as they did so. Then they began pulling away, and by 5.30 were beyond range – 24 knots against 18. Scheer remained confident that he could still add to the damage Hipper had done to the British heavy scouting forces. He had no idea that, less than 50 miles away, the entire Grand Fleet was racing towards him.

Just one hour after the four British 15-inch-gun battleships made off to the north-west and disappeared from sight, look-outs in the *König* and the other leading German battleships sighted the faint silhouettes of dreadnoughts to the north, one, then another, and another.

The most fierce and
terrifying combats
occurred during the
night after the main
fleet action at Jutland,
when the torpedo
craft on both sides set
about the giant
battleships with
sublime courage.

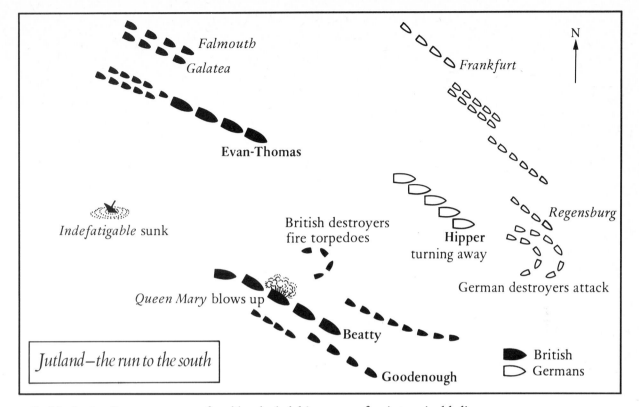

Jutland—the run to the south

Suddenly the German van was faced by the belching guns of an interminable line of heavy ships extending from north-west to north-east, while salvo followed salvo without intermission, an impression which gained in power from the almost complete inability of the German ships to reply to this fire, as not one of the British Dreadnoughts could be made out through the smoke and fumes. . . .

The German official historian continued his narrative by detailing Scheer's appalling dilemma, 150 miles from his base, with three hours to go before the shelter of darkness could aid him, and a fleet that was out-gunned and out-paced by an enemy that was already within range and scoring hits on his leading ships.

With the British deployment into a single line, and both fleets now on an approximately easterly course, this was the moment when Scheer ordered the *Gefechtskehrtwendung*, the battle reversal, simultaneously, ship by ship. The High Seas Fleet had practised this difficult evolution many times, but never under such adverse circumstances, with the van already losing its formation, with heavy shells sending up masthead-high waterspouts, and the noise and 'fog of war' as a further distraction for every commander.

Scheer was late again, but again not quite too late. With skill, and luck, the entire High Seas Fleet, nine miles long, completed the evolution in thirteen minutes from the hoisting of the signal, and was proceeding on a westerly course with the 'five-minute ships' now in the van. In order to reach the security of his minefields and base he would eventually have to turn south. But when?

Scheer maintained after the battle that he was not fleeing from the enemy but only manoeuvring in order to extricate himself from an unfavourable position and place his fleet more favourably in order to commit more damage on the enemy. As an expression of pride, this is acceptable. It is unacceptable as history. Doubtless, if he had chanced on an inferior British force on the way home, he would have engaged it and done as much damage to it as possible, so long as it did not delay his progress.

Anticipating that Jellicoe would turn west after the German destroyer attack and attempt to bar his passage south, Scheer reversed his course again in the hope of getting behind the British battle fleet, and then turning south, close to the Danish coast, the dark sky of the east obscuring him from his searchers. It was a good idea but his timing was imperfect, and when he found himself again facing the British line, this time silhouetted against the last of the light, his second *Gefechtskehrtwendung* was more precipitate and untidy than the earlier turn, and he felt it necessary to risk the destruction of his already severely mauled battle cruisers in their 'death ride' attempt to stay the British attack.

Scheer's return home through the hours of darkness was like that of a drunk man under intermittent attack from small boys. He had as little idea of his enemy's whereabouts as had Jellicoe. Sometimes the Grand Fleet was to the east of him, sometimes the south-east, and for a period it was dead ahead, barring his way, though neither commander knew it. But there was plenty of evidence that the Grand Fleet was in close proximity, and there were in all seven valiantly pressed-home attacks from the British light forces, in the finest traditions of Nelson's time. Whatever had happened to the spirit of high command, there was no lack of initiative and courage amongst the officers and men of the light cruisers and destroyers.

All this was evident to Scheer, just as his own light forces fought off the attacks with equal courage. One destroyer rammed the German battleship *Nassau*, reducing her speed by 6 knots. Another put a torpedo into the *Pommern* – one of the pre-dreadnoughts – and it did not last five seconds, never mind five minutes. Far to the north, Hipper's flagship, the new battle cruiser *Lützow*, torn to shreds by shellfire and with thousands of tons of water onboard, could keep under way no longer, and after evacuating her survivors, she was sent to the bottom by a German torpedo. Two more German battle cruisers were in little better shape and also lagged far behind.

The last British destroyer attack occurred at 2.30 am. The only casualty was one German destroyer. Scheer was by then only a few miles from the Horns Reef lightship and knew that he was safe.

The German communiqué on the battle, which Scheer helped to prepare within hours of his return, made extravagant claims of victory – 'The victory of Skagerrak' – and caused consternation in England and jubilation at home. At Wilhelmshaven, the kaiser boarded Scheer's flagship, embraced him emotionally, and cried out that 'the spell of Trafalgar has been broken'. The High Seas Fleet had indeed sunk more ships than had the Grand Fleet – three battle cruisers against one, and nine light cruisers and destroyers against eight. The German *Pommern* and three British armoured cruisers were further losses but only the crews were of any value.

The battle, and the conduct of the commanders at all levels, has been debated and analysed for 60 years. But Scheer's claim of a victory was a hollow one. Within twenty-four hours of its return to base, Jellicoe reported to the admiralty that the Grand Fleet was operational and ready to proceed to sea. Scheer had only ten undamaged dreadnoughts ready for action, Jellicoe 24, against 21 and 37 before the action. Moreover, all the damaged British heavy ships were repaired within eight weeks. The last German battle cruiser did not rejoin the fleet until December.

It is an indisputable truism that the army that holds the field at the end of the day is the victor. Scheer had retreated from Jellicoe and escaped, battered but largely intact. Britain controlled the world's sea lanes before the battle, and after it, when the blockade of Germany was as tight and damaging as ever.

Scheer never risked a fleet action again. After the embracing at Wilhelmshaven was over, he had to 'remind the Emperor that actions with a fleet so much more powerful as the British might end in success, though never in victory'. As Arthur Marder reminds us in his definitive account of the battle,

The *Seydlitz* was so badly damaged at Jutland that she could not rejoin the fleet for three and a half months.

from the tactical point of view Jutland was inconclusive. 'From the strategical point of view, which is what really matters – that is, the effect on the
outcome of the war – the Grand Fleet was, beyond a shadow of a doubt, the
winner.'[22] By this valid definition, Jellicoe defeated Scheer. But it does not
take into account the profound results if Jellicoe, as he could and should have
done, had put Scheer's fleet out of action.

Because the first reason why he failed to do so was fear of the torpedo, the
torpedo may reasonably be declared the real victor at Jutland. And yet it had
done trivial damage. The massed flotillas on both sides scored a negligible
number of hits. The submarine 'trap' had been a total failure. But the fear
the torpedo instilled was crucially influential. Another failure, except for that
single sighting by one British seaplane, were the air arms of both fleets. The
Zeppelins, in which Scheer had placed so much trust, did not even partici-
pate. Five became airborne late, reported poor visibility, and were soon
recalled. Thus the air arm and the submarine arm, soon to be the real arbiters
of power and supremacy at sea in place of the battleship, utterly failed on
their first major outing, deceiving the world into thinking that the battleship
still counted in the preparations for a second world war 20 years later.

Now that Scheer had convinced the kaiser and the high command that it
was impossible to reduce the power of the British fleet by gunfire without
unacceptable losses to the German fleet, he began to press more strongly than
ever for a return to unconditional U-boat warfare. The rate of sinking had
been so encouraging when it had been briefly tried before, that he and many
others believed that it could not fail to bring the Allies to their knees. He won
his way. But not until 1 February 1917 did Scheer's orders come through
to pursue unrestricted submarine warfare 'with the utmost energy'.

The proponents had maintained that Britain could be brought to her
knees within five months, and that it did not matter what the United States
thought or did as the war would be all over before her power could be
mobilized. It very nearly worked, too. Allied losses at sea soared, and
Britain was brought to a condition of imminent starvation.

But Scheer was once again too late. If the U-boat fleet had been unleashed
with a free hand six months earlier, his prediction could have come true.
However, America was in the war by April, the worst month for sinkings,
and from then onward new vigour of action and new methods of counter-
attack, followed by the introduction of convoys, gradually paid off.

Even in the spring of 1918 when it was clear that the U-boat had finally
been overcome, the spirit of aggression in Scheer was still alive, and on 23
April, at a time when the German armies were advancing on their last-fling
offensive on the Western Front, he took the High Seas Fleet to sea. His
intention was to intercept and destroy one of the Scandinavian convoys
which frequently crossed the North Sea to Britain with an escort of variable
strength. Another strong motive was to put some muscle back into the
fleet's morale which was at a low ebb because of inaction and the failure of

the U-boats, to which many of the battle fleet's best personnel had been drafted.

The operation was a fiasco due to faulty intelligence and the almost complete breakdown of the machinery of one of the battle cruisers. It was an inglorious end to operations of the once-proud High Seas Fleet. The next time it was ordered out, on a last desperate and near-suicide sortie, the crews of a number of the ships mutinied. Then came the humiliation of surrender, and the scuttling in Scapa Flow in June 1919.

Long before this, Scheer had given up his command. But he was able to comment cheerfully on the scuttling that it wiped out the stain of surrender and that it was in the best traditions of the German navy – a curious observation, but in character with an admiral who believed he had won a great victory at Jutland.

Scheer's retirement allowed him to return to the modest bourgeois life he had always enjoyed at home. But one last act of violence remained to be played out. On 9 October 1920 a shell-shocked and deranged ex-soldier managed to secrete himself in the cellar of Scheer's house in Weimar. On being discovered by a maidservant, he shot her. Frau Scheer, curious at the long absence of the maid, looked for her in the cellar, and was in turn shot. This shooting aroused Scheer's daughter, and she too descended the stairs and was shot. At last – and too late again – Scheer was alerted to the danger. He arrived in time to save his daughter, but not his wife. And then the old soldier committed suicide.

Admiral of the Fleet Earl Beatty
1871–1936

In him, as in Nelson, the fire burned as a passion for victory. . . . When any tidings came that the enemy was coming out, he was like one of his own hounds set from the leash. His signal at the Dogger Bank, 'Keep closer to the enemy', *though it miscarried at the time*, expressed the very spirit of the man.

The Archbishop of Canterbury at
Beatty's funeral (author's italics)

After all the years of expensive naval rearmament, and the expectation of mighty clashes of arms in the North Sea, during the four and a quarter years of the First World War the German and British battle fleets were in contact only twice, both times on that mist-and-smoke-shrouded evening of 31 May 1916. The exchange of fire lasted only minutes, and the British battle fleet was scarcely touched.

Among the big ships at Jutland, only the battle cruisers and British armoured cruisers were seriously engaged. By far the largest number of casualties was suffered in these ships. Not a single dreadnought battleship was lost.

The most famous remark made on either side at Jutland was spoken by Sir David Beatty, the admiral commanding the British battle cruiser force, after the second of his great ships had blown up within half an hour of the first. Beatty was, characteristically, standing unprotected on the bridge of his flagship when he saw the *Queen Mary* break in two and disappear in an enormous cloud of smoke, taking down with her all but 20 of her company of 1266. 'There seems', he remarked to his flag captain in his quiet, patrician voice, 'to be something wrong with our bloody ships today.' He then ordered his four surviving battle cruisers to alter course *towards* the enemy.

David Beatty was born on 17 January 1871 of wealthy, aristocratic, Anglo–Irish parents for whom hunting, racing and polo were all. He was the second of four sons, all of whom were fearless steeplechase riders and polo players. Intellectualism was not a consideration in the family, but David's mind was not exclusively concerned with horses, although he rode to hounds as rashly as the rest. He had a streak of romanticism in him, which made him his mother's favourite son. From a very early age he wanted to go to sea; and at the age of twelve he was sent to Burney's Naval Academy at Gosport, and then on to the training establishment of HMS *Britannia*.

By a combination of favouritism, merit, charm, luck and ability, things at once went well with him. Like Nelson a hundred years earlier, he enjoyed and deserved rapid promotion, the most rapid since the Hero, and enjoyed risks both in his personal and professional lives as Nelson did. Moreover he

managed to find action and acquire the DSO for extreme gallantry at a time when few officers ever heard a shot fired in anger throughout their career.

Beatty had excellent and natural leadership qualities, and was early wounded in action. Again following Nelson, he married for love a woman who had been married before, and although at first happy, the marriage was not a success. His wife, Ethel Tree, heiress to the Marshall Field fortune in America, divorced her first husband in order to marry Beatty. For most officers, to marry a divorcee meant resignation and a severely restricted social life. By a combination of remarkable discretion and bravado Beatty got away with it, was knighted by George V and even became one of his ADCS.

When he was the brightest rising star in the navy, he refused an appointment to a high command because he preferred to wait for something better. He got away with this, too, against all precedent; was made naval secretary to Winston Churchill when he became first lord (they had been together in the Egyptian campaign in 1896); and was given the Battle Cruiser Fleet, the most romantic and the second most responsible seagoing appointment in the navy, at a time when war with Germany seemed inevitable.

Beatty commanded the Battle Cruiser Fleet as if he were a master of fox-hounds, with dash and *élan*. He was admired by all ranks, achieved a great *esprit de corps*, and created a band-of-brothers spirit among his commanders as Nelson did.

As a hard-hitting aggressive fighting force, the battle cruisers – Fisher's 'ocean greyhounds' – were allowed to take risks considered unacceptable to the main fleet. With their speed and firepower, they formed the spearhead

These are the only two commanders who experienced the realities of a dreadnought gunnery duel in the age of steel and cordite: Beatty (LEFT) and Hipper (ABOVE), both men of supreme courage. Beatty saw two of his ships blow up, and Hipper was forced to abandon his sinking flagship.

189

of scouting and offensive operations. In the first six months of war, Beatty's battle cruisers with their attendant light cruisers and destroyers won a clear victory over German light forces in the Heligoland Bight, pursued Hipper's battle cruisers several times, and caught them at last in January 1915 when they were attempting to raid the Dogger Bank fishing fleets. The battle cruisers gravely damaged several German heavy ships and sank Hipper's most powerful armoured cruiser, while two of Beatty's ships, detached to the South Atlantic, all but annihilated Admiral von Spee's powerful squadron off the Falkland Islands.

At the time of Jutland, eighteen months later, Beatty's battle cruisers had gained considerable ascendancy over Hipper. In this first action with his antagonist in which the German did not at once retreat, Beatty was at a considerable tactical disadvantage, with the light behind him and the German battle cruisers scarcely visible in the darker haze of the east. His higher speed, also dictated by the tactical circumstances, put him at a gunnery disadvantage.

In the opening stages, moreover, although Beatty could muster six heavy ships against Hipper's five, two of the British vessels were early and obsolescent battle cruisers, with inferior gunpower and sketchy protection. The German shooting, assisted by superior optical equipment as well as better shells and much practice, was brilliant, as it had been at earlier battles. But Beatty's gunnery improved as the duel warmed up, while Hipper's seemed to tire, and it deteriorated markedly when Beatty's supporting fast battleships belatedly added their 15-inch fire – which was beautifully accurate from the first salvos.

There is, however, no arguing that the Germans had the better of the exchange of fire on what came to be known as 'the run to the south', when Hipper was drawing Beatty on to Scheer's battleships. Beatty lost two heavy ships, Hipper none, though Hipper later said that nothing could have saved him from disaster if the British shells had not been of such poor quality, breaking up on impact instead of penetrating the German armour, as they were perfectly capable of doing.

Beatty's achievement in reversing the trap into which he had so nearly fallen, and bringing the High Seas Fleet into gun range with Jellicoe's superior strength of battleships, was of the highest order. Moreover, his success without suffering further serious damage led to Hipper's conversely being savagely mauled and losing his flagship.

Beatty had carried out his first task successfully, and expressed deep bitterness after the battle was over that, having presented Jellicoe with the High Seas Fleet for dinner, his c-in-c failed to gobble it up. The Jellicoe–Beatty controversy soon burst into flames but neither admiral took any part in fanning them. Reputations as well as traditions were at stake, and the search for scapegoats was bitter and long-drawn-out. The disillusionment of all ranks, both at the failure to destroy the enemy and at the British public's initial belief that it had been a German victory, was expressed by Beatty's flag-lieutenant in a letter to his mother:

It was probably one of the most fiercely contested and bloodiest naval battles in history, and the most powerful fleet but one was put to flight in exactly ten minutes, and escaped annihilation by the skin of their teeth. We have returned and are told there has been a disaster! Our losses are grievous! and our Admirals fools![23]

But there was no denying that there *had* been British failures, including failures by this young officer's admiral.

Beatty's leadership and aggressive style, as exemplified by his remark to his flag-captain about the quality of his ships, were incontestable. The gunnery of his ships, by contrast with the shells they fired, was shown to be good except during the early, almost impossible conditions.

Beatty's failure lay in poor signalling. Poor signalling led to a misunderstood distribution of fire for the first vital ten minutes of the gun duel, with four of Beatty's ships firing at two of Hipper's, leaving one German battle cruiser without the distraction of being fired upon. Poor signalling led to the delay in the arrival of Beatty's fast battleships. What these 15-inch guns might have done during the first phase can be judged by the execution they committed when they did get within range.

There were other cases of signalling failure in the Battle Cruiser Fleet, the most important of all being the failure to report more frequently, more fully and more accurately the course and position of the High Seas Fleet and of Beatty's own fleet. Jellicoe was left in exasperated silence for long periods. If he had known more fully when and where he was likely to encounter Scheer, he could have manoeuvred the Grand Fleet to a more favourable position for his reception, and possible destruction.

The German battle cruiser *Seydlitz* and Beatty's flagship *Lion* had both come close to destruction eighteen months earlier at the Dogger Bank engagement. Both sides had failed to appreciate the risk of a flash from a gun turret penetrating to the magazine below if its doors were left open for speed and convenience in action. All the German battle cruisers then took proper precautions against this danger. British battle cruisers remained vulnerable, and but for a Royal Marines' officer's bravery the *Lion* would probably have met her destruction at Jutland just as the *Queen Mary* and *Indefatigable* did blow up.

The signalling failure of David Beatty as a commander stems more from the failure of a system and a standard than from the individual. It is one thing to fight a battle, giving all your attention to the destruction of the enemy. It is conduct within another dimension to fight a battle skilfully and bravely and remember that others are fighting beside you. Nelson, when engaged in warfare that was much more personal than twentieth-century naval fighting, always remembered that his ship and its contest was only one of many engaged or about to be engaged about him, and that it was his duty to command them all and keep them informed as far as possible.

HMS *Indefatigable*, blown up by the *von der Tann* at Jutland.

The failure of reporting and signalling at Jutland was general throughout the fleet, with one or two notable exceptions. It is especially difficult to forgive Beatty, who commanded a scouting force, for not keeping his superior properly informed. Lack of imagination was the root cause, and this in turn originated in the British navy's arrogance and disregard for and suspicion of intellectualism. A naval staff did not even exist at the admiralty until 1912, when Churchill pressed home the demand for one, against strong opposition. There were numerous brilliant officers in the Grand Fleet, but almost everywhere philistinism ruled.

In contrast to its effect on Jellicoe, the Battle of Jutland in no way tarnished Beatty's reputation. On the contrary, he was widely regarded in the fleet and in the country as the hero. 'If only Beatty had been in command,' people said, 'the result would have been different.'

Beatty succeeded Jellicoe as C-in-C, and in spite of possessing an even greater advantage in strength over the enemy, especially when the American battleships arrived, he demonstrated as cautious a policy and as great a reluctance to risk his heavy ships.

But at the surrender of the High Seas Fleet, it was Beatty who, in the eyes of the public, personified the triumph once again of British seapower. Later he became first sea lord, and remained in that high office for eight years of peace, a record period.

There were two tragedies in Beatty's life, the professional tragedy of what he regarded as the failure at Jutland, and the personal one of his marriage, his wife suffering a mental breakdown which among other agonizing manifestations led her to accuse him of neglect. She died of acute melancholia in 1932, four years before he succumbed to heart failure.

David Beatty, Britain's most romantic and celebrated admiral since Nelson, was buried with full honours in St Paul's Cathedral close to the Hero.

OPPOSITE HMS *Lion*, grievously damaged at Jutland.

6
To Control the Narrow Seas

Admiral of the Fleet Earl Cunningham of Hyndhope
1883–1963

He was the best sailor we had.
Lord Attlee

Andrew Browne Cunningham ('ABC' to his intimates) lacked entirely the flamboyancy and style which drew the public's admiring attention to David Beatty. But his success as an administrator and fighting admiral was quite as notable as Beatty's. A half-generation younger, Cunningham won his spurs and decorations for gallantry in the little ships in the First World War, and became a fleet commander and then first sea lord in the Second World War.

At the renewal of world war in September 1939, Britain was no longer the paramount naval power. The days when there were anxious parliamentary debates if the two-to-one parity of the Royal Navy over any other navy was threatened were long since past. The intervention of the USA in the First World War, the build up of her military and naval strength, the impoverishment of the British economy after more than four years of struggle, the rise of Japanese naval power, all resulted in both a relative and actual reduction of her fleet to a size approximately equal to that of America, and with a marked inferiority to the combined fleets of her likely opponents, Japan, Germany and Italy.

The dependence of Britain and the empire on commerce and trade was as total as in 1914, but the means to secure them were no longer adequate. The economic recession of the 1930s had diminished further Britain's seapower, and although the belated recognition of the relentlessness of Nazi German ambitions had accelerated naval shipbuilding from 1935, only the first few ships were coming into active commission by 1939. The British navy was still relatively strong in battleships and battle cruisers. The naval air service, which had been a pioneer in the First World War, had been bedevilled by inter-service competition. Its equipment was antiquated, its spirit and skill of compensatory high quality.

The British navy's near-fatal weakness lay in its failure to appreciate that the concept of the big gun as the first weapon had been blown up with the *Invincible*, *Indefatigable* and *Queen Mary* at Jutland. The final but agonizingly expensive defeat of the German U-boats from 1917 had convinced policy-makers that the torpedo could be tamed. In the eyes of all but a small number of less myopic officers, the battleship remained the final arbiter. The usefulness of airpower for reconnaissance and for attack in the narrow seas was accepted. But the threat of the bomber to heavy ships, especially heavy ships

PREVIOUS PAGES With the *Tirpitz*, the *Bismarck* was the most formidable battleship Germany built. Although as nearly 'unsinkable' as a warship could be made, the *Bismarck* was sunk by shellfire and torpedoes, the *Tirpitz* by bombs.

in the open sea with accompanying carriers, was not taken seriously. Judged by the destructive power of British fleet air arm bombs, this was a reasonable assumption.

The role of the Royal Navy in September 1939 was exactly the same as in August 1914: to keep the seas open to British shipping and closed to German shipping, to attack the German fleet whenever opportunity occurred, and to cover the transport of the British army to France. *Plus ça change, plus c'est la même chose....* The soldiers even sang 'Mademoiselle from Armentières' on the way up to the front, and their equipment was very nearly the same as before; and all but two of the British heavy ships had been built during the First World War.

In June 1939 Andrew Cunningham, now an admiral, had been appointed C-in-C of the Mediterranean Fleet with his flag in the Jutland battleship *Warspite*. He was fifty-six years old, with forty-two years of service behind him, including useful staff posts ashore. He was much loved and respected in the service. He was modest, yet firm in his convictions, and decisive in action, exemplified by the way he invariably sprang up stairs and gangways at full speed. Like so many highly successful British admirals, Cunningham was short in stature. His eyes were piercing and shining with intelligence, and his ruddy complexion suggested a fit body – kept so by energetic and competitive tennis and golf.

The role of his fleet was at first a mainly passive one, far from the struggles in the North Sea and the Atlantic, and from the moment it became clear that Italy was not yet going to join her axis partner, Cunningham suffered a steady reduction in the number of his vessels. However, with the defeat of France and the declaration of war by Italy on 10 June 1940, the function of the Mediterranean Fleet at once became of crucial importance and Cunningham received reinforcements. Now lacking the support of the considerable French fleet, Cunningham was responsible for destroying communications between Italy and her North African army, for attacking her fleet whenever opportunity occurred and keeping communications open to the isolated but vital British base of Malta.

With the Italian superiority in surface vessels and submarines, and immense superiority in aircraft, the British high command was reconciled to eastern trade and army supplies having to make the long voyage round the Cape rather than through the Mediterranean. To compensate for the loss of the French fleet, a new squadron called Force H had been formed and based on Gibraltar. To Force H fell the unhappy task of bombarding and neutralizing a large part of the defeated and now neutral French fleet at Mers el Kebir.

The Italians demonstrated as marked a reluctance to face up to a gun duel with the British fleet as the Germans had shown in the First World War. Only the Italian air force showed any aggression, but their bombing was atrocious.

In North Africa General Wavell, with 30,000 troops, soundly defeated

The grave, responsible countenance of one of Britain's greatest admirals, Andrew Cunningham.

Cunningham's flagship *Warspite* as rebuilt before the Second World War. Her fighting career extended from 1916 – gravely damaged at Jutland – to 1945, and from Pearl Harbor to the North Atlantic.

Cunningham was supreme commander of all naval forces for the North African invasion of 1942. *The Great Convoy to North Africa*, painted by R. Eurich.

Marshal Graziani's army of 200,000. In the air 190 British machines faced the whole weight of the Regia Aeronautica, and never yielded control of the air. At sea Cunningham continued to cause casualties to superior forces whenever his commanders could get within range.

Then, on 11 November 1940, at the height of the bombing of open cities in Britain when civilian morale badly needed a fillip, Cunningham devised a sort of overture to Pearl Harbor. With the support of a modern aircraft carrier, but using the antiquated aircraft with which the fleet air arm had for so long been saddled, he sent his torpedo bombers and dive bombers against a strong force of the Italian battle fleet in Taranto harbour at night. The pilots' success, signalled Cunningham, 'may well have a most important bearing on the course of the war in the Mediterranean'. And indeed it did! For the loss of two aircraft, the aircrews disabled three out of Italy's six battleships.

Defeated on land and by sea, the Italians had now to look to their allies to redress the balance of success. The German air force hurried to Sicily, the Germany army moved into Greece where an Italian invasion was faltering in the face of fierce patriotism, and German influence obliged the Italian navy to offer a less timorous profile. The effect of these first two moves was highly damaging to the British cause. The third led to the annihilation of three Italian heavy cruisers and two destroyers in a night action with Cunningham's battleships. Prince Philip, controlling the *Valiant*'s searchlights at Matapan, commented laconically, 'When the enemy had completely vanished in clouds of smoke and steam we ceased firing and switched the light off.'

The surprise of the Italian heavy cruisers was brought about by air reconnaissance, the destruction by old-fashioned gunfire – and also by Cunningham's decision to risk torpedo attack and turn *towards* his enemy by contrast with Jellicoe at Jutland. He reaped his just reward.

But the real meaning of airpower, when correctly handled by a skilful

and well equipped air force, was spelled out by the Germans over the following weeks. The British army had come to the rescue of the hard-pressed Greeks, but had been forced to withdraw, first to Crete and then back to North Africa. It was Cunningham's responsibility to cover these evacuations. He did so, but at the cost of grave losses in cruisers and destroyers, nearly all torn apart by the Luftwaffe's bombs. His carrier was put out of action by a direct hit. The Italian losses at Matapan seemed trivial by contrast.

The navy had achieved great glory in the eastern Mediterranean. The army commander, General Wavell, sent Cunningham a message expressing 'the deepest admiration and gratitude of the Army in the Middle East for the magnificent work of the Royal Navy in bringing the troops back from Crete'. But the loss of ships and lives was grievous. Later in the year one of Cunningham's battleships was sunk by a U-boat, and two more were disabled in harbour by a daring Italian frogman attack.

The Mediterranean, which had in the past been regarded as 'a British lake' now seemed as seriously at risk as in Nelson's worst days. But in 1941 far more was at stake than in the 1790s. Malta had to be kept supplied, and the hard-pressed land forces in North Africa supported until a counter-offensive could be mounted against the fresh and formidable new German army.

These were grave days for British arms in the Middle East. But Cunningham never relaxed his offensive spirit. He relentlessly attacked Italian convoys, on one occasion wiping out every merchantman; and he even succeeded in getting a convoy through to Malta.

With the American entry into the war after Pearl Harbor, the tide of battle through 1942 swung slowly to the advantage of the Allies. It was only just that, when the command was set up for the landings in North Africa from the west, and then for the invasion of Sicily and Italy itself, Cunningham should be appointed to the naval command of the combined forces.

His greatest moment came in September 1943 when the surviving battle-

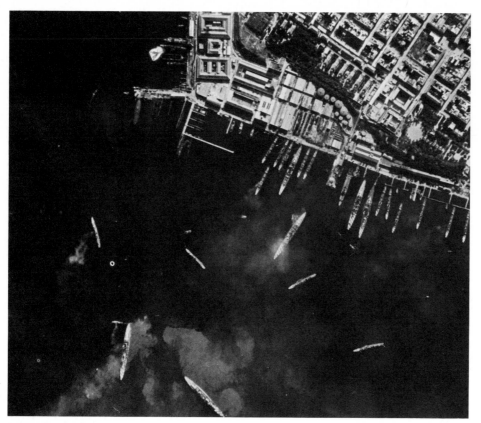

ABOVE Italian warships disabled and resting on the bottom of Taranto harbour in November 1940.

RIGHT Cunningham's greatest moment. Surviving units of the Italian fleet surrendered in Malta.

ships, cruisers and destroyers of the Italian fleet surrendered to him. It was like November 1918 when Beatty had accepted the German surrender. Cunningham signalled London: 'Be pleased to inform Their Lordships that the Italian Battle Fleet now lies at anchor under the guns of the fortress of Malta.' A month later, he was ordered home to continue in supreme command as first sea lord at the admiralty in the tradition of so many of the great admirals of the past.

'ABC' died at the age of eighty in 1963 and was buried at sea off Portsmouth. His memorial service was conducted by the former Bishop of Portsmouth, who concluded: 'Thank God for giving our people and nation such a man at such a time.'

Grand Admiral Erich Raeder
1876–1960

Hitler launched into a spiteful ... attack on the Navy. He started from its foundation and went on to describe the insignificant role that it had played since 1864.
Erich Raeder on the cause of his resignation

Raeder's career extended from the glory of serving in the first scouting group – the battle cruisers – at Jutland, to imprisonment for war crimes after the Second World War.

In the early hours of 1 June 1916, there took place on board the battered *Lützow* a crucial discussion between the admiral commanding the Battle Cruiser Squadron, Admiral Franz Hipper, and his chief-of-staff, Erich Raeder. Hipper was inclined to remain with his ship; Raeder was adamant that the flag should be shifted without delay because the battle cruiser was doomed.

The *Lützow* had been hit by no fewer than twenty-four shells, her guns were unworkable, her casualties numerous, and she had taken in thousands of tons of water. Hipper eventually took his chief-of-staff's advice and shifted his flag via a destroyer to the less badly damaged *Moltke*.

Erich Raeder was born in Wandsbek, Silesia, in 1876, and joined the German navy in 1894, shortly before its first period of intense expansion. He had a certain talent for writing, and found himself seconded for some time to the staff of the journal of the German Navy League.

As so often happened, Raeder's luck changed when, in 1910, he was appointed to the royal yacht. As navigating officer of the *Hohenzollern* he met not only that arch-navalist, Kaiser Wilhelm II, but Hipper, who later appointed him his chief-of-staff when he took command of the Battle Cruiser Squadron.

In this capacity, Raeder shared all the action with his admiral, and after the war contributed the volumes covering cruiser warfare to the German official history of the naval war.

In the grey, demoralizing years for Germany following the Versailles Treaty, which had reduced the navy to a token force no greater than before Tirpitz's time, Raeder commanded the Light Forces, North Sea (two small cruisers and a half flotilla), and the Baltic Naval District. His promotion to supreme commander came suddenly and unexpectedly in 1928. He was to hold the post for an unprecedented fourteen years – years as exciting from a naval standpoint as those leading to the First World War and its opening months.

A highly prized characteristic in the German Navy at this time was deviousness, and Raeder was blessed with it in abundance. Sly methods were necessary if the treaty limitations for the navy were to be circumvented. Versailles prohibited submarines: Raeder saw that these were built. Battleships were limited to 10,000 tons: a year after his appointment, the first

A photograph taken
before Raeder's luck
broke and he was
succeeded by Doenitz,
seen with him here.

heavy armoured ship since the scuttling of the High Seas Fleet was laid down
and others of the same class followed. The design was an ingenious com-
promise between a fast heavy cruiser and a battleship, and attracted the
designation 'pocket battleship'. The pocket battleships were all well above
the defined limit of 10,000 tons.

With the accession to power of Adolf Hitler in 1933, and Germany's
unilateral abrogation of the Versailles Treaty the following year, the last
shackles were removed and Raeder felt no compunction in laying down
heavy ships beyond even international agreements. For a few heady years

it was like the Tirpitz period again. Raeder found in Hitler as eager an amateur navalist as the Kaiser had been. 'His detailed knowledge was often greater than that of the experts themselves,' Raeder observed. 'He always had a good factual basis on which to form his own judgements.'[1]

Also in common with the earlier period of rearmament, Germany constantly emphasized that the new navy was in no way intended to provoke Britain, and, with a straight face and a steady pen, Raeder put his signature to an agreement with Britain promising that the new U-boat fleet would never be used, as the last one had been, for commerce warfare outside international law.

Raeder's real designs against Britain, to avenge 1918 and bring her to her knees, were defined in his memoirs, *Struggle for the Sea*, published in English just before he died. The 'Z Plan', which Raeder presented to Hitler for his approval in January 1939, provided for everything from giant super-battleships through carriers to submarines, to be completed by 1945.

This was to be no new High Seas Fleet to fight in the line of battle. It was to be a commerce-destroying fleet. 'In addition to submarines and auxiliary cruisers, task forces consisting of battle cruisers and ordinary cruisers were to be used against Britain's overseas supply lines,' Raeder wrote. Britain would have to counter by providing heavy naval escorts. But, Raeder claimed, 'Our fast cruisers would be supported by battle cruisers which would themselves be speedy enough to avoid action with British battleships.'[2] His grandiose plan was based on the premise that Britain would in no way react to the construction of this vast new armada, and that there would be no war before 1945. To Raeder's chagrin, war came instead in eight months. German surface raiders were no more effective in the Second World War than 25 years earlier, although they gave a great deal of anxiety and called for the attention of a large proportion of the British battle fleet.

Raeder succeeded in despatching two of his pocket battleships into the Atlantic undetected to prey on British commerce. He soon recalled one of them, after it had committed negligible damage, and the *Graf Spee* had little more success before it was attacked by an inferior force of British cruisers and cravenly retreated to the neutral port of Montevideo, where it was scuttled in the mistaken belief that a much reinforced British squadron was just over the horizon. This was hardly in the spirit of the admiral after whom the ship was named, and the destruction of this heavy ship was a sorry blow to German naval prestige.

Raeder kept his small but modern and highly efficient navy as inactive as the High Seas Fleet had been in the First World War, limiting its activities to minelaying and U-boat raiding, which of course was unrestricted from the outset. One notable U-boat commander succeeded in accomplishing what Admiral Jellicoe had feared and entered Scapa Flow, where he torpedoed and sank the battleship *Royal Oak*.

It was not until the Norwegian invasion of April 1940 that the German

OPPOSITE The battle cruiser *Scharnhorst* in Arctic seas.

Navy was fully employed. Raeder succeeded in escorting German army units in seven separate groups, two destined for Denmark and the other five for Norway, from Oslo to as far north as Narvik. Good staffwork, speed and security ensured the success of the expeditions, but the price paid was high. In a series of desperate and mainly close range contests, Raeder lost many of his large and powerful destroyers, one heavy and two light cruisers, and the battle cruisers *Gneisenau* and *Scharnhorst* suffered serious damage, leaving Raeder with just one heavy cruiser operational. British losses were also serious, but, as at Jutland, could more easily be borne in view of the superiority in numbers. The blockade of Germany was as tight as before, and it remained so for the rest of the war, though the vital Scandinavian ore and armaments could still get through by way of the Baltic and the Norwegian inshore waters.

The career of Erich Raeder during the first three and a half years of the Second World War was linked with the fortunes of Germany's surface fleet. Although he was a strong advocate of U-boat warfare, this was run (with increasing severity and success) by his subordinate, Karl Doenitz, whose name was almost synonymous with the submarine service.

After the Norwegian operations, however, the German navy did not conduct itself with dash, or even with much style. The two most powerful units in 1940 shied away when surprised by a single aged Royal Navy battle cruiser.

As he rebuilt the strength of his surface fleet, Raeder again contemplated operations on the 'z Plan' principle, though necessarily on a muted scale. Before long, he had in commission two brand new, highly efficient and very fast battleships, the *Bismarck* and *Tirpitz*, several new cruisers, and the *Gneisenau* and *Scharnhorst* again. Raeder recognized that the threat of a mass

Scharnhorst's sister ship, *Gneisenau*. These two formidable battle cruisers were named after Admiral von Spee's armoured cruisers, sunk by gunfire in 1914.

breakout and descent upon the Atlantic shipping routes of this force would pose the enemy with great problems.

The British replied by using old battleships as additional support for large convoys. Not all the advantages lie with the raider on the high seas, especially if there are no bases in which to seek shelter and supplies, and repair damage. Even minor damage can slow up the raider and increase his vulnerability, and modern radar and radio works against him too.

The pocket battleship *Admiral Scheer* was despatched by Raeder into the North Atlantic in October 1940. The first convoy she found was protected by an armed merchantman, the *Jervis Bay*, which fought so ferociously with her pop-guns that almost the entire convoy escaped. In five months, all that the *Scheer* could show for her expensive and hazardous effort was 16 merchantmen sunk.

The cruiser *Hipper* did no better, and when the *Scharnhorst* and *Gneisenau* at length reached the French port of Brest preparatory to conducting a *guerre de course* of their own, they were harassed from the air so unremittingly that they had to be brought back to the fatherland – where they were promptly bombed again, one of them being put out of action for the rest of the war.

The two big battleships gave the Royal Navy a lot of worry, though. The British had nothing to match against them on equal terms and had to rely on numbers, and on airpower. This was just how one of them was done for in the end, after sinking an old British battle cruiser. In an exciting and pro-longed hunt, the *Bismarck* was struck first by a heavy shell which caused an oil leak and fuel contamination, and later by an airborne torpedo which damaged her steering. These two small injuries were enough to seal the *Bismarck*'s fate. Helplessly circling in the Atlantic, she was hammered to pieces by heavy shells from two British battleships and more torpedoes. Her sister ship continued as a hidden threat, rarely emerging from the Norwegian fjords, for a further three and a half years, when she was at last sent to the bottom by RAF 12,000-pound bombs.

By this time, November 1944, Raeder had long since resigned as supreme commander of the German navy. The failure of his big ships as commerce raiders, the heavy losses sustained off Norway, and the absence of aggressive spirit among the commanders as well as in high command, had all prejudiced Hitler against armoured ships, and against Raeder himself. The real damage was again being committed by the U-boats, which were cheap and easy to build, and economical to run in men and fuel – and by airpower.

Norway had given a false sense of security to the heavy warship, which suffered little from the bomber or the torpedo bomber. Taranto told another story. So did Pearl Harbor and the loss of the *Prince of Wales* and *Repulse*, and all the Royal Navy ships sunk by dive bombers in the eastern Mediter-ranean. Hitler ordered work on large fighting ships to cease.

All through 1942, Raeder fell steadily from grace. He had many enemies,

ABOVE *Tirpitz*: German naval architects deliberately designed their heavy ships with similar silhouettes to confuse their identity. On many occasions heavy cruisers were reported from the air as battleships.

OPPOSITE The same ship hiding deep in Altafjord, Norway. She was sent to the bottom by RAF Lancasters in November 1944.

too, who were working ardently for his downfall, notably Hermann Goering, whom Raeder described as 'unimaginably vain, immeasurably ambitious, impractical and selfish'. Then, in December, Raeder received news of the departure of a large and vitally important convoy from Britain to Russia. In Norwegian waters he had a U-boat flotilla based at Narvik, a dozen big destroyers, two light and one heavy cruiser, a pocket battleship, and the mighty *Tirpitz*.

On the last day of the year, far to the north in the Barents Sea, the German commander, Vice-Admiral Kummetz, with a pocket battleship, a heavy cruiser and six destroyers, sighted the 14 merchantmen of this convoy and moved in to the attack. But by superior tactics and valorous conduct the much inferior British escorts succeeded in sinking one of the German destroyers, badly damaging a heavy cruiser, and forcing the pocket battleship and the rest of the German squadron to retire. Not one of the merchantmen was sunk, and the only British naval losses in the desperate exchange of gunfire were a small minesweeper and one small destroyer.

After this humiliating result the end came rapidly for Raeder. In the words of Captain Stephen Roskill,

When Hitler learnt how five British destroyers supported by two 6-inch cruisers had held off a pocket battleship, an 8-inch cruiser and six far more powerful destroyers for four hours, and had finally forced them to withdraw, he flew into an

ungovernable rage, and so insulted Raeder and his service that the Grand Admiral tendered his resignation.[3]

Little more was heard of Erich Raeder until the end of the war, when he was captured by the Russian army. At the Nuremberg Trials he was found guilty of 'planning and waging aggressive war' and several other charges, and, in the eyes of some people, was harshly dealt with when he was given a life term of imprisonment. Raeder was, in fact, released from Spandau after serving only nine years because of his age and the poor state of his health. He lived for a further five years, dying on 6 November 1960.

Raeder employed his exceptional administrative and organizational powers in creating for Germany a new navy to challenge British supremacy for a second time in forty years. His failure to inspire it with the fighting spirit of his old commander, Franz Hipper, and his inept tactical handling of the vessels under his command from 1939 until the end of 1942, stemmed from his age and the poor state of his health.

It was an immense blessing for Britain, and later for her allies, too, that Raeder was not superseded by Karl Doenitz on the outbreak of war. The resulting concentration on U-boat construction and the pursuit of all-out submarine commerce warfare might well have been fatal in 1942, before air-power and new counter-measures could be brought into the Battle of the Atlantic.

7
The Pacific 1941-5
The Greatest
Naval War

Admiral Isoruku Yamamoto
1884–1943

The fiercest serpent may be overcome by a swarm of ants.
Japanese proverb quoted by Yamamoto in his advocacy of torpedo planes

After the heroic but hollow victory at Tsu-Shima, the Japanese navy continued to build up its strength, challenging American naval power in the Pacific as blatantly as Germany competed with British naval power in European waters. The 1920s threatened to be a decade of mighty and crippling battleship competition for eventual control of the Pacific. Both the United States and Japan had plans for super-super-dreadnoughts which would make Jellicoe's flagship at Jutland appear puny.

This insane extravagance was halted by the Washington Treaty of 1922, which restricted capital ship strength of the three greatest naval powers, the USA, Britain and Japan to 15:15:12 respectively, with other classes in proportion, and restrictions in displacement. Once again, Japanese ambitions had been nipped in the bud: at least, that was how Tokyo saw it, and determined to find loopholes in this treaty.

Within the high command of the Imperial Japanese Navy there was a strong body of opinion in favour of building up the fleet's air arm in order to compensate for the inferiority in battleships. A number of officers had shrewdly observed that Britain, during the First World War, had been taking seriously the future influence of air upon naval power, and that the Royal Navy had developed torpedo bombers of a design in advance of any others, had converted dreadnoughts into aircraft-carriers and, a year after Jutland, had laid down the world's first purpose-built aircraft-carrier. The Japanese, as was their practice, went shopping. Britain was only too anxious to oblige, just as she had helped to build Togo's fleet that had defeated the Russians. In 1923, an advisory British naval mission, with experienced naval pilots, visited Tokyo.

Throughout the 1920s and 1930s Japan built up the largest and most efficient naval air service in the world. 'The China Incident', as it was euphemistically defined, provided it with battle experience. By 1941, this élite service possessed superb planes for every role in air-sea warfare, and brilliant aircrews who flew from the navy's ten carriers and from shore bases. It was ready to strike anywhere in the Pacific in a new form of battle at sea as remote from Jutland as from Trafalgar or Lepanto, with the distance between the adversaries limited only by the range of their aircraft.

It was indicative of Japan's belief in the relative importance of her air arm that the supreme commander of the fleet was one of the earliest advocates of airpower. Admiral Isoroku Yamamoto had been born in 1884 at a time

PREVIOUS PAGES Pearl Harbor, 7 December 1941, temporarily broke the back of the American battleship fleet yet later sealed the fate of the attack's leader, Yamamoto, and the Japanese navy he led into war.

Yamamoto as a young
naval officer who knew
that one day he would
fight against the
United States fleet.

when his nation was flexing her muscles for her first Western-style wars.
As a young man of twenty he had fought with Togo at Tsu-Shima, and had
studied with infinite care the lessons of the First World War, in which his
own country had played only an insignificant part.

As early as 1915, with a prescience that Admiral Fisher would have
admired, Yamamoto was predicting that 'the most important ship of the
future will be a ship to carry aeroplanes'. Convinced that war with the USA
was inevitable, Yamamoto studied at Harvard, served as Japanese naval
attaché in Washington and travelled the nation widely. He knew better than
anyone else in high command the strengths and weaknesses of the USA. Its
first weakness was its lethargy, its pacifism and its unpreparedness. On the
other hand, its ultimate strength, its natural resources and industrial capacity,
were far beyond the reach of the Japanese.

Before the final decision for war was made, Yamamoto is supposed to have

Zero fighters escorted the bombers to Pearl Harbor and added to the destruction with their strafing attacks.

confided to his premier, Konoye, 'If I am told to fight regardless of the consequences, I shall run wild for the first six months or a year, but I have utterly no confidence for the second and third years of fighting.' Fate, and American battle prowess, were to allow him only the shortest of these estimates. But Yamamoto had always been a gambler, as a number of Americans knew who had played and lost at bridge and poker with him. 'People who don't gamble aren't worth talking to,' claimed this inscrutable officer.

Yamamoto's other gamble, shared by the whole of the Japanese high command, was that Hitler would have overwhelmed Russia, and the British in North Africa, in the first half of 1942 – an odds-on chance it seemed – with the consequence that the USA would be forced to turn first to the danger to Europe.

The decision to make a surprise attack on the United States Pacific Fleet at Pearl Harbor was made early in 1941, but not finally confirmed by the Japanese Supreme War Council until 6 September. It was designed to knock out enough of the enemy for long enough to allow the Japanese main attack to develop.

This drive south was directed towards the oil and rubber and other resources of British Malaya, Sumatra, Java, Borneo and the Philippines. A defensive perimeter across the Pacific and the western boundary of the Burma frontier was to be established and made sufficiently strong to deter the enemy, at least for long enough for Japan to complete her conquest of the rest of China. By then she would command the world's greatest empire.

In this way, according to a top secret operation order issued by Yamamoto on 1 November, 'the vast and far-reaching fundamental principle, the goal of our nation – *Hakko Ichiu* – will be demonstrated to the world'. Such were the fantastic aspirations of this modern, recently Westernized power as recently as 36 years ago.

The British Navy had demonstrated what a handful of obsolete aircraft could accomplish against battleships confined in their base. Yamamoto conceived his attack on the Americans as a super-Taranto, and prepared his plans with immense care, speed and secrecy. The advance force consisted of 20 submarines, some carrying midget submarines which were to penetrate the defences and operate against moored or anchored ships within Pearl Harbor. The main striking force, under Vice-Admiral Chuichi Nagumo, consisted of four fleet carriers and two light carriers carrying some 450 aircraft, screened by a cruiser and a flotilla of destroyers. The support force consisted of two old battleships and a pair of cruisers in company. The proportion of six carriers to two battleships signified the Japanese scale of priorities in the Pacific naval war upon which they were about to embark.

On 2 December Yamamoto radioed from his flagship in the Inland Sea the code word to proceed with the attack: *Niitaka Yama Nobore* – 'Climb Mount Niitaka'.

As a practical demonstration of the new role of airpower in sea warfare, the attack by 354 bombers, torpedo bombers and fighters on the American Pacific Fleet early on the morning of 7 December 1941 could not have been bettered. And it all went off as efficiently and swiftly as one of the last rehearsals Nagumo had put his pilots through during recent weeks. At the conclusion of the brief attack the battle fleet was shattered and powerless, all at the trivial cost of 29 planes.

But amid the thunder of exploding bombs and torpedoes, Yamamoto had also sealed the eventual fate of his fleet and destroyed the extravagant dreams of *Hakko Ichiu*. For, when Commander Mitsuo Fuchida led the first wave of bombers down through the overcast into the clear sky above Pearl Harbor, he saw that their first targets, the American carriers, were not there. You could call it bad luck, or weak intelligence, but the fact was that the new American capital ships of ocean warfare were scattered about the Pacific, the *Saratoga* at San Diego in California, the *Lexington* near Midway Island, and the *Enterprise*, the newest and most valuable of all, a mere 200 miles distant from Pearl Harbor.

That evening, the Japanese pilots celebrated their victory. The same signal that Togo had hoisted before Tsu-Shima had been signalled by Nagumo before the attack, and they had every reason to believe that they had lived up to the highest traditions established by the father of the Japanese navy, and had served their emperor proudly.

In fact, Pearl Harbor was a Japanese disaster and a triumph for the democracies. Admiral Morison has described it as 'a strategic imbecility. One can search in vain for an operation more fatal to the aggressor.'[1] The USA had been driven into war alongside the British and Russian empires, and no matter how long it might take and what losses might be suffered by the forces of freedom, the industrial strength, resources and manpower of the United States must prevail in the end.

So powerful was the traditional omnipotent image of the battleship that it still had not faded after Pearl Harbor. Even that far-sighted and brilliant 'man of war' Winston Churchill could not accept that the carrier was the new arbiter, that the torpedo and bomb had replaced the big gun and shell, and that future decisive actions would be fought between fleets that would never sight each other. A few days later, after Britain had lost her only two capital ships in the Pacific, the new *Prince of Wales* and the old battle cruiser *Repulse*, also sent to the bottom by Japanese aircraft, Churchill wrote to his foreign secretary: 'It will be many months before effective superiority [at sea] can be regained through completion of British and American *new battleships*.'[2] (Author's italics.)

In fact, the United States Navy lost no more battleships throughout the Pacific war, and the new ones that joined the fleet filled a most useful role as bombardment ships and as anti-aircraft gun platforms to protect their successors, the carriers – the new 'ships-of-the-line', the new dreadnoughts. A number of the older battleships, crippled at Pearl Harbor, were modernized when they were repaired and provided with numerous batteries which avenged Pearl Harbor by shooting down many hundreds of Japanese aircraft.

From Pearl Harbor, Yamamoto's 'swarm of ants' swept south to support invasion forces at Rabaul, and then west into the Indian Ocean, where they raided the British base at Colombo, sank with consummate ease two British heavy cruisers and the carrier *Hermes*, and withdrew to the east again. As a striking force they seemed invincible, the fastest and most deadly instrument of maritime warfare ever conceived, before which 'the fiercest serpent' was helpless.

The first months of 1942 were heady days for Yamamoto's navy. A combined British–American–Australian–Dutch force was virtually annihilated at the Battle of the Java Sea. An American carrier, the *Saratoga* – the richest prize of all – was torpedoed, and it was many months before she could be repaired and made battle-worthy again.

Then, suddenly, the navy had nothing left to do. It had, seemingly, accomplished all that had been expected of it, while the conquest of the Philippines, Malaysia and the Dutch East Indies had been completed in half the predicted time. Yamamoto knew that the two US carriers which had escaped the fate of the rest of the Pacific Fleet at Pearl Harbor were lurking somewhere in the wastes of the Pacific, but he had no doubt that he would in due course bring them to battle and destroy them with his overwhelmingly more powerful carrier fleet.

The opportunity seemed to have arrived when the Japanese attempted the occupation of Port Moresby and Tulagi in May 1942, drawing the two American carriers and their escorts down into the Coral Sea area of the south-west Pacific. In the battle that resulted from this intervention, one of the two big American carriers was sent to the bottom at the cost of a small Japanese carrier. Yamamoto was well pleased with his pilots, who had claimed both American ships, and Adolf Hitler cabled his allies in Tokyo, 'After this new defeat, the United States warships will hardly dare to face the Japanese Fleet again, since any United States warship which accepts action with the Japanese naval forces is as good as lost.'

OVERLEAF At the receiving end. Breakfast time, 7 December 1941.

'Battleship row', Pearl Harbor, at the start of the attack. The carnage was fearful. But the event confirmed that the carrier was the new arbiter of naval power, and the US carriers were absent.

If the speed of the Japanese conquests had agreeably surprised Yamamoto, the speed of the American recovery from the early disasters came as an unpleasant shock. At the time of the Coral Sea engagement, plans had already been completed for the invasion and occupation of the tiny island of Midway, one of the few American Pacific bases outside the Hawaiian islands. Although contingency planning allowed for as many as three US carriers in the Midway area to oppose the invasion fleet, under the direct command of Yamamoto himself, the Japanese staff believed that there would be only nominal opposition from aircraft stationed on the island, and they would be dealt with very rapidly.

The Battle of Midway has been described as the turning-point of the Pacific naval war. But it was a very shallow turn and the hardest and most bloody struggles still lay ahead for the US Navy after Yamamoto, with his carrier force wiped out, ordered the cancellation of the invasion and the withdrawal of what was left of his fleet at 2.55 am on 5 June. The gambler had lost when the stakes were at their highest.

It can never be known whether Isoroku Yamamoto recognized in his heart that all chances of a Japanese victory had been shattered at the time of his death ten months after Midway. There had been substantial successes for his navy during that intervening period, but every day that passed the enemy was gaining power in men and *matériel* at a steadily compounding rate, much faster than Japan could hope to equal. Perhaps, as a gambling man, he believed that a streak of luck could still bring about an American fleet action defeat by his brave pilots that would reverse the tide of war.

Certainly, when he set out on a tour of inspection of the Upper Solomons to praise his pilots and inspect installations, Yamamoto was under the completely false impression that great successes had recently been achieved in offensive air operations against targets like Port Moresby and Milne Bay in Papua. The aircraft carrying him and his staff was intercepted by long-range American fighters on 18 April 1943, and one of the most ardent and earliest prophets of naval airpower was killed in the air. His death was a major blow to the Japanese navy, and he was deeply mourned, especially by the pilots of the naval air service to whom he was very much their personal leader.

For all his personal qualities, his fine tactical leadership and his percipience, energy and thoroughness, Yamamoto was a disaster as a strategist. But for his powerful persuasion, his navy would never have been allowed to attack Pearl Harbor. The earlier and long-agreed strategy was to carry out the southern conquests while the battle fleet and the carriers lurked in home waters awaiting the arrival of the Americans, already savaged by submarine and air attack on the long and hazardous voyage, threading between the outer Japanese bases. Yamamoto alone was responsible for the reversal of this sound strategy. The man who best knew America had turned out to be America's best friend.

Fleet Admiral Chester W. Nimitz
1885–1966

It is important for all Americans and their friends in all lands to understand
how the United States and her allies used the sea to win the victory in
World War II ....
Chester W. Nimitz[3]

O n Christmas morning, 1941, a depressing day of rain and low
cloud, there arrived at Pearl Harbor by flying boat a fifty-five-
year-old American admiral, an alert, broad-shouldered man
with grey hair and keen grey eyes. He had come to take over
supreme command of the United States Pacific Fleet, most of which was
displayed before him in a sunken or crippled condition, capsized or showing
only fighting tops above the water of the inner harbour.

Admiral Chester W. Nimitz later told his staff – as if the whole world did
not know it – 'We've taken a terrific wallop.' His duty was to pick up the
remaining pieces of a once great fleet, put them together again, and delay
the tide of the enemy's advance until his country could assemble a fleet
capable of taking the offensive against Admiral Yamamoto.

Like his adversary, Nimitz had been a great admirer of Admiral Togo,
and had met him long ago, when both he and Yamamoto were young naval
officers. It was the summer of 1905. All Japan was celebrating the nation's
great victory over the Russians. Nimitz was serving as a midshipman in the
American Asiatic Fleet's flagship *Ohio*, and was one of a small party from the
ship to be invited to a garden party given by the emperor of Japan. Moreover,
it was Nimitz who was elected to invite Togo to the American table in order
to congratulate him on his victory at Tsu-Shima. Togo smilingly agreed,
drank captured Russian champagne with the young Americans and chatted
to them. Thirty years later, Nimitz was deputed to attend Togo's funeral in
Japan. If Yamamoto was familiar with American naval practice, and the
strengths and weaknesses of the USA, Chester Nimitz knew at least as much
about the oriental mind and the devious ways of the Imperial Japanese
Navy.

Nimitz came from good Nordic stock, which was at once evident in his
physique and appearance. His ancestors had moved first to Hanover in
Germany, and then to the USA in the 1840s. Nimitz's grandfather built a
hotel in Texas in 1852. It was, appropriately, designed in the shape of a ship,
and is today a memorial museum to his grandson.

Nimitz's father died before he was born, and his mother married her
brother-in-law. The joint family was numerous, penurious and steady. As a
young boy, Chester worked about the hotel, and joined the navy as a cadet
in 1901. At the time when Tirpitz's U-boats were bringing the Allies close to

Nimitz points at the heart of the matter. He is at his Guam headquarters, and the end is not far off.

defeat in the First World War, Nimitz was appointed to the staff of the Submarine Force, US Atlantic Fleet. His first love had been for the battle-ship, but he had been appointed to the submarine service years before the outbreak of war. His knowledge of submarine warfare and understanding of its importance was, much later, to have a strong bearing on his strategy in the Pacific. The spectacular carrier warfare was to attract the lion's share of the publicity; but the damage committed by US submarines, especially against Japanese merchant shipping, was to have profound consequences.

Between the wars, Nimitz undertook the customary duties, ashore and afloat, that are the lot of promising officers ascending the promotion ladder. He attracted the favourable attention of the naval hierarchy when he was appointed head of the Bureau of Naval Personnel (at that time still inappro-priately called the Bureau of Navigation) in 1939. His balanced judgement, calmness, keen mind and distinctive authority were soon made evident to the secretary of the navy, Frank Knox.

Although the Pearl Harbor débâcle had numerous causes, and it was difficult and unjust to pin the blame on to only a few senior officers, it soon became evident that the unfortunate c-in-c would have to be replaced. The appointment of Chester W. Nimitz in his place, however, came as a surprise to Nimitz and to a number of the two dozen and more flag officers senior to him. But it was to prove an inspired choice, by the President himself, which at once became evident when the fighting spirit of the navy in the Pacific was quickly restored, as Winston Churchill had inspired the British after the catastrophe of Dunkirk in 1940.

Both these war leaders went over to the offensive with the limited weapons at their command in order to prove to the enemy (and themselves) that they were undismayed and eager for renewed battle. Nimitz had his submarines, and his carriers, all formidable and all undamaged. Within a few weeks of assuming his new duties, he organized raids on a wide range of targets, from the newly conquered Japanese outposts to the very heart of the enemy's empire.

The story of those early months of US Navy endeavour in the Pacific is as inspiring and fascinating as that of any of the vast and brilliantly executed operations of the later stages of the war. From the first tentative darts against the Marshall Islands to the first direct confrontation between the Japanese and American air fleets at Coral Sea, the Americans learned fast and some-times expensively many of the lessons which more prudent preparation might have made unnecessary.

It appears to be an inevitable price of democracy that faults in *matériel* become evident only under combat conditions. The usual reason for this is peacetime parsimony. Lack of imagination is another cause. A third is defensive rather than offensive thinking. How else could British naval shells have been so consistently faulty and ineffectual in the First World War, and American torpedoes as bad in 1941–2? American carrier aircraft were almost

The American carrier
Lexington goes down at
the Battle of Coral Sea.
But the tide would
soon turn. . . .

as obsolete at the outset of the Pacific war as were the British two years earlier in European and Mediterranean waters. American torpedo bomber pilots were not tested under near-combat conditions as were Japanese pilots, with the result that US Navy pilots at first tended to drop their 'pickles' too high and too distantly from their target under the stress of accurate anti-aircraft fire. Dive bomber pilots found their screens and bomb sights misting up with the sharp change of temperature in their dives. Why had this not been discovered years before?

Among Nimitz's numerous early tasks was the correction of these faults, the replacement of obsolete aircraft by new types as quickly as possible, and the sustainment of aircrew morale in the meantime. At Midway, for example, of the first attack force of 15 Devastator torpedo bombers, not one scored a hit and not one survived. The Japanese Zero fighters, best in the world for their job, shot them out of the sky.

The Japanese 'Kate' torpedo bombers were twice as efficient and deadly as the American Devastators. Their torpedoes could be dropped from such a height that they were sometimes mistaken for level bombers, and the 'pickles' had a very low failure rate. Japanese ship-borne torpedoes included the devastating 'Long Lance', which could run more than 20 miles at 36 knots or at shorter range up to 50 knots. Its warhead charge was twice that of Allied torpedoes.

Like their torpedo planes, these Japanese 'Long Lances' stemmed from

RIGHT . . . and even the *kamikaze* suicide planes could not reverse it.

'Marianas turkey shoot': one of the bag of 315. Many of the victims had only a few hours' flying experience.

Anglo-Japanese naval consultation during the period of the alliance. The British navy had been experimenting with liquid oxygen as a propellant instead of compressed air after the First World War and had passed on their findings though rejecting the principle as too dangerously volatile. This was not a consideration of importance to the Japanese, and by 1941 oxygen-powered torpedoes were a deadly and completely secret weapon.

Nimitz's fleets benefited from British know-how and experience in another field. The Japanese had no shipboard radar in 1941, the Americans did, though at first of only a crude design, and unfortunately its existence caused visual slackness. The Japanese had look-outs specially selected for their exceptional night vision. They were equipped with huge and magnificent binoculars, which were originally thought to compensate for their reputed myopia but were later highly prized when captured. Consequently, the Japanese were at first much superior at night fighting. At the Battle of Savo Island on 9 August 1942 the Japanese sank four heavy cruisers with little damage or loss to themselves. The Americans hardly knew what had hit them.

American radio was marginally superior to Japanese but Japanese radio discipline was much superior. Warnings and information were often missed by the Americans through over-excitement and verbosity.

To set against these disadvantages and handicaps, Nimitz could credit himself with one incalculably valuable asset. American Intelligence had cracked the Japanese code, and, from the opening of hostilities, the US Navy knew more about Japanese movements and the order of battle than the Japanese themselves could have believed possible. While the Japanese had no idea, until it was too late, that the US carriers were absent from Pearl Harbor on 7 December 1941, and that they would be facing substantial enemy carrier strength in the Coral Sea, the Americans were fully fore-warned of Japanese strength, movements and intentions at Midway.

Throughout the entire campaign, American commanders enjoyed superior Intelligence, not only as a result of knowledge of the Japanese code but also from information radioed from 'coast watchers' on Japanese-controlled islands.

While it took time for Yamamoto to become aware of superior American Intelligence, he knew from the start that the rate of American replacements and improvements in *matériel* and personnel must soon take effect. The loss of carriers and planes at Coral Sea, Midway and Guadalcanal was serious enough for Yamamoto. The loss of professional, highly skilled aircrews was much more serious, just as it had been for the British in the Battle of Britain two years earlier. Nimitz had time on his side and knew it.

In the first two years, the Japanese lost 8000 naval aircraft and almost all her regular pilots. The callously named 'Marianas turkey shoot' at the Battle of the Philippine Sea in June 1944 was all too tragically true for the Japanese: 315 Japanese planes were shot down in one day, most by anti-aircraft

Roosevelt with Nimitz and MacArthur. Who claimed most of the President's attention?

gunners who found the amateurishly flown enemy planes easy targets.

Guadalcanal, the Gilberts, the Marshalls, the Marianas, Leyte Gulf, the Philippines, Iwo Jima, Okinawa – wielding forces of ever-growing strength organized in fleets and fleet trains of logistical complexity which American talents relished, the pincers implacably closed on the increasingly disadvantaged but never demoralized and often fanatical enemy forces. But it was never, for the Americans, only a matter of weight of numbers and organizational skill. Nerve and strategical ingenuity were also called for, as well as individual courage. When the marines suffered 3000 casualties in the conquest of the tiny atoll of Tarawa, Nimitz's commanders advised caution in the next island-hopping stage, the Marshalls. Not a bit of it, said Nimitz. That is just what the enemy will surmise and prepare for. We shall bypass all the outer islands and go straight for their headquarters at Kwajalein. It worked like a dream. Nimitz's next leap-frog was 1000 miles.

In the closing stages of the campaign, Nimitz was obliged to accept British reinforcements. It was only a token force, like the US Navy contribution to the vast British Grand Fleet in the First World War. There were French and Australian contributions, too, and Nimitz regarded them all with a suspicious eye, remembering the chaos of the multi-national and multi-lingual mixed fleet which the Japanese had chopped to pieces in the Java Sea.

He need not have worried, and soon ceased to do so, and the US Navy's allies rightly took a modest part in the victory ceremonials when the Japanese, threatened with annihilation by nuclear fission, finally surrendered.

On 2 September 1945 there occurred the culminating occasion in the history of the US Navy, and the life of its greatest admiral. On board the battleship *Missouri* ('the Mighty Mo': you could not very well use anything as undignified as a carrier even if they had won the war), Nimitz for the United States and General Douglas MacArthur on behalf of the Allied

ABOVE Nimitz signs
the Japanese surrender
document on board the
USS *Missouri*. Halsey
stands between
MacArthur and Sherman.

OPPOSITE The genesis
of naval power in
World War II. British
Fleet Air Arm planes
in 1924.

Powers signed the Instrument of Surrender, their personal standards floating above them in Tokyo Bay.

Chester W. Nimitz, modest and unassuming even on this solemn and triumphant occasion, returned home at last in October to take up a two-year spell as chief of naval operations. Then he retired quietly to California, living close to the Pacific, an ocean which would remember his influence on its history and affairs alongside those of Magellan and Drake, Bougainville, Cook and Darwin before him. And here he completed his four score years, dying shortly before his eighty-first birthday in 1966. It was typical of him that he never wrote his memoirs, nor authorized a biography.

Admiral Raymond Ames Spruance
1886–1969

You will be governed by the principle of calculated risk.
Admiral Nimitz to his carrier admirals before the Battle of Midway

There is no better proof than in the fighting record of Raymond Spruance that an able commander will fight successfully anywhere in any class of ship. Spruance has been credited with possessing the best tactical mind of any naval commander in the Pacific theatre. He was nicknamed 'Electric Brain' for the speed of his thinking as well as for his specialist knowledge of electrical engineering. Although he commanded much greater forces and participated in many greater battles later in the war, Spruance's name will always be associated with the Battle of Midway.

Raymond Spruance was born at Baltimore, Maryland, on 3 July 1886, and graduated from the Navy Academy just 20 years later. For the greater part of his career, his twin special interests were engineering and the navy's big ships, the 'battlewagons', and their gunnery control. As a young man he served in the battleships *Iowa* and *Minnesota*, and was on the China Station when Admiral von Spee commanded the ill-fated German Far East Squadron there. His interest in electrical engineering led to his appointment as a machinery inspector at Newport News, Virginia, where the battleship *Pennsylvania* was being fitted out. At this time, the US Navy was experimenting with a revolutionary form of turbo-electric drive in their big ships.

In 1917, after serving as electrical engineering supervisor at the New York navy yard, Spruance visited Europe to study British fire control methods after the experience of the Jutland engagement. Between the wars, he commanded battleships and was for some time on the staff at the Naval War College at Newport, Rhode Island. He was recognized as a future commander of unusual quality for his quiet and modest competence as well as for his agile, razor-sharp mind.

Chance brought Raymond Spruance new and heavy responsibilities early in the Pacific war. He was commanding the cruiser division in Task Force 16 (carriers *Enterprise* and *Hornet*) when the C-in-C was taken ill. Although Nimitz was well aware of Spruance's lack of experience with carriers, he did not hesitate to make him task force commander – 'A happy choice indeed,' as Admiral Morison commented, 'for Spruance was not merely competent; he had the level head and cool judgement that would be required to deal with new contingencies and a fluid situation; a man secure within.'[4]

After the indecisive engagement in the Coral Sea (4–8 May 1942), the Japanese high command was in a quandary about future policy. Except for

PREVIOUS PAGES
LEFT Smoke and destruction at Pearl Harbor, 7 December 1941.

RIGHT The attack on Pearl Harbor struck deep into the heart of every American.

OPPOSITE Below decks during the Battle of Midway, painted by the American war artist Dwight Shepler.

Keen, decisive, percipient and fast-thinking: Raymond A. Spruance on board his flagship.

Pearl Harbor and the massive invasions south which followed it, incredible as it may seem, they had projected virtually no forward planning. Conflicting interests and intentions led to navy plans to invade Ceylon and army refusal to provide the troops. No one knew what to do about Australia. Should it be invaded, depriving the Allies of this enormous southern base? Or should it be isolated?

When plans were agreed, they were, as always, devious and oriental, involving the splitting of forces, the laying of traps and dummies, and tortuous evolutions. Between January and June 1942, from dilatoriness and indecisiveness, the Japanese threw away countless opportunities for exploiting their early successes.

Admiral Yamamoto was at least decisive in that he wished, single-mindedly, to complete the destruction of the American Pacific Fleet. His plan was to draw a weakened and greatly outnumbered enemy towards the base he knew the Americans could not afford to lose, and there pounce upon them with overwhelming weight.

Midway is about as mid-Pacific as it can be – as its name implies – just

1134 nautical miles west-north-west of Honolulu. A line from Pearl Harbor through Midway passes also close to the heart of Japan. This atoll of two islets and a reef was America's Verdun, from which she could not retreat, neither strategically nor morally; at once pivot, front line and unsinkable carrier. In peacetime it had been a staging post for Pan-American flying boats. By June 1942 it was a fortress, defended by guns, aircraft and a contingent of marines.

Yamamoto intended to invade and destroy the American ships that must come to its rescue. His plans were convoluted, slow in gestation and completely un-Nelsonian. A massive carrier force was to approach from the north-west, bomb Midway, destroy its aircraft and soften up the defences for the landing, which would be made from the south-west, by 5000 crack troops of the Occupation Froce. A line of submarines was to take up position to intercept and torpedo American ships as they steamed rapidly from Pearl Harbor. The Japanese carriers would then pounce on the survivors, and anything left would be gobbled up by the main body of battleships pounding in from the west.

Battleships no longer filled their intended role in the Pacific war, but it took ten torpedoes and 23 bombs to send the massive 18-inch gunned *Yamato* to the bottom.

239

That was not all. As a diversion, another carrier task force would strike at the Aleutian Islands far to the north, landing invasion troops on several of them. So buoyed up with self-confidence was Yamamoto that he was not in the least concerned that his widely scattered forces could never be mutually supportive in another carrier battle like the Coral Sea. He even ordered the name Midway to be changed. In future the atoll was to be known as 'Glorious Month of June'.

At Pearl Harbor, Nimitz's Intelligence, busily decoding Japanese signals, was well aware of enemy intentions. The advantage this gave to high command was immeasurable. The c–in–c early decided not to split his forces, ignoring the Aleutians' trap or diversion except for the despatch of some cruisers and destroyers. He had little enough with which to oppose the Japanese threat without dividing his forces: nil battleships to Yamamoto's eight, including the new and biggest-ever flagship *Yamoto*; two undamaged carriers to the Japanese eight; and a massive disparity in smaller ships, too.

On 28 May, Spruance took his two carriers, *Enterprise* and *Hornet*, down Pearl Harbor Channel, noting that the wreckage of the 7 December holocaust had not yet all been cleared, a rust-red inducement for revenge. In dry dock was more evidence of Japanese destruction: the carrier *Yorktown*, badly battered at Coral Sea, and now the object of frantic day-and-night repair work by welders, shipwrights and electricians. Weeks of work was being accomplished in days. Would she be made ready in time for the imminent battle? A third 'flat-top' could add fifty per cent to existing American strength and marginally redress some of the balance.

Spruance's orders included the injunction 'to hold Midway and inflict maximum damage on the enemy by strong attrition tactics'. Two carriers with inferior planes, six cruisers and a thin destroyer screen against almost the entire Japanese navy!

On the afternoon of 2 June, Spruance to his relief was joined by the *Yorktown* and Task Force 17. The carrier had been patched up well enough for the fight that lay ahead. This task force was commanded by Rear-Admiral Frank J. Fletcher and included two more cruisers and half a dozen destroyers. But its planes were of the same type and vintage as Spruance's, and the pilots had never previously flown together as a unit.

Fletcher was, in fact, a senior admiral to Spruance, and officer in tactical command. But, unlike Spruance, he had no aviation staff, and the two task forces therefore exercised what amounted to close and mutually informative but independent commands.

A stratosphere view of the opening stages of the Battle of Midway would have revealed the combined American task forces steaming north-west, carriers flanked by their thin shield of cruisers and destroyers, towards Midway, while the three main Japanese forces hastened towards the same area of Pacific Ocean, Admiral Nagumo's strike carriers in the van from the west. Both sides had reconnaissance planes out on search patrol, more

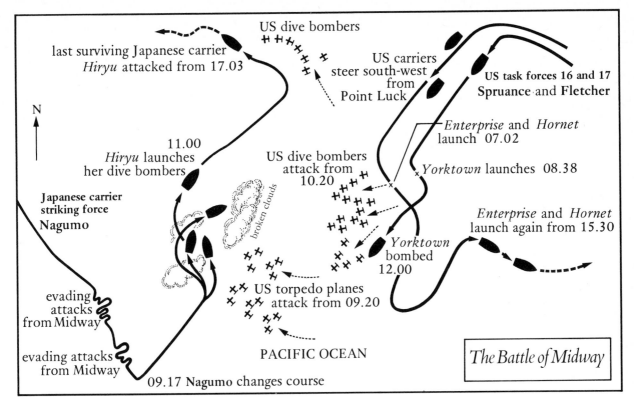

US dive bombers

last surviving Japanese carrier
Hiryu attacked from 17.03

US carriers
steer south-west
from
Point Luck

US task forces 16 and 17
Spruance and Fletcher

N

Enterprise and *Hornet*
launch 07.02

11.00
Hiryu launches
her dive bombers

US dive bombers
attack from
10.20

Yorktown launches 08.38

**Japanese carrier
striking force
Nagumo**

broken clouds

Enterprise and *Hornet*
launch again from 15.30

Yorktown
bombed
12.00

evading
attacks
from Midway

US torpedo planes
attack from 09.20

PACIFIC OCEAN

The Battle of Midway

evading attacks
from Midway

09.17 Nagumo changes course

American planes were ranging far over the ocean from the airfield on Midway, and American radar aerials were rotating on shipboard and ashore.

In spite of these sophisticated means of scouting, all through 2 June Spruance remained as blind as Jellicoe before Jutland, and much less informed than Drake before the Armada battles. Then at nine o'clock the next morning, a flying boat pilot on dawn patrol some 700 miles from Midway, sighted tiny shapes on the ocean thirty miles ahead and far below. For two more hours he tracked them on their easterly course, reporting details as he and his crew identified them.

The operations that followed were an anti-climactic overture to the real action. Midway-based aircraft flew out to attack, but committed negligible damage. And it was only the Occupation Force anyway. The position of Nagumo's four big fleet carriers remained unknown at 6 pm on 3 June as dusk fell over the mid-Pacific. Neither side knew that the gap was only four hundred miles and rapidly closing.

At dawn on 4 June, both commanders studied the weather with anxious care. For the first time for more than a century, wind had again become an important factor in sea warfare. A light breeze meant carriers had to work up to high speed for launching. Carriers could only launch into wind and this could mean a time-consuming or hazardous turn at a critical moment. Wind also affected the speed and range of the aircraft themselves. It had

even been known, in the Mediterranean, for very fast light cruisers and destroyers almost to outpace slow and heavily loaded aircraft bucking a strong headwind.

On 4 June there was a light 5-mph breeze from the south-east. Spruance and Fletcher would therefore have to turn their carriers away from the enemy in order to launch, effectively reducing their aircraft's range to the west and increasing their own distance from the scene of combat.

Before 6 am the news was received that Nagumo's carriers had been spotted, and that they had already launched a big attack towards Midway. For the American commanders, confident that they themselves had not been seen, events were following the predicted pattern with comforting precision.

There was, however, nothing comfortable about the position on Midway itself half an hour later as the Japanese level and dive bombers spread their explosive over the American base. Much damage was done and the defending fighters were outfought by the Japanese Zeros. Japanese pilots reported that they had destroyed Midway, proving themselves as susceptible to exaggerating the damage they caused as all bomber pilots throughout the war. The airfield was intact and the American bombers had been got away in time. As soon as they landed on the smoking islet, they were bombed up and alerted for a counter-attack.

It was a brave but, by later standards in Pacific fighting, hopelessly inept performance. Heavy level bombers, torpedo bombers, dive bombers, all missed, though claiming hits, and suffered grievous casualties themselves. And so it came about that by breakfast-time on that eventful 4 June, the balance of destruction was strongly in favour of the Japanese. A decision made by Admiral Spruance, after much heart-searching, was shortly to tip the balance fatally in the opposite direction.

Spruance had readied his planes for launch at 9 am. But rapid calculations made with his staff suggested an earlier start by two hours might catch the Japanese carriers with the returned planes from the Midway strike below decks or on deck refuelling and rearming, the moment when every carrier commander dreads an attack. Spruance therefore decided to start launching at 7 am. He also decided to throw in everything he had, except for a force of fighters for his own protection, making up a strike force of 96 bombers and 20 fighters.

The decision was 'governed by the principle of calculated risk' as laid down in Nimitz's message. What would be the outcome if they all failed to locate the enemy, who could strike back as they themselves were landing on again? And what about endurance? The attack force would now have to fly farther to find the Japanese carriers, and fly farther back to their carriers.

Spruance shrugged aside these considerations and stood on his bridge wing to watch the lumbering Devastator bombers taking to the air with their torpedoes, the Dauntlesses with their single 500-pound or 1000-pound bombs, and the tubby little Wildcat fighters to protect them. After six

OPPOSITE
SBD Dauntless dive bombers, seen here over Midway, sealed the fate of the Japanese carriers at the Battle of Midway.

months of Pacific war, Spruance and every one of his pilots now knew that the enemy possessed strong anti-aircraft defences, and fighters that were better than anything that the US Navy was operating. The old comforting peacetime illusion that the Japanese naval air arm was composed of silk and bamboo Wright brothers' machines, manned by little amateur airmen with thick glasses, had been shattered along with the Pearl Harbor battleships and the *Lexington* at Coral Sea.

As the last machine lifted off the *Enterprise*'s flight deck and climbed into the clear blue sky to join its squadron, there was nothing more that Spruance and his staff could do except take in the intercepted radio calls and the plots from the radar operators. In this war of electronics and gadgetry and fearsome weaponry that, three years later, would culminate in nuclear bombs, time had in some respects made a paradoxical slide back over the centuries to simpler principles. The wind was as important as at Gravelines in 1588; Spruance and Fletcher, and Nimitz back at Pearl Harbor, had no more control over events than King Philip of Spain, or Lord Barham after Horatio Nelson embarked for Trafalgar.

The position of these three American commanders was closer to that of a gunnery control officer after a broadside has been fired. To them, those flights of warplanes climbing away from the morning sun westwards in search of their target were like shells in their trajectory.

As well, in this new and ultra-sophisticated naval warfare, individual valour and initiative suddenly counted again. What could be more different from directing 12-inch shells into gun breeches in the anonymity and cacophony of a battleship's turret at Jutland than aiming a Dauntless or Kate dive bomber towards a thin, swerving rectangle 18,000 feet below – then, seconds later, spraying the gun crews and lined-up aircraft with machine-gun fire as a parting present?

At Midway there was massive courage on both sides among aircrews and gunners alike. And the price paid was high, especially at first among the Americans. The aircrews from Midway had already lost half their number when the slow Devastators from *Yorktown*, *Enterprise* and *Hornet* steadied low over the wave tops and held their 'pickles' for as long as they dared, knowing that every second that passed increased their chances of hitting as well as of dying. Their courage was sublime, and few of them survived. In most cases the Zeros cut them to ribbons even before they were within light anti-aircraft gun range. Out of 41 only 6 returned, and not a hit was made.

Yamamoto and Nagumo had every reason to be proud and confident. Had Spruance known of his torpedo bombers' fate, he might have regretted his brave decision to send out everything, and must have doubted that his forces could prevail.

By 10 am in the fighting area of sea north of Midway there had been much destruction of American aircraft, and much confusion among those not yet committed. Escorting fighters lost their charges. Bombers failed to find their targets. Extemporization was the order of the day. Individual fighting initiative had not been so exercised since Lepanto.

But if in that massive galley battle the courage and fighting skill of almost everyone present influenced the outcome, at Midway a handful of dive bomber pilots turned the tide of battle, all within six minutes. Not until 10 am did Spruance learn that the Japanese carriers had even been found. Three-quarters of an hour later, his antagonist Nagumo was scrambling from the flaming, exploding remains of his huge fleet carrier flagship, *Akagi*.

The American dive bombers' success was as swift and spectacular as the torpedo bombers' failure had been drawn out and dreadful. But the Devastator crews had not died needlessly. Their attacks had brought down all the Zeros to sea level, leaving the sky above clear for the dive bombers. The most highly trained and powerful fleet air arm had failed to take the elementary precaution of guarding against successive or simultaneous forms of attack, at which they themselves were past-masters. Even the ships' gunners seemed bemused or distracted by this sudden descent from above.

Not all the Dauntless pilots hit their targets. It did not matter. Two bombs were enough to knock out the *Akagi*, though there was a third for good measure. One bored through into the aircraft hangar and exploded more torpedoes than all the poor Devastators had carried. The *Kaga* became a holocaust after four bomb hits, the fuel from the planes lined up on deck adding to the flames.

The four carriers had formed into a defensive circle eight miles across, all steaming flat out, their white wakes, like a child's wild brushstrokes, marking the ocean with their evading turns. When Lieutenant-Commander Maxwell F. Leslie arrived at 14,500 feet from the *Yorktown* with his squadron of 17 dive bombers, the other Dauntlesses from Spruance's Task Force 16 were already going about their deadly business. Leslie selected for his target the untouched carrier *Soryu*, new like his own ship and of about the same size. He ordered his pilots to dive down-sun, from different quarters and in three close-spaced waves.

As they went in at 70 degrees, they could see the carrier turning to launch the newly fuelled and armed planes lined up on the flight deck. Seconds later, a 1000-pounder fell into the midst of these machines, a second plumb in the centre of the flight deck forward of the superstructure, exploding in the hangar below. Morison recounts: 'The entire ship burst into flames, and within twenty minutes the crew were ordered to abandon by Captain Yanigimoto, whom they last saw bellowing "*Banzai!*" on the bridge.'[5]

Leslie's squadron was lucky and got away unscathed. Many of the dive bombers were harried relentlessly by the faster and more manoeuvrable Zero fighters, often at wave-top height.

Spruance's information on the progress of the battle far beyond the horizon was as scrappy as Jellicoe's or Scheer's during the Hipper–Beatty duel at Jutland. And what there was of it was exclamatory, the language of

The USS *Yorktown*
takes a direct hit.

men tensed up in personal combat, like 'Wow! Look at that bastard burn!'[6] He would not get the full picture until his planes returned.

There was no sign of the *Enterprise*'s dive bombers until 11.50 am, when most of them must have been almost out of fuel and some had actually already ditched. Then one and a second and third appeared from the west and began to land on in succession. Most were damaged and some barely made it. Eighteen in all failed to return, and only 4 of 14 torpedo bombers survived. Japanese shells and bullets had done for most of them, but the sea had claimed many of the dive bomber crews who ran out of fuel. It was a hard fate to die of thirst or drowning after hitting the enemy and successfully braving his fire.

The first of the survivors to touch down was the *Enterprise*'s air group commander, Wade McClusky, and it was from him that Spruance at last received the encouraging news that he had been awaiting for so long: three Japanese carriers burning.

But one remained undamaged. And if half a dozen American bombs could put three Japanese carriers out of action, the more modern and powerful dive bomber force from this surviving enemy carrier could still send *Enterprise*, *Yorktown* and *Hornet* to the bottom. Moreover, the Japanese had reserves to draw upon; the Americans had none. (In fact, the two carriers on the Aleutians' operation were ordered to hasten south and rendezvous with Yamamoto at nine o'clock the following morning.)

Just as McClusky was being sent down to the sick bay to have his wounds tended (he was dripping blood on Spruance's deck) his commander's attention was drawn to smoke on the horizon from the direction of the *Yorktown*. As Spruance had anticipated, one carrier was enough – enough to turn the tide again.

In spite of the most strenuous and courageous defence, including the firing of heavy shell into the sea ahead of the Japanese torpedo bombers to blind or destroy them, Admiral Fletcher's flagship was rapidly and fatally damaged by bombs and torpedoes.

Unlike Yamamoto's carriers, *Yorktown* had few aircraft on board when the attack began. Amongst those airborne were ten reconnaissance machines, one of which gave the precise position, course and company of the surviving Japanese carrier, from which this punishing attack had come: the *Hiryu*, with two battleships, three cruisers and four destroyers, was steaming north in a position 110 miles west by north of *Yorktown*.

The quality of scouting reports at Midway was excellent, in contrast to the vague and infrequent messages received by the commanders at Jutland, and this report enabled Spruance immediately to take this monstrous game of tit-for-tat across the wastes of the Pacific to its next stage.

Within minutes of its receipt, and as his fellow task force commander was abandoning the *Yorktown*, Spruance ordered off 24 dive bombers, some of them *Yorktown*'s own machines, whose pilots were more eager than ever for

247

revenge. They climbed away without fighter support – there were none to spare – and headed for the calculated position of the last of Nagumo's 'flat-tops'.

With just four direct hits, and for the loss of only three planes, the dive bombers wrecked the *Hiryu* with the same business-like efficiency which had accounted for the other three carriers. They also, incidentally, killed one of Japan's finest flag-officers, Rear-Admiral Yamaguchi.

The reality of the disaster which had overwhelmed his enormous fleet – all four fleet carriers and every one of their aircraft – overcame Yamamoto slowly, and it was not until the early hours of the following morning that he ordered the cancellation of the invasion of Midway and the withdrawal of his forces.

At 1 pm Spruance radioed to Fletcher, who had shifted his flag to the cruiser *Astoria*, the news that the last Japanese carrier was being attacked. 'Have you any instructions for me?' he asked. Fletcher replied that he would in future conform to Spruance's movements. This meant, in effect, that over-all control was now firmly in Spruance's hands, and when he had recovered the planes from their last successful mission of the day, he ordered the two task forces to steer east.

Once again, Spruance's decision and timing were correct. His two carriers were all that the Pacific Fleet had available and they were totally vulnerable at night to the vast armoury of weapons, from 18-inch guns to Long Lances, that Yamamoto could bring to bear.

At midnight, Spruance reversed course to the west again in preparation for a renewal of battle if the enemy could be found. There were few pickings left, and it was not until the following day, 6 June, that two damaged Japanese heavy cruisers were located. One was repeatedly hit but limped home; the second was sent to the bottom by dive bombers.

The fact that Admiral Yamamoto, in the most powerful battleship in the world, had retreated because he had lost his fighting planes, revealed to the world once again that the carrier was now the real arbiter in sea warfare. The lesson had taken many strategists a long time to learn, but its validity could no longer be doubted.

After the victory at Midway, for which he was awarded the DSM, Admiral Spruance was appointed Nimitz's chief of staff in order to organize the future operations he was to lead. It took more than a year to formulate in full the planning, to assemble and train the personnel, and to take delivery of the new ships that emerged from the American shipyards at a volume which was far above even Admiral Yamamoto's direst predictions. While Japanese yards laboured to produce a handful of converted auxiliaries, merchantmen and even converted battleship-carriers to augment the magnificent and purpose-built craft like the 25,000-ton *Zuikaku*, the Americans mass produced carriers as if they were cars on a Detroit line. Aircraft of a design to make obsolete the Japanese Vals, Kates and Zeros poured from the American west

OPPOSITE The morning after. The smouldering hulks of the Japanese carrier *Hiryu* and heavy cruiser *Mogami*. The cruiser was nursed to safety.

coast plants to fill these carriers' hangars, and new pilots, eager and competently trained, graduated from the numerous new flying training schools.

A year after Midway, Raymond Spruance was promoted vice-admiral to command the US Central Pacific Fleet, or Fifth Fleet as it was later termed: a vast armada comprising 19 carriers, 12 battleships, 14 cruisers and 56 destroyers, all formed into flexible carrier groups based on the Yamamoto-conceived principle, but with seemingly limitless power and reserves. With amphibious components to match, Spruance's fleet began operations against the Gilbert Islands in November 1943. The pace and stress of events increased as the daring, island-hopping amphibious American operations became more and more ambitious, and the enemy more and more desperate. Time and again, at Kwajalein, Truk, Tarawa, Eniwetok, Saipan, and dozens more Japanese islands and bases, American superiority in the air and at sea overcame the skilful and fanatical fighting prowess of the Japanese, the great majority of whom chose death to surrender.

It was a weary, burdensome business, a precursor of the Vietnam war 30 years later. Sometimes it seemed that superior *matériel* and numbers counted for little in the face of suicidal defence tactics. But, in contrast to their attitude in Vietnam, the American will to win was always strong, and the whole American nation was working with dedication for victory.

On 31 March 1945, Spruance witnessed uncomfortably at first hand the desperation of Japanese defence when his flagship *Indianapolis* was struck by a *kamikaze* bomber. He was unharmed, but was forced to transfer his flag, appropriately to one of his old loves, the battleship *New Mexico*, which had begun life in 1915 when he was still a young officer, the battleship was queen of the seas, and the term *kamikaze* had not been coined.

The Okinawa operations in 1945, under his supreme command, were Spruance's final formidable responsibility in the Pacific war. Although he controlled forces that made Task Force 16 in 1942 seem negligible by comparison, it was the tactical precision and inspired timing at Midway for which Raymond Spruance always preferred to be remembered.

At the end of the Pacific war, to the success of which Spruance had contributed so much, he was promoted to the supreme naval command in Japanese waters, and on 20 November 1945 succeeded Chester Nimitz as c-in-c Pacific. He returned to the scene of so much of Pacific war activity when he was appointed US ambassador to the now independent Philippines in January 1952 for three years. Like his old friend and contemporary, Nimitz, Spruance settled in California, and died there on 13 December 1969.

Fleet Admiral William F. Halsey
1882–1952

A forceful and inspiring leader who indoctrinated his command with his own fighting spirit and invincible determination to destroy the enemy.
From the citation for the second of Halsey's four DSMS

Anyone witnessing the loading of big twin-engined army bombers on to the flight deck of a US Navy carrier in San Francisco Bay on 1 April 1942 could be excused for thinking that this was a giant April Fool. In fact, it was the first stage in the cheekiest and one of the most strategically important air raids of the war.

On the following day the carrier sailed, and when she was well clear of land her crew were informed of the planes' destination: Tokyo. The news was greeted at first with incredulity and then with cheers. Eleven days later the carrier rendezvoused with the carrier *Enterprise*, and together with four cruisers, eight destroyers and a couple of tankers, formed Task Force 16.

The force's commander was Vice-Admiral William F. Halsey, the David Beatty of the Second World War. In style, manner and aggressiveness of spirit, no one in the US Navy was better suited to the hazardous task that lay ahead. To bomb Tokyo when the Japanese people believed that they now owned the Pacific and had almost won the war was in perfect keeping with the flamboyant defiance of this leader.

William Halsey, Jr, was born to the navy. His father was a captain USN; Halseys had been in the whaling or the privateering business back in the eighteenth century. He graduated from the Academy in 1904 and served as ensign in the battleship *Missouri*, predecessor to 'the Mighty Mo', his flagship 41 years later, on board which the Japanese surrender was to be signed.

In his early years, Halsey was a destroyer man. In 1910 he commanded the little *Charles W. Flusser* of 700 tons. Franklin D. Roosevelt, assistant secretary of the navy, used her as a survey ship. This marked the beginning of a long and close association with the future president. In the First World War, Halsey continued to serve in destroyers, mainly on escort and anti-U-boat work in the Atlantic, for which he was awarded the Navy Cross.

It was not until 1927 that Halsey was bitten by the aviation bug. From that year, like Yamamoto in Japan, Halsey worked for the cause of the navy's air arm, eating, drinking and breathing aviation, as he himself put it. He tried to take a course in flying, was turned down for inadequate eyesight, then paradoxically was appointed commander of a carrier on condition he took a flying course as an observer. Somehow this was converted into a pilot's course, with Captain Halsey wearing special goggles. At the age of fifty-one he earned his golden wings.

'Bull' Halsey broods on the imminent end of the Pacific war he has done so much to win.

By the time war came in Europe, with the ever-growing likelihood of Japan joining in, Halsey was the most experienced and best-informed carrier commander in the US Navy. He was also one of the most popular. Everyone loved his bluff, direct style, his ferocious language when aroused; and aviation men warmed to his enthusiastic espousal of the carrier and her planes. When the new 20,000-ton carriers *Enterprise* and *Yorktown* joined the fleet in 1938, Halsey was appointed to command them as Carrier Division 2.

It was typical of Halsey luck that he was away delivering fighter planes to Wake Island at the time of Pearl Harbor. For twenty-four hours he searched for the retiring Japanese force, then was forced to return to base to refuel. Like so many navy men, the sight of the wrecked vessels, with more than

1000 fellow sailors entombed for ever in one of the capsized battleships, inflamed the spirit of revenge. Never a lover of the Japanese race, Halsey was heard to say on this occasion, 'Before we're through with 'em, the Japanese language will be spoken only in hell!'

These were good days for fire-eaters, and Nimitz soon had Halsey on the rampage, his planes striking at Japanese bases and ships. It was essential to keep alive the offensive spirit during this period when the Japanese were announcing daily their victories on land and sea and in the air and the Allies had so little with which to reply.

The Tokyo raid in April 1942 was the most widely publicized of these American offensive strikes. The Army pilots had never before taken off from the narrow, heaving deck of a carrier, and if anything went wrong they could never land back on again. They were to be launched as close to the Japanese mainland as possible, fly to Tokyo and three other Japanese cities, drop their bombs and try to make it to a friendly airfield in Chiang Kai-shek's China.

When the task force was spotted and reported by a Japanese patrol, Halsey took the chance of ordering the launch farther out than had been planned. The bomber commander, Colonel James Doolittle, and every one of his pilots, made a successful take-off in heavy seas. They all dropped their bombs, 13 over central Tokyo. Most of the crewmen survived their hazardous flight, but eight were captured and three put to death by the Japanese for their 'crime'.

Halsey withdrew his force safely, and when he reached Pearl Harbor again on 25 April he learned of the sensation the raid had caused. Although such a small-scale attack had not resulted in any substantial damage, it had struck a hard blow at Japan's pride. Having virtually wiped out the American Pacific Fleet only four months earlier, what size raid could they expect in another 4 or 14 months, the Japanese commanders asked themselves?

As Morison wrote of the results: 'Four Japanese Army fighter-plane groups, urgently needed elsewhere, were pinned down in Japan. The higher command, disconcerted, expedited plans for an over extension which led directly to the Battle of Midway.'[7] Above all, the Halsey–Doolittle raid reduced the always vulnerable Japanese self-confidence and range of vision.

The news of the raid acted like a shot of adrenalin to the spirit and industry of the American people, and was fortuitously timed after the American surrender at Bataan in the Philippines.

But for Halsey, the aftermath was disappointing and frustrating. Nimitz ordered him to take his task force towards New Guinea and the Solomon Islands where the Japanese were preparing assaults. But instructions to remain within the protection of land-based aircraft handicapped his progress and resulted in his being too late for the Coral Sea engagement – or so he believed, and so he said, in his inimitable 'goddam' and 'Jesus' vituperative style.

Task Force 16 returned to Pearl Harbor on 26 May 1942 with Halsey suffering from shingles, no doubt brought on by the strain of the past weeks. This resulted in another and even greater disappointment. Something really big was brewing up around Midway, and now, of all times, Halsey found he had to hand over his command to Raymond Spruance. From his hospital bed he watched his beloved *Enterprise* and *Hornet* steaming out of Pearl Harbor and head for what turned out to be the most crucial carrier fight in history.

For more than three months Halsey remained unfit for duty. It was a period when his tactical skill and aggressive spirit were sorely needed. The war was not going well for the Allies in the South Pacific. There had been a number of defeats, and the situation, especially at Guadalcanal, was highly unsatisfactory.

As soon as he was fit, Halsey flew down on what he thought was no more than a trouble-shooting tour. When he arrived, he was handed secret orders, which, to his astonishment, contained his appointment as supreme commander of the South Pacific area which included control over the Australian, New Zealand and Free French as well as American land forces. 'My reactions were astonishment, apprehension, and regret, in that order,' Halsey put it with uncharacteristic mildness.

There was nothing at all mild about his policy, however, which was instantly reflected at every level. He knocked together quarrelling heads, sacked the flabby, promoted the strong. But it was very hard going, and there was no fiercer fighting on land and at sea than during the last months of 1942 in the South Pacific. Japanese battleships bombarded the vital American base of Henderson Field, destroying runways and half the aircraft. Among the Santa Cruz islands on 26 October, Japanese navy bombers sank the *Hornet* and three more bombs ploughed up the flight deck of the *Enterprise*.

But Japanese losses were heavy, too, especially in precious and irreplaceable seasoned pilots. Then, in four days of furious day and night and often close-action fighting, with blind mêlées reminiscent of hand-to-hand galley combats, Halsey's dogged forces got the upper hand off Guadalcanal, sinking in all 2 battleships, a heavy cruiser, 3 light cruisers, 7 destroyers and 10 packed troopships, and thus frustrating the landing of 13,500 Japanese reinforcements...

As after the Tokyo raid, the congratulations poured in from his old friend and admirer, President Roosevelt, the secretary of the navy, Nimitz at Pearl Harbor, and Admiral King in Washington. Halsey, a man of deep compassion and religious conviction beneath his crustiness and volatility, concluded his reply: 'To the glorious dead: Hail heroes, rest with God.' On 18 November, Roosevelt promoted him to full admiral.

As Halsey first consolidated and then extended the Allied position in the South Pacific, he found himself becoming ever closer to General MacArthur's strategic area, a situation which a commander weaker than Halsey might

face only with misgivings. Although nicknamed 'Bull' by the men of the media, Halsey was no 'heads-down-and-charge' man. He could be subtle in diplomacy, and now informed Nimitz that all was well between them. Privately, he put it thus: 'I can work for Doug MacArthur, but he sure as hell could never work for me.'

The mutual respect between these two men, who seemed to have so little in common, became an invaluable asset in the final, climactic stage of the Pacific war. On 15 June 1944 Halsey gave up the southern command, his job magnificently completed, and returned once again to Pearl Harbor.

Admiral Spruance had completed successfully the operations which had resulted in the conquest of the Marianas. He was now due for 'rest and refit', and Halsey took over from him the Central Pacific Force, renaming it Third Pacific Fleet. Flying his flag in the battleship *New Jersey*, and with an armada so vast and so well equipped that the whole of his old Task Force 16 could have been swallowed up by it unseen, Halsey's future operations were – no less – to co-operate with MacArthur in the liberation of the Philippines, and (as he put it himself) 'jumping from there to the home islands of Japan, via Iwo Jima and Okinawa'.

The combined chiefs of staff in Washington had wanted to bypass the Philippines, except for a small toe-hold on Mindanao for the purpose of checking enemy air attack, and to approach the Japanese mainland via

The reality of American sea power and industrial might. Thirty months earlier, the navy was down to two serviceable carriers. Now it has over 90. These are Super Essex class (right).

255

Formosa and the Chinese coast. MacArthur, determined to clear up the Philippines first, had talked them out of this policy. He had Halsey's firm support. Halsey, who had seen more of the action than any other American admiral, was certain that the Japanese were weaker than was generally believed, and that the Allies should cut clean into the core of the Philippines, where they would find the fruit soft for the picking.

As a preparatory operation before the invasion of stepping-stone islands *en route* to the Philippines, Halsey took his fleet out in mid-September 1944 on a lightning raid deep into the enemy-held islands. His planes destroyed hundreds of enemy aircraft, in the air or on the ground, and shore bases, airfields and shipping proved as open to attack as he had suspected.

Here was the 'vulnerable belly of the Imperial dragon', as he characteristic-ally put it. Speed up the plans, attack now, forget the stepping stones, was the burden of Halsey's report to Nimitz. MacArthur agreed and the invasion of Leyte was advanced by two months. Some of the preliminary operations were bloody in the extreme, and there were also American losses at sea. But the Leyte invasion was almost unopposed, and by 20 October more than 60,000 troops were safely landed. MacArthur waded ashore, too, as all the world witnessed, along with the president of the Philippines. 'This is the voice of freedom,' MacArthur boomed. 'People of the Philippines, I have returned. . . . Rally to me!'

The Japanese reacted sharply. High command knew that if the Americans consolidated their position, and then overwhelmed the islands, it must mean eventual defeat. The fuelling of the giant Japanese war effort had been dependent from the beginning on acquiring and holding the sources of energy and raw materials in Malaysia and the East Indies, and on bringing it home. American submarines were already sinking tankers at an alarming rate. From the Philippines, the Americans could wield a knife to sever completely the Japanese southern lifeline.

The battle that followed, the Battle of Leyte Gulf, and, in effect, the battle for Japan itself, was complex and extended. In terms of the number and power of ships and aircraft involved, it was the greatest battle at sea of all time.

In the long straggle of islands running north–south and separating the main Philippine islands of Luzon and Mindanao, the most strategically central is Leyte, upon which American invasion forces had landed and consolidated themselves. Their arrival attracted the inevitable Japanese response from as far south as Lingga to the Japanese home islands.

Four separate squadrons closed in on Leyte. The northern force, under Admiral Ozawa, consisted of two hermaphrodite battleship–carriers, a heavy carrier, three light carriers, three light cruisers and destroyers. Ozawa was the bait, to tempt the most powerful American task forces north while the other Japanese squadrons destroyed the invasion forces. From Brunei and Lingga in the south, Admirals Kurita and Nishimura raced up with 7

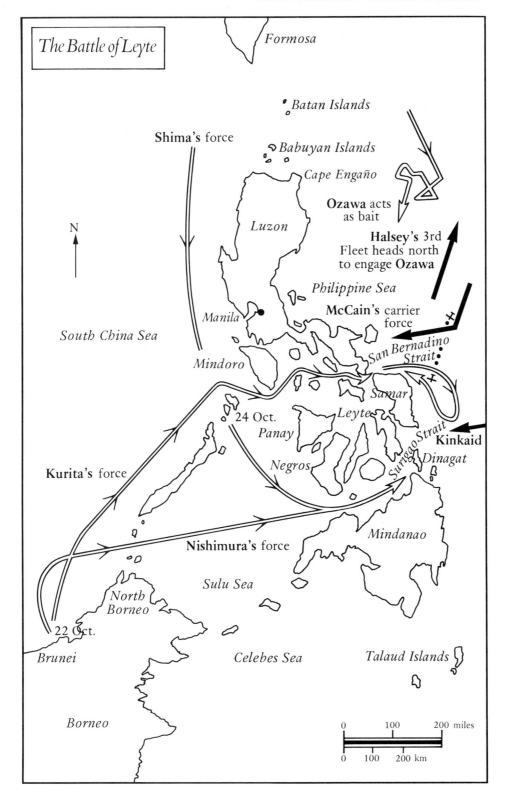

The Battle of Leyte

Formosa

Batan Islands

Babuyan Islands

Cape Engaño

Shima's force

Ozawa acts
as bait

Luzon

N

Halsey's 3rd
Fleet heads north
to engage **Ozawa**

Philippine Sea

Manila

McCain's carrier
force

South China Sea

San Bernadino
Strait

Mindoro

Samar

24 Oct.
Panay

Leyte

Surigao Strait

Kinkaid

Kurita's force

Negros

Dinagat

Nishimura's force

Mindanao

Sulu Sea

North
Borneo

22 Oct.

Brunei

Celebes Sea

Talaud Islands

Borneo

0	100	200 miles

0	100	200 km

battleships, including the giant *Yamato* and *Musashi*, 11 heavy cruisers, and light cruisers and destroyers. Finally, Admiral Shima hastened down from the Ryukyus with cruisers and destroyers.

The intended pattern was for Kurita to fall upon the invasion forces from the north, Shima and Nishimura from the south. They would have no carrier air cover, only limited protection from land-based aircraft. The reason for this was that the precious reserves of operationally trained naval pilots and planes, and effective carriers, were being held in reserve for the expected assault on Japan.

By contrast with Pearl Harbor three years earlier, when they attacked by air ships undefended by carrier aircraft, the Japanese were now intending to attack with ships enemy ships that were themselves heavily defended by carrier aircraft: a certain formula for suicide as well as a measure of America's war output. (Before the end, America would have 100 carriers in commission!)

Admiral Kurita, with almost no air support, was doomed to defeat at Leyte Gulf.

The defending American forces consisted of Admiral Kinkaid's Seventh Fleet (six battleships, 18 escort carriers and cruisers and destroyers to match) all loaned to the MacArthur command by Halsey for the purpose of the invasion. Halsey's Third Fleet was approaching the islands from the west with four task groups, each on average consisting of 2 new battleships, 2 heavy and 2 light carriers, with accompanying cruisers and destroyers.

By any reckoning, and especially after taking into account the nature and quality of the *matériel*, the American strength was overwhelming. The one American potential weakness lay in the division of command. To have one half of the American defending forces under the command of an admiral ashore at Pearl Harbor, with the volatile Halsey as his subordinate, and the other half under a volatile general at sea and serving under him an admiral (Kinkaid) who had recently been Halsey's subordinate, looked like a formula for anarchy. That it did not turn out quite as bad as that says much for the skill, quality and quick thinking of those involved in command responsibility.

First blood went to the submarines, those easy-to-forget yet deadly vessels which had been doing such execution recently, and, in the judgement of Halsey himself, were more responsible than any other factor for the eventual defeat of the Japanese. In quick order, two submarines sank two of Kurita's heavy cruisers and sent a third limping home.

Airpower was, inevitably, the next weapon to go into action. Halsey despatched five air strikes on the next day, 24 October. Another cruiser was disabled; and then, like some Wagnerian epilogue to the golden years of the dreadnought, his dive bombers and torpedo bombers roared in on the mighty and supposedly invulnerable *Musashi*, and struck her again and again with torpedoes and heavy bombs until at length she capsized.

The Japanese struck back with all the land-based planes they had. So poorly trained were their pilots, however, that they lost the greater number of their machines and sank only one light carrier, Halsey's *Princeton*.

Reconnaissance reports now coming in to Halsey told of Ozawa's carrier force steaming down from the north. It required little skill to identify it, so much smoke and so many signals was it making in its efforts to be seen. Halsey concluded that this squadron was intended to reinforce Kurita with sorely needed carrier planes, and that it must be his duty to cut it to pieces before it could do so.

Halsey's operation plan orders from Nimitz were not as clear as they could have been. On the one hand, they ordered him to cover and support 'forces of the south-west Pacific [Kinkaid]'; on the other hand, they directed, 'In case opportunity for destruction of major portion of the enemy fleet offers or can be created, such destruction becomes the primary task.'

'My job was offensive, to strike with the Third Fleet,' Halsey commented later. Immediately after Pearl Harbor, in reply to a question Halsey had put to Nimitz's predecessor, he had received the sharpish reply, 'Goddamit, use your common sense!' By going north after these carriers, Halsey reckoned that he was doing just that. Under the circumstances, in the false belief that his pilots had done more damage than they had to Kurita, and that Kinkaid could easily cope with the undamaged remnants of the Japanese squadrons, Halsey was right to take the offensive step he did. Where he was undoubtedly wrong was in failing to inform fully and properly his commander, Nimitz, at Pearl Harbor, and Kinkaid himself, for whom his absence was highly relevant. This failure can again be traced back to the unsound division of command agreed to by the joint chiefs of staff in Washington.

Kinkaid was not at first alarmed at Halsey's departure north, believing that he had left behind his fast battleships to cover the vulnerable convoys and deal with Kurita, Shima and Nishimura. The Japanese were delighted that their trick was working. Their light carriers were for the sacrificial pyre anyway, a small price to pay for the chance of destroying the enemy invasion forces.

Halsey made radar contact with Shima's northern force in the early hours of 25 October. By 8 am his attack planes were going in, brushing aside the few defending fighters and striking the carriers and escorting ships. Halsey, in the *New Jersey*, steaming at flank speed, was looking forward with keen satisfaction to finishing off with his guns whatever his airmen had left him.

Earlier that morning he had answered an anxious signal from Kinkaid with the message that he had his battleships with him: 'Task Force 34 is with carrier groups now engaging enemy carrier force.'

Shortly after his planes dived down through thick anti-aircraft fire on to the hapless Japanese carriers, Halsey received another radio call. This time it was an appeal from the commander of one of the small escort carrier units off Leyte Gulf for the big guns of Halsey's fast battleships.

Halsey was still not worried. He reckoned that Kinkaid's battleships on their own, and much nearer than he was, could cope, along with the carrier aircraft. He became rattled, however, when more appeals for help came in over the ether. What was the matter back at Leyte? he asked himself. They had big guns and air cover in abundance, hadn't they?

At this point, drama turned to black comedy. At Pearl Harbor, Nimitz was listening in with increasing anxiety to the flurry of messages which suggested an increasing absence of liaison and growing hints of real trouble. 'Where is, repeat where is Task Force 34?' he demanded peremptorily. It was customary for the encoder to add an irrelevant phrase as an additional security precaution. It was comically unfortunate that the four words he added to this message were, 'All the world wonders.'

This implied insult was too much for the choleric Halsey, and he precipitately ordered his battleship force to reverse course and return south, turning 'my back on the opportunity I had dreamed of since my days as a cadet. ... At that moment the Northern Force, with its two remaining carriers crippled and dead on the water, was exactly 42 miles from the muzzles of my 16-inch guns.' Once again, poor signalling – in this case comically poor signalling – had radically influenced the course of a naval battle.

Halsey's guns were not needed down south anyway. In his absence, Kinkaid and his subordinates had, with luck and some peerlessly brave and skilful evasion, escaped serious damage. In spite of what he regarded as interference from above – and from his flank, too – Halsey's force had additionally destroyed four Japanese carriers, a cruiser and two destroyers, also damaging battleships, cruisers and more destroyers, all at negligible loss. Together with Kinkaid's record of destruction, the total tonnage of American sinkings at what came to be known as the Battle of Leyte Gulf was over 300,000. Roosevelt pinned on Halsey's third DSM at the White House for his brilliant and daring work in the liberation of the Philippines.

For the closing stages of the Pacific war, Halsey commanded an immense Allied fleet which included a British combined force of battleships and carriers under Vice-Admiral Sir Bernard Rawlings.

'We will attack the Japanese home islands,' Halsey claimed, 'destroy what is left of her navy and air force, destroy factories and communications. Our planes will strike inland. My only regret', he is reported to have added, 'is that our ships don't have wheels, so that when we drive the Japs from the coast we can chase them inland.'

Halsey was a tidy as well as a ruthless commander. He was not going to have the Japanese claiming at the time of their surrender that they could still wield considerable power in order to temper the terms. His cleaning up was thorough. He dealt smartly with what was left of Japanese surface ships at Kure, and destroyed over 400 planes at airfields in the Tokyo area. Time and again he extracted revenge for Pearl Harbor with bombardments of Japanese coastal military targets.

Halsey never believed that the atom bomb was the reason for the Japanese surrender; its function was to act as a facesaver for the Japanese. The sub-

marines, and the naval airpower he had done so much to create and support and then to command, had brought Japan to her knees.

William Halsey was sixty-two when the Japanese surrender was formally effected on board his flagship, the evidence of the immense naval power he commanded – the greatest in history – anchored about the *Missouri* in Tokyo Bay.

America's best-known admiral in the Second World War, and perhaps in all her history, lived another fourteen years, dying on 16 August 1959 at the age of seventy-six.

Was this the biggest smoke screen of all time? The US Navy conceals its massive strength in Leyte Gulf.

'The strife is o'er, the battle done;/Now is the Victor's triumph won. . . .' After two successive atomic bomb explosions have done their terrible work, Halsey's Third Fleet heads for Tokyo Bay and the surrender ceremony.

Notes

CHAPTER I
1. G. Slocombe, *Don John of Austria* (London, 1935), p. 12.
2. R. C. Merryman, *The Rise of the Spanish Empire* (London, 1934), Vol. IV.
3. G. K. Chesterton, *Lepanto*.
4. 'The appointment of the Duke of Medina Sidonia to the command of the Spanish Armada', I. A. A. Thompson, *Historical Journal*, XII, 2 (1969), pp. 197–216.
5. *Ibid.*
6. Michael Lewis, *The Spanish Armada* (London, 1960), p. 99.
7. Cited Evelyn Hardy, *Survivors of the Armada* (London, 1966), p. 168.
8. State Papers, Vol. II, p. 183. Cited J. F. C. Fuller, *The Decisive Battles of the Western World* (London, 1955), Vol. II, pp. 65–6.

CHAPTER 2
1. Richard Hannay, *Admiral Blake* (London, 1886), p. 114.
2. *Ibid*, pp. 129–30.

CHAPTER 4
1. Nelson emulated his father in his reading, and *Henry V* was his favourite play.

CHAPTER 5
1. G. Dewey, *Autobiography* (London, 1913), pp. 47–8.
2. *Ibid*, p. 63.
3. *Ibid*, p. 105.
4. *Ibid*, p. 164.
5. *The Spectator*, 7 May 1898.
6. Dewey, p. 196.
7. *Ibid*, p. 223.
8. *Ibid*, p. 225.
9. *Ibid*, p. 29.
10. These included *The Influence of Sea Power upon History (1660–1783)* and *The Influence of Sea Power upon the American Revolution*.
11. Grand Admiral von Tirpitz, *My Memoirs* (2 vols, London, 1919). I, p. 63.
12. *Ibid*, p. 64.
13. Jonathan Steinberg, *Yesterday's Deterrent* (London, 1965), p. 20.
14. *Ibid*, p. 201.
15. Tirpitz I, p. 139.
16. A. Temple Patterson, (ed), *The Jellicoe Papers* (Navy Records Society, 2 vols, 1966), I, p. 57.
17. *Ibid*, p. 97.
18. *Ibid*, p. 106.
19. Admiral of the Fleet Earl Jellicoe, *The Grand Fleet* (London, 1919), p. 359.
20. The total complement was 200.

21. Broadlands Archives, by permission of Admiral of the Fleet Earl Mountbatten of Burma.

22. A. J. Marder, *From the Dreadnought to Scapa Flow* (5 vols, London, 1961–70), III, p. 205.

23. *Ibid*, p. 195.

CHAPTER 6

1. Erich Raeder, *Struggle for the Sea* (London, 1959), p. 94.

2. *Ibid*, p. 128.

3. S. W. Roskill, *The Navy at War 1939–1945* (London, 1960), p. 269.

CHAPTER 7

1. S. E. Morison, *History of US Naval Operations in World War II* (15 vols, Boston, 1948–62), III, p. 132.

2. W. S. Churchill, *The Second World War* (6 vols, London, 1948–54), III, p. 554.

3. From Nimitz's introduction to *The Great Sea War* (London, 1961), which he co-edited with E. B. Potter.

4. Morison, IV, p. 82.

5. *Ibid*, p. 128.

6. W. Lord, *Incredible Victory: The Battle of Midway* (New York, 1967), p. 190.

7. Morison, III, p. 398.

Select bibliography

BLOND, G., *Admiral Togo* (New York, 1960).

BOWEN, F. C., *The Sea: Its History and Romance* (2 vols, London, 1925).

CHALMERS, W. S., *The Life and Letters of David, Earl Beatty* (London, 1951).

CLOWES, W. L., *The Royal Navy: A History from the Earliest Times to the Present* (5 vols, London, 1897–1903).

CURTIS, C. D., *Blake: General at Sea* (Taunton, 1934).

DEWEY, G., *Autobiography* (London, 1913).

FULLER, J. F. C., *The Decisive Battles of the Western World* (3 vols, London, 1955).

GRENFELL, R., *The Art of the Admiral* (London, 1937).

HANNAY, R., *Admiral Blake* (London, 1886).

HOUGH, R., *The Fleet that had to Die* (New York, 1958).

HOUGH, R., *Dreadnought: a History of the Modern Battleship* (New York, 1964).

KEMP, P., (ed), *History of the Royal Navy* (London, 1969).

LORD, W., *Incredible Victory: the Battle of Midway* (New York, 1967).

MARDER, A. J., *The Anatomy of British Sea Power* (New York, 1940).

MARDER, A. J., *From the Dreadnought to Scapa Flow* (5 vols, London, 1961–70).

MORISON, S. E., *History of United States Naval Operations in World War II* (15 vols, Boston, 1948–62).

NAISH, G. P. B., (ed), *Nelson's Letters to his Wife* (London, 1958).

OMAN, C., *Nelson* (London, 1947).

PACK, S. W. C., *Cunningham the Commander* (London, 1974).

PATTERSON, A. Temple, (ed.), *The Jellicoe Papers* (2 vols, London, 1966–8).

POCOCK, T., *Nelson and his World* (London, 1968).

POTTER E. B., and NIMITZ, C. W., (eds), *The Great Sea War* (New York, 1960).

POWELL, J. R., *Robert Blake, General at Sea* (London, 1972).

RAEDER, E., *Struggle for the Sea* (London, 1959).

ROSKILL, S. W., *The Strategy of Sea Power* (London, 1962).

ROSKILL, S. W., *The Navy at War* (London, 1960).

STEINBERG, J., *Yesterday's Deterrent* (London, 1965).

WARNER, D. and P., *The Tide at Sunrise* (London, 1974).

WARNER, O., *Nelson* (London, 1975).

WARNER, O., *Cunningham of Hyndhope* (London, 1967).

WARNER, O., *Great Battle Fleets* (London, 1973).

Acknowledgments

Endpaper National Maritime Museum

Title pages Imperial War Museum (photo Eileen Tweedy)

10–11 Science Museum

13 Prado, Madrid

15 National Maritime Museum

18 National Maritime Museum

20–21 Science Museum

23 Museo Navale, Madrid

24 National Portrait Gallery

28–9 Weidenfeld and Nicolson Archive

31 Radio Times Hulton Picture Library

37 British Museum

40–41 National Maritime Museum

42 National Maritime Museum

46 Science Museum

48–9 National Maritime Museum

50–51 National Maritime Museum

52 National Maritime Museum

52 National Maritime Museum

53 National Maritime Museum

54–5 National Maritime Museum

55 *above* Escorial, Madrid (Michael Holford)

55 *below* National Maritime Museum

56 National Maritime Museum (Michael Holford)

58–9 Wallace Collection

60 Mansell Collection

62 Radio Times Hulton Picture Library

64 Mansell Collection

65 Radio Times Hulton Picture Library

69 Mansell Collection

70–71 Mansell Collection

72 Mansell Collection

76–7 Royal Library, Stockholm

79 Gryssholm Castle, Sweden

80 Sjöhistorika Museum, Stockholm

81 Sjöhistorika Museum, Stockholm

82–3 Parker Gallery, London

85 Radio Times Hulton Picture Library

86 National Maritime Museum

88 *above* Weidenfeld and Nicholson Archive

88 *below* Weidenfeld and Nicolson Archive

89 *above* Weidenfeld and Nicolson Archive

92–3 British Museum

96–7 National Maritime Museum

98 Nelson Museum, Monmouth

103 National Maritime Museum

106 National Maritime Museum

110 Nelson Museum, Monmouth

110–11 National Maritime Museum

115 National Maritime Museum

116–17 National Maritime Museum

120–21 Imperial War Museum

123 Victory Museum, Portsmouth

124–5 Süddeutscher Verlag

127 Radio Times Hulton Picture Library

128 Vickers Ltd

129 Bulloz

130 Palace of Versailles

131 National Maritime Museum

132–3 National Maritime Museum

134 *above* author

134 *below* US Navy/ National Archives, Washington (Orbis)

135 *above* author

135 *below* National Maritime Museum

136 National Maritime Museum (Michael Holford)

139 Radio Times Hulton Picture Library

140 Shizuo Fukui

145 Robert Hunt Library

148–9 Radio Times Hulton Picture Library

152 Weidenfeld and Nicolson Archive

155 *left* Bildarchiv

155 *right* Radio Times Hulton Picture Library

158 Ullstein

159 Imperial War Museum

160–61 Bildarchiv

162 Bildarchiv

164 Radio Times Hulton Picture Library

168 Public Record Office

168–9 Radio Times Hulton Picture Library

172 Imperial War Museum

174–5 W. P. Trotter

178 Bildarchiv

179 Ullstein

182 Bildarchiv

185 Imperial War Museum

189 *left* Popperfoto

189 *right* Bildarchiv

192 Public Record Office

193 Imperial War Museum

194–5 Ullstein

197 Keystone

198–9 Keystone

200–201 Imperial War Museum (photo Eileen Tweedy)

202 Imperial War Museum

202–3 Imperial War Museum

204 Ullstein

205 Keystone

207 Imperial War Museum

208 Imperial War Museum

210 Ullstein

211 Popperfoto

212–13 Weidenfeld and Nicolson Archive

215 Associated Press

216 Robert Hunt Library

219 US Navy/National Archives, Washington

220–21 Imperial War Museum

224 Associated Press

226–7 Popperfoto

227 Popperfoto

228–9 Orbis

231 Associated Press

232 Keystone

233 author

234 US Navy/National Archives, Washington

235 Imperial War Museum

236 US Navy/National Archives, Washington

238 Associated Press

239 Imperial War Museum

242 Imperial War Museum

246–7 US Navy/National Archives, Washington

249 *above* Photri

249 *below* US Navy/ National Archives, Washington

252 US Navy/National Archives, Washington

255 Keystone

258 Morison History Project

261 Keystone

262–3 US Navy/ National Archives, Washington

Index